D1159553

INTRODUCTION TO HEBREW

MOSHE GREENBERG
Professor of Biblical Studies
University of Pennsylvania

Prentice-Hall, Inc.
Englewood Cliffs, New Jersey

PRENTICE-HALL INTERNATIONAL, INC. *London*
PRENTICE-HALL OF AUSTRALIA, PTY., LTD. *Sydney*
PRENTICE-HALL OF CANADA, LTD. *Toronto*
PRENTICE-HALL OF INDIA (PRIVATE) LTD. *New Delhi*
PRENTICE-HALL OF JAPAN, INC. *Tokyo*

Current printing (last digit):
12 11 10 9 8 7 6 5

Library of Congress Catalog Card No.: 64–10135

Printed in the United States of America
48446-C

ACKNOWLEDGMENTS

I am happy to acknowledge the generous attention of the following persons whose comment and criticism have done much to lessen the imperfections of this work.

Dr. Haim Blanc went over an earlier draft of the grammar with me; the benefit of his comments to that draft continues into the present revision.

My father, Dr. Simon Greenberg, criticized the work from a pedagogic viewpoint; whatever merit it possesses on that count derives largely from his criticism.

The Hebrew parts underwent the careful scrutiny of Dr. Svi Rin.

Drs. D. N. Freedman and E. A. Speiser were good enough to review the philological material and supply many helpful observations.

I am indebted to the Department of Oriental Studies of the University of Pennsylvania and its chairman, Dr. Speiser, for having enabled me to publish and teach from successive drafts of the work and thus to accumulate precious classroom experience that I trust has accrued to its advantage.

I have dedicated this work to my parents, who instilled in me the love of the Hebrew language and its literature.

MOSHE GREENBERG

ON THE USE OF THIS BOOK

The plan of the work

The aim of this book is to teach the fundamentals of Hebrew grammar and to enable one to acquire a mastery over a basic vocabulary of Biblical Hebrew. The grammatical material has been selected on the basis of frequency, less common phenomena being omitted. Vocabulary and readings are based on a self-contained part of the Joseph story in Genesis 37–45, and illustrations of the grammar and the material for the exercises are drawn almost exclusively from these readings. The last stage of the course is the study of five chapters of Genesis. The essentials of Biblical Hebrew grammar, and roughly a third of the words of highest frequency in Biblical Hebrew (fifty occurrences and more) are included.

The order of study

The grammar and readings have been interlaced so as to illustrate and reinforce one another. Grammar sections 1–8 are to be studied consecutively. Thereafter, two readings (pp. 139–169) are to be covered before each grammar section, as indicated at the end of each grammar section and reading.

Sections 27–30 are for reference only and are not integrated with readings. Following section 26, then, reading — which has now reached Genesis 44:10 — may proceed uninterruptedly. A convenient division of the remaining material into units is Genesis 44:11–23, 24–34; 45:1–15, 16–28.

Just before beginning the study of the biblical text the Orientation in the Hebrew Bible (pp. 173–179) may be read. To aid the student during this study, Notes on the Hebrew Text of Genesis 37, 42–45 (pp. 180–192), and a Glossary (pp. 197–207) are supplied. As each chapter is finished, the Questions for Review pertaining to it (pp. 193–196) may be utilized. The Index (pp. 219–224) brings together all the topics and grammatical terms in the book.

Abbreviations and signs

abs	absolute
apoc	apocopated form
art	the article
B.C.E	before the Common Era
c	common gender
C.E	Common Era
coh	cohortative
cond	condition(al)
conj	conjunction
cs	construct form, state
di obj	direct object
du	dual
f	feminine
fs, fpl	feminine singular, feminine plural
impf	imperfect
impf cons	imperfect consecutive
imv	imperative
inf	infinitive
juss	jussive

m	masculine
ms, mpl	masculine singular, masculine plural
MH	Modern Hebrew (Israeli)
neg	negative
part	particle
pass	passive
pers	person
pf	perfect
pf cons	perfect consecutive
pl	plural
pron	pronoun
pt	participle
s	singular
suf	suffix
term	terminitive
w	with
1	first person
1cs, 1cpl	first person common gender singular, " " " " plural
2	second person
2m, etc.	second person masculine
3	third person
3m, etc.	third person masculine
*	hypothetical form
>	becomes, became
<	(is) derived from
§	section
_́	stressed syllable; used as a rule only when stress is not on the final syllable

CONTENTS

INTRODUCTION
TO
HEBREW

לאבא ולאמא

- - ישעיה נט, כא

INTRODUCTION: THE HEBREW LANGUAGE

The Semitic languages

Hebrew belongs to a family of languages whose speakers anciently inhabited the area of present-day Iraq, Syria, Lebanon, Israel, Jordan, and the Arabian peninsula. In the eastern part of this region — the territory of modern Iraq — lived the ancient peoples of Assyria and Babylonia, who spoke dialects of *Akkadian.*[1]

In the west, the area from Syria to Israel comprises roughly the original home of the *Aramaic* and *Canaanite* languages (one of the latter being Hebrew). To the south, in the Arabian peninsula, the *Arabic* dialects originated. A branch of South Arabic later crossed the water to Africa, where it developed into *Ethiopic.*

Most of the peoples who lived in this area in biblical times were believed by the Israelites to have descended from Noah's son Shem

---

1 The Babylonians' own name for their language. Akkad was the chief city of the first Semitic empire in Mesopotamia (about 2300 B.C.E.); it is mentioned in the Bible in Genesis 10:10.

(written Sem in Greek and Latin Bibles). Modern scholars have accordingly found it convenient to refer to the languages spoken by them as Semitic languages, though, to be sure, the notions of filiation held by the ancient ethnographer (see Genesis 10) do not always agree with those of the modern student of these languages.[2]

"The language of Canaan"

To the Israelite of the monarchic period (10th–6th centuries B.C.E.) the language he spoke was "the language of Canaan" (Isaiah 19:18), which his ancestors had adopted from the natives of old Palestine (at that time called Canaan) well before it was conquered by Israel in the 13th century B.C.E. The language of the Bible is, in fact, a dialect of Canaanite, differing little from the languages spoken by Israel's neighbors– the Phoenicians, the Moabites, and the Edomites. Modern discoveries have furnished us with specimens of the languages of Canaan from as early as the 15th century B.C.E., in Palestinian forms, which are close to biblical Hebrew,[3] as well as in Syrian form, which is somewhat further removed.[4] In language, as in several aspects of their culture,

---

[2] A striking example of disagreement concerns the filiation of Canaanite. According to Genesis 10:6, "Canaan," along with "Mizraim"(Egypt) and others, was a "son" of Ham. Yet we class Canaanite as a Semitic, not a Hamitic, language; i.e., Canaanite belongs rather with the languages spoken by the "sons of Shem" than with Egyptian and the other Hamitic tongues.

[3] For example, Canaanite glosses in the Akkadian el-Amarna letters. These letters, discovered in Egypt in 1887, date from the 15th-14th centuries B.C.E.; they are directed to the Egyptian court from Egyptian officials and vassals in Canaan.

[4] The reference is to Ugaritic, the language of a large treasure of documents unearthed at Ugarit, an ancient coastal city of Syria. The site, presently called Ras Shamra, has been yielding written documents since excavations began there in 1929.

the Israelites borrowed from their environment, though here, as in much else, the borrowed vessels were filled with new content.

The language of Canaan was the spoken and literary language of Israel to the end of the monarchy (6th century B.C.E.). The great bulk of biblical literature is composed in it, and a few contemporary extra-biblical inscriptions recovered by archaeologists in Palestine attest that the language of the Bible was really in current, vulgar use and is not an artificial literary creation. Traces remain of regional differences in the language, but these have been mostly effaced by the leveling process of later tradition.

Hebrew during the Second Temple period (5th century B.C.E.–1st century C.E.)

The Babylonian exile (586–538 B.C.E.) hastened a process that was already beginning during the last generations of Israelite independence: the coloring of Hebrew by Aramaic, the *lingua franca* of the Near East in the 6th century B.C.E. and for several centuries thereafter. We hear that the returning exiles — a minority in a non-Jewish milieu — were hard put to preserve their native language. Children of mixed marriages "spoke half in the language of Ashdod [probably a Canaanite or Aramaic dialect], and none of them could speak in the Jews' language [i.e., the language of the people of Judah], but according to the language of each people" (Nehemiah 13:24). From this time on the influence of Aramaic grew, especially in cosmopolitan Jerusalem and among the aristocratic and commercial classes.

Hebrew[5] continued as the vernacular of the rural population, which

---

5 The earliest datable use of "Hebrew" for the name of the language is found in a work of the 2nd century B.C.E. In the Bible, "Hebrew" is an ethnic appellation, infre-

comprised the bulk of the Jewish people. With the success of the Hasmonean revolt against Syrian–Greek domination and the subsequent regaining of Jewish independence under the Hasmonean dynasty (166-67 B.C.E.) Hebrew letters experienced a renascence. Court histories were composed in Hebrew, imitating biblical style, and official and administrative documents were issued in Hebrew, thus laying the groundwork for the legal language that was later to be fashioned into a fine tool in the rabbinical academies of Palestine.

At the end of the era Hebrew and Aramaic were both freely used in Jewish Palestine. It is a point of dispute among scholars as to which of the two was the original language of books written then that have survived only in non-Semitic translations (e.g., the Apocrypha). Even in the academies of Torah study both languages were employed, though the proceedings were summarized and transmitted almost exclusively in Hebrew.

Rabbinic Hebrew

After the Bible, the second great monument of the Hebrew language

---

quently used, and then chiefly to set off Israelites from other national groups. It first occurs in Genesis 14:13 in the phrase "Abram the Hebrew"; the later Jewish usage of "Hebrew" as the name of the language is based on the ethnic connotation of the word and on the idea that it was the language spoken by Abram "the Hebrew" and his descendants. Jewish etymologies carry the word back either to Eber, the ancestor of all the "Eberites" (Hebrews) of whom Abraham was a descendant (Genesis 10:21 and 11:14-26), or to a like-sounding Hebrew word meaning "the other side (namely, of the Euphrates River)," whence Abraham came (Joshua 24:3). The derivation of the word is still obscure; a connection with a flotsam element of the Near Eastern population of the 2nd millennium B.C.E. called "Hapiru" in cuneiform and "'Apiru" in Egyptian and Ugaritic sources has been widely accepted.

is Tannaitic literature — the product of scholars of the 1st century B.C.E. to the 3rd century C.E. whose commentaries upon and enlargement of the laws of the Bible crystallized in the great compendia of the Mishnah, the Tosefta, and the early Midrashim.[6] The Hebrew of the Tannaim, usually termed Mishnaic Hebrew but preferably Rabbinic Hebrew, represents a marked change from Biblical Hebrew. Its vocabulary is many times greater, doubtless including many words that accidentally failed to be recorded in the Bible, and in addition it borrowed freely from Aramaic, Greek, and Latin. Its structure is quite Aramaized; its capacity for precision remarkably augmented. Presumably originating in Hasmonean times, this Hebrew is the final stage reached in the organic growth of the ancient "language of Canaan" on Jewish soil. It represents the vernacular of the centuries just before and after the turn of the era, preserving the spiritedness and vigor of an earthy folk, but distilled and refined by scholars.

The natural base of the Hebrew language — the rural peasantry — was destroyed by the terrible bloodlettings that accompanied the two Jewish revolts against Rome (66-70, 132-135 C.E.). The second (Bar-Kochba) rebellion particulary ravaged Judaea; its population was slaughtered or deported into slavery by the hundreds of thousands. The center of Jewish life moved north into Galilee, a region of mixed population where Aramaic and Greek were the prevailing tongues. From the 3rd century even the rabbinical academies in which the study of the Mishnah was pursued adopted Aramaic as the medium of

---

6 The Mishnah and its supplement, the Tosefta, are two parallel systematizations of Jewish law. The Midrashim (pl of Midrash) are homiletic and legal commentaries to the Torah and various other biblical books. The period in question is called Tannaitic after the title of its scholars — Tanna ("reciter, teacher"), pl Tannaim.

discourse. Hebrew continued as the language of spiritual life — the synagogal liturgy and liturgical poetry, the study of Scripture and its traditional midrashic commentaries — and efforts were made to keep it up as a vernacular in some circles. But the organic life of the language as the vernacular of the Jewish people had come to an end. All further creativity in Hebrew — and there was a great deal of it — was based on a language learned from books and in schools. Rabbinic Hebrew continues even today as a literary medium for traditional scholars. Its bearers are fully capable of carrying on epistolary, and even conversational, intercourse in this medium, and in that sense Rabbinic Hebrew has never been a dead language. The point being made here is that it was a language lacking a natural linguistic habitat; it was not acquired by children as the spoken idiom of the community in which they grew up.

During the Middle Ages

The persistence of Hebrew as a vehicle of Jewish culture provided the foundation for the rise of varieties of the language during the Middle Ages, each adapted for special use. Under the influence of Islamic culture, the Jews of the Iberian peninsula developed a remarkable Hebrew literature during the 10th to 13th centuries. Poets and thinkers reflected the fulness of the Judaeo-Moslem civilization of the times, its secular as well as its religious sides in a rich and multifaceted creativity. In the hands of the best writers of the age Hebrew was as pliable an instrument as it had been in the hands of the psalmists; the latter do not eclipse the former in felicity of expression and boldness of invention.

Islamic culture also stimulated the rise of science among the Jews: it was the milieu in which Jewish philosophy, medicine, and grammar flourished. Accordingly, we find a distinct scientific-philosophic idiom developing from about the 10th to the 15th centuries. The character of this idiom was determined by the fact that its classic, early representatives were translations from the Arabic (for the classic Jewish philosophers and scientists wrote in the language of their environment: it was chiefly for the edification of Jews living outside the Moslem world — notably in Christian Europe — that their works were translated into Hebrew). Scientific-philosophic Hebrew of medieval times has, therefore, a very marked Arabic flavor in its vocabulary, word structure, and syntax.

The modern Hebrew renascence

The renascence of Hebrew as a modern language took its rise in the 18th-century movement of enlightenment; its first object was the westernization and acculturation of the Jews of the European ghetto. The leaders of the enlightenment disdained the Yiddish vernacular of the masses, the Judaeo-German "jargon" as they contemptuously called it, and preferred to employ Hebrew as a medium of instruction and propaganda. The style they chose reflected their break with tradition; not the Rabbinic Hebrew of the religious authorities of the ghetto, but the old Biblical Hebrew — inadequate as it was for their purpose — was called into service. Thus the very language bespoke the ideal of the enlightenment: a return to the pristine source of inspiration — the pure, rational religion of the prophets (for so it was believed to have been).

The movement arose in central Europe, where it resulted in a significant literary and journalistic productivity in Hebrew. In eastern Europe the enlightenment prepared the ground for the birth, in the 19th century, of a vigorous nationalistic movement. While here, too, the linguistic situation reflected a rejection of tradition in the tendency to prefer Biblical to Rabbinic Hebrew, east European Jewry's deeper roots in tradition showed themselves in the richer blend of all styles and epochs in the language they employed. It was in eastern Europe that the first classics of modern Hebrew literature were produced in the last years of the 19th and the first of the 20th centuries.

The revival of Hebrew as a spoken language is connected with the Zionist colonization of Palestine that began in the last decades of the 19th century. The prophet of the revival was Eliezer Ben Yehuda (1858–1922), whose tireless advocacy of resuscitation of Hebrew as a vernacular and whose monumental assemblage of the resources of the language in a *Complete Dictionary of Ancient and Modern Hebrew*[7] entitle him to be called the father of Modern Hebrew. The necessity for a common language to unify the diverse elements of the Jewish immigration helped Ben Yehuda and his colleagues persuade the leaders of the Palestinian community of the rightness of their cause. After a critical "war of languages" in 1913-14 the primacy of Hebrew in Jewish Palestine was firmly established. By the time the British Mandate was instituted Hebrew had come along far enough to be recognized, alongside Arabic and English, as one of the official languages of the Government (1922).

Thus, well before the State of Israel came into being in 1948, Hebrew had proved capable of serving as the vehicle of a modern culture as well as of a modern state. Cultivated lovingly by scholars and adopted by a dedicated population, the language had, in the course of but a half-century, spanned the gulf between medieval and modern times with astonishing success. To be sure, it is a far cry from Modern Hebrew to "the language of Canaan." Not only is the vocabulary of Modern

---

[7] Completed in 16 volumes after Ben Yehuda's death.

Hebrew greatly augmented, not only does it throw together all historical varieties of Hebrew in bewildering juxtaposition, but its entire idiom and structure has undergone a radical Europeanization — inevitable, due to the European origin of most of its creators. But the chief agent of change has been the restoration of the language into the mouths of children. Hebrew has lost the timeless stability of a book language as it has re-entered the living organism of a community of generations. It is again transmitted from mouth to ear and has thus become subject to all the vicissitudes of organic life. The unpredictability of the course that Modern Hebrew has embarked upon is the sure sign that Hebrew has been reborn.

§ 1

THE ALPHABET

1.1 The Hebrew alphabet consists of 22 letters, all consonants.

Letter	*Name*		*Transcription*	*Remarks*
א	אלף	*'ålɛf*[1]	'	§1.3
ב	בית	*beṯ*	*b v*	§1.5
ג	גמל	*gimɛl*	*g g̱*	§1.5
ד	דלת	*dålɛṯ*	*d ḏ*	§1.5
ה	הא	*he*	*h*	
ו	וו	*wåw* (MH *våv*)	*w* (MH *v*)	
ז	זין	*záyin*	*z*	
ח	חית	*ḥeṯ*	*ḥ*	§1.3
ט	טית	*ṭeṯ*	*ṭ*	§1.4
י	יוד	*yoḏ*	*y*	
כ ך	כף	*kaf*	*k ḵ*	§1.5
ל	למד	*låmɛḏ*	*l*	
מ ם	מם	*mem*	*m*	
נ ן	נון	*nun*	*n*	

1 Vowels are to be pronounced as in Spanish, Italian, or German; ɛ is the *e* in *set*, *å* is the *a* in arm or the *o* in soft; see § 2.5.

Letter	*Name*		*Transcription*	*Remarks*
ס	סמך	*sȧmɛk̲*	*s*	
ע	עין	*ʿȧyin*	ʿ	§1.3
פ ף	פא	*pe*	*p f*	§1.5
צ ץ	צדי	*ṣȧd̲e*	*ṣ*	§1.4
ק	קוף	*qof*	*q*	§1.4
ר	ריש	*reš*	*r*	trill or flip of tongue-point against back of upper gums, or of uvula [cf. §1.4 (ק)] against raised back of tongue
שׂ	שׂין	*sin*	*ś*	=s
שׁ	שׁין	*šin*	*š*	*sh* as in *shoe*
ת	תו	*tåw* (MH *tåv*)	*t t̲*	§1.5

1.2 Hebrew is written from right to left, hence the predominantly leftward orientation of the letters.

Final forms are employed for the letters כ, מ, נ, פ, צ when they stand at the end of a word. In the case of כ, נ, פ, צ the downstroke is carried beneath the line (ך, ן, ף, ץ) instead of terminating in a leftward horizontal leading into the next letter of the word. The two forms of *mem* are variant developments of the earliest form (see §1.7).

The laryngals

1.3 The consonants א, ה, ח, ע are produced in the larynx and are therefore called laryngals.

The *larynx* is the "voice box" visible externally as the Adam's apple.

א is a glottal stop, produced by closing the glottis momentarily and then letting it spring open under the pressure of the breath.

The *glottis* is the opening between the vocal cords. Its extreme positions are: wide open during ordinary breathing, firmly closed when one holds one's breath with the mouth open.

ה, like English *h*, is made by narrowing the glottis so as to make the outgoing breath produce a friction noise.

ח is a very strongly whispered ה produced by tightening the throat muscles.

ע is a voiced ח.

A *voiced* sound is one in which the vocal chords are set vibrating by the outgoing breath, producing the musical sound which we call the voice.

Nonoriental speakers of MH do not usually distinguish ח from spirantized כ (see § 1.5), or ע from א.

The emphatics

1.4 The emphatics, ק ,צ ,ט, are produced further back in the mouth than are their nonemphatic correspondents. Precisely how they were sounded in antiquity is not certain; speakers of MH who pronounce emphatics distinctively sound them like their Arabic correspondents.

ט is a nonaspirate *t* sound produced with the back of the tongue approaching the soft palate.

An *aspirate* is a sound followed by a puff of breath. The *t* of *top* is an aspirate; the *t* of *stop* is not.

צ is an *s* sound produced with the back of the tongue raised toward the soft palate, the tip of the tongue not quite touching the back of the upper gums.

ק is a nonaspirate *k* sound produced with the back of the tongue touching the uvula.

The *uvula* is the fleshy lobe that hangs down in the center of the mouth at the back end of the soft palate.

Nonoriental speakers of MH do not usually distinguish ט from ת, or ק from כּ. צ is sounded as *ts* in *pits*.

The letters begad̲ kefat̲

1.5 The letters ב, ג, ד, כ, פ, ת (mnemonic: *b^e^gad̲ k^e^fat̲*[2]) each represent two sounds, a stop and a spirant.

A *stop* is produced when the outgoing breath is stopped momentarily by a closure of some part of the vocal organs. If the closure is effected by pressing the back of the tongue against the soft palate, the resultant stops are *k* or hard *g*; if by pressing the tip of the tongue against the back of the upper gums, the resultant stops are *t* or *d*; if by the closure of the lips, *p* or *b*. The first of each of these pairs (namely, *k, t, p*) are unvoiced stops; the second (namely, hard *g, d, b*) are voiced.

If, instead of completely stopping the exit of breath, the tongue and the lips leave it a very narrow passage, the outgoing breath produces a friction noise. This sound is called a *spirant*. Spirantized *t*, for example, is like the *th* of *thin*; spirantized *d*, like the *th* of *then*.

In writing, the stop sound is indicated by placing a dot, called in Hebrew *dåg̲eš qal* "gentle dagesh," within the letter: בּ *b*, גּ (hard) *g*, דּ *d*, כּ *k*, פּ *p*, תּ *t*. To indicate the spirant, the dagesh is left out: ב *v*, ג *g̲* (unrolled French *r*), ד *d̲* (*th* as in *then*), כ *k̲* (German *ch* as in *ach*), פ *f*, ת *t̲* (*th* as in *thin*).

B^e^gad̲ k^e^fat̲ are primarily stops; they become spirants after a vowel [except when they are long consonants (§ 2.11)] or mobile *š^e^wå*, a slurred vowel [§ 2.7 (b)]. Spirantization is the effect of the open position of the vocal organs in the pronunciation of the vowel being carried into the pronunciation of *b^e^gad̲ k^e^fat̲*. Thus פ is a stop in the name of the letter פא *pe*, but it is spirantized in אלף *'ålɛf*, since here it follows upon a vowel.

In the pronunciation of MH ג, ד, ת are never spirantized, but are always pronounced as the stops (hard) *g, d, t*.

---

2 A raised ^e^ indicates a hurried vowel, like the *e* of *stupefy*.

The development of the alphabet

1.6 The Hebrew alphabet, like the language, is Canaanite. It represents the crowning achievement of a long history of writing in the ancient Near East; the traces that remain of its development suggest that its Syro-Palestinian inventors were inspired by both Egyptian and Mesopotamian methods of writing.

Writing began in the 4th millennium B.C.E. both in Egypt and in Sumer. In both lands, pictographs gradually gave way to syllabic and logographic symbols that were numbered in the hundreds at any given time and so demanded long training to master. Some time in the first part of the 2nd millennium B.C.E., an anonymous genius living in Syria-Palestine — the crossroads of Egypt and Mesopotamia — hit upon the idea of reducing the number of symbols to the number of consonants in his language. The idea may have been stimulated by the development in Egyptian hieroglyphics of signs used purely as consonants, though in Egypt itself this never led to alphabetization.

Starting from the first half of the 2nd millennium, the glimmerings of alphabetic writing appear in Palestine in short inscriptions on tablets, potsherds, and household objects. Related to these are other inscriptions found at ancient Egyptian copper mines in the Sinai peninsula, dating from the 16th–14th centuries B.C.E. and commonly believed to be Canaanite.

Solid evidence for the achievement of an alphabet are the alphabetic texts from the ancient Syrian town of Ugarit (modern Ras Shamra) from the 15th-14th centuries B.C.E. Here in a simplified cuneiform script (showing Mesopotamian influence) the Canaanite dialect of Ugaritic is represented in hundreds of literary, religious and administrative texts. Even the present order of the letters was known at Ugarit — and all signs point to the fact that the Ugaritic alphabet was not an original invention. By the 15th century, then, the Canaanites had already a long history of alphabetic experimentation behind them.

1.7 The direct ancestor of the Hebrew alphabet is the Phoenician, used by the Canaanites, the Israelites, and such neighbors of Israel as the Arameans and Moabites. This script, along with the Canaanite names and order of the letters, passed to the Greeks, probably through the agency of traders, in about the 9th century B.C.E.

As time went on the Phoenician script was gradually modified by the Arameans in the direction of simplicity and greater cursiveness. By the 6th century it had assumed a shape in which the present Hebrew letters can easily be recognized. During the 6th-4th centuries Hebrew scribes adopted the Aramaic "square letters," as they are called, abandoning the old Phoenician script for good [save in the case of some sectaries and for sporadic nationalistic purposes (e.g., for inscriptions on Jewish coins)].

The following specimens show the relationship of these scripts to one another.

Phoenician—Old Hebrew	*Greek*	*Aramaic*	*Hebrew*
𐤀	Α	𐡀	א
𐤃	Δ	𐡃	ד
𐤄	Ε	𐡄	ה
𐤈	Θ	𐡈	ט
𐤊	Κ	𐡊	ךכ
𐤌	Μ	𐡌	מ
𐤔	Σ	𐡔	ש
𐤕	Τ	𐡕	ת

Assignment:

1. Learn the names of the letters in their proper order. Know how to read and write the names in Hebrew.

2. For each occurrence of the *bᵉg̱aḏ kᵉfaṯ* letters in the names, determine why it is a stop or spirant, as the case may be.

§ 2
VOCALIZATION

2.1 The chief bearers of meaning in Hebrew, as in the other Semitic languages, are the consonants; the vowels serve merely to specify more particularly the meaning conveyed by the consonants. For example, the consonant group אכל carries the general sense of *eating*. Vowels particularize the meaning as follows: *'ọḵɛl* "food," *'åḵal* "he ate." *'ᵃḵilå* "eating." Because of this the inventors of the alphabet ignored the vowels, relying on the native reader of the language to determine from the context which of these possibilities best fit the situation.

The vowel letters

2.2 To keep the possibilities within a reasonable range, however, it was desirable to limit their number as far as possible. If, in addition to the three words above, *'åḵᵉlå* "she ate," *'åḵᵉlu* "they ate," *'iḵli* "eat!" (fs), *'oḵel* "eater" are also candidates for the proper reading of the group אכל, the variables become too many to be handled with ease. Some method for indicating vowels — at least the major, long vowels — was early felt to be needed. From the 9th century B.C.E., Hebrew writing began to indicate final long vowels by the signs for consonants which were formed with the same vocal organs as the vowel sound: י for final *i* (and later *e*), ו for final *u* (and later *o*), and ה for final *å* and other vowels. This usage soon became consistent and standard.

Some centuries later the use of vowel letters to indicate long vowels within the body of a word came into vogue: י stood for *i* and certain *e*'s, ו for *u* and certain *o*'s. This stage is reflected in biblical spelling, but while the usage of vowel letters to indicate final vowels was standardized early, there is no consistency in the use of internal vowel letters in the Bible.

The abovementioned forms of אכל appear in biblical spelling as follows:

1.	*'ōḵɛl* "food"	אכל	4.	*'åḵ^{e}lå* "she ate"	אכלה
2.	*'åḵal* "he ate"	אכל	5.	*'åḵ^{e}lu* "they ate"	אכלו
3.	*'^{a}ḵilå* "eating"	אכילה or אכלה	6.	*'iḵli* "eat!" (fs)	אכלי
			7.	*'oḵel* "eater"	אוכל or אכל

2.3 Where the vowel letters appear, the writing is said to be *full*. When the vowel letters are absent in words in which they may be expected to appear, the writing is said to be *defective*. In the above words, the alternative spellings of 3 and 7 are defective.

As a rule, the later a text the fuller the spelling. In Rabbinic Hebrew texts vowel letters are often used even for short vowels.

Systems of vocalization

2.4 Needless to say, the use of vowel letters was not a final answer to the problem of representing the vowels. The ambiguity of each vowel letter, the frequency of defective spelling, and the complete lack of representation of the short vowels made it desirable to invent another, more exact method of vocalization. The need became acute after Hebrew ceased as a vernacular and the tradition of the correct pronunciation of the sacred text of the Bible became more and more removed from life.

Several systems of diacritical marks were gradually developed to indicate the vowels with greater exactitude. Three main systems are known, of which the Tiberian — developed by the 10th century in the city of Tiberias in Palestine — finally prevailed, to become the standard vocalization of Hebrew.

The vocalization marks do not replace the old vowel letters, which had been fixed in the biblical text centuries before and were regarded as sacrosanct by the vocalizers. They merely add precision to them. Accordingly, the vocalizers never changed the spelling of any word, but rather added their diacritical marks above, below, and inside of the letters. Thus the present biblical text displays two systems of vocalization: the primitive vowel letters (normally representing only long vowels), and the new, Tiberian vocalization marks superimposed upon them.

The Tiberian vocalization

2.5 The Tiberian vocalization consists of the following signs:

Sign	*Name*[1]	*Transcription*	*Quality*
◌ָ	קָמֵץ *qåmeṣ*	*å*	*a* as in *arm*
◌ָ	קָמֵץ חָטוּף *qåmeṣ ḥåṭuf*[2]	*ŏ*	*o* as in *soft*

The *Ashkenazic* (central and east European) pronunciation of both *qåmeṣ*'s is as *o* in *soft*. That the Tiberian vocalizers also pronounced both alike is indicated by their failure to distinguish them graphically. Their pronunciation was probably similar to the Ashkenazic.

1 Variant pronunciations of each of these names exist; e.g., *qåmɛṣ, qåmåṣ; s^{e}gol; ḥiriq.*

2 Called also קָמֵץ קָטָן *qåmeṣ qåṭån.*

The *Sephardic* (Spanish-Portuguese) pronunciation of *qåmeṣ* differs from that of *qåmeṣ ḥåṭuf* as indicated above. MH pronunciation is in this case patterned after the Sephardic, and thus does not distinguish *qåmeṣ* from *pa̍ṯaḥ* (see the next sign).

Qåmeṣ ḥåṭuf is a phonetic variant of *qibbuṣ* (see below). As distinguished from *qåmeṣ*, it occurs only in syllables that are closed [§ 2.7 (a), § 25.2 (b)] and unstressed; e.g., אָזְנַיִם *'ŏz-na̍yim*. (See further § 28.2[2].)

Sign	*Name*		*Transcription*	*Quality*
◌ַ	פַּתַח	*pa̍ṯaḥ*	*a*	*a* as in *arm*
◌ֶ	סֶגוֹל	*sɛg̱ol*	*ɛ*	*e* as in *set*
◌ֵ	צֵרֵי	*ṣe̍re*	*e*	*e* as in *grey* (MH *ṣe̍re* often = *sɛg̱ol*)
◌ִ	חִירֶק	*ḥi̍rɛq*	*i*	*i* as in *siesta*
◌ֹ	חוֹלֶם	*ḥo̍lɛm*	*o*	*o* as in *mold*
וּ	שׁוּרֶק	*šu̍rɛq*	*u*	*u* as in *rule*
◌ֻ	קִבּוּץ	*qibbuṣ*	*u*	*u* as in *rule*

(a) All the vowel signs, except *ḥo̍lɛm* and *šu̍rɛq*, are sublinear. *Ḥo̍lɛm* is placed above and to the left of its consonant, as in כֹּל *kol* "all," or directly over an already present vowel letter ו, as in חוֹלֶם. *Šu̍rɛq* is a dot placed within an already present vowel letter ו to designate it as *u*, as in שׁוּרֶק.

Vowels are pronounced after the consonant beneath which (in the case of *ḥo̍lɛm*, above which) they are written; see the names of the vowels for examples.

(b) The laryngals ע ,ח ,ה when they are final[3] cannot be preceded by any but an *a* vowel. Should another vowel precede them, a brief *a* sound glides in between the laryngal and that vowel. This *a* is indicated by *pa̍ṯaḥ* written beneath, but pronounced before, the laryngal; e.g., רוּחַ

[3] When final ה is consonantal it is marked with a dot called מַפִּיק *mappiq* to distinguish it from final ה as a vowel letter: תָּמַהּ *tåmah* "he was astonished."

rúaḥ "spirit," שׁוֹמֵעַ *šoméaʿ* "(one who) hears." Such a *páṯaḥ* is called a "furtive *páṯaḥ*."

2.6 The vowel signs were designed to indicate the quality (sound) of the vowels, not their quantity (the length of time taken to utter the sound). Most of the signs are, in fact, ambiguous as to quantity, representing sounds that are now long, now short. The determinants of the quantity of vowels will be discussed later (§25). For the present it may be noted that ◌ָ, ◌ֵ, and ◌ֹ represent vowels that are often a lengthened modification of short *a*, *i*, *u* (represented by ◌ַ, ◌ִ, ◌ֻ), respectively.

Distinctions of length are not observed in the pronunciation of MH, but they are significant for understanding various grammatical phenomena.

The šewå

2.7 To mark a consonant that has no full vowel the Tiberian system uses a special sign ◌ְ called שְׁוָא *šewå*.

(a) The *šewå* indicating complete vowellessness is called *quiescent šewå*. It occurs at the end of a syllable and closes the syllable; e.g., שִׁמְעוֹן *šim-ʿon* "Simeon," יִשְׁמֹר *yiš-mor* "he will guard."

(b) The *šewå* pronounced as a slurred vowel — like the *e* of English *stupefy* — is called *mobile šewå*. Mobile *šewå* derives from a full vowel that has become slurred owing to a shift in the word stress. For example, the feminine of גָּדוֹל *gåḏol* "big" is גְּדוֹלָה *geḏolå*, in which the mobile *šewå* represents a slurred *a*-vowel. Again, the plural of שָׁמַר *šåmar* "he guarded" is שָׁמְרוּ *šåmeru* (syllabified: *šå-meru*) "they guarded," in which the mobile *šewå* represents the slurred *páṯaḥ*. Every *šewå* at the beginning of a word (or a syllable) is a mobile *šewå*.

(c) Mobile *šewå* retains enough of the force of its original vowel to cause a following *begad kefat* to be spirantized. Thus, for example, when the particle -לְ *le* "to" is prefixed to בֵּן *ben* "son," the result is לְבֵן *leven* "to a son."

The distinction between quiescent and mobile *šewå* is fundamental for understanding the vocalization. In the pronunciation of MH, however, mobile *šewå* tends to be elided; the two examples of (b) are normally sounded as *gdolå*, *šåmru*.

2.8 Vowellessness at the end of a word is not marked by a *šewå*; thus בַּ֫יִת *bayit* "house." Chief exceptions to this rule are (a) final *kaf*, which, when vowelless, bears in it a *šewå* in order to distinguish it from final *nun*; thus הָלַךְ *hålak* "he went"; and (b) final *tåw* of 2 fs pronominal elements; e.g., אַתְּ *'att* "you" (fs), שָׁמַרְתְּ *šåmart* "you (fs) guarded."

2.9 With the laryngals (א, ה, ח, ע), and occasionally with other consonants, *šewå* may be combined with *pataḥ*, *sɛgol*, or *qåmeṣ ḥåṭuf* to form the composites ֲ חֲטָף פַּ֫תַח *ḥaṭåf pataḥ*, ֱ חֲטָף סֶגוֹל *ḥaṭåf sɛgol*, and ֳ חֲטָף קָמֵץ *ḥaṭåf qåmeṣ*. The purpose of the *ḥaṭåfs* is chiefly to facilitate the articulation of the laryngals: יַעֲקֹב *Ya'aqov* "Jacob," אֱלֹהִים *'elohim* "God," צָהֳרַ֫יִם *ṣŏhŏrayim* "noon."

The dågeš

2.10 To mark certain peculiarities in consonants, the Tiberian vocalization places a dot, called דָּגֵשׁ *dågeš*, inside the letters.

(a) To indicate that *begad kefat* are to be pronounced as stops, a dot called דָּגֵשׁ קַל *dågeš qal*, "gentle *dågeš*," is placed within them (§ 1.5).

(b) Long (doubled) consonants are indicated by a dot called דָּגֵשׁ חָזָק *dågeš ḥåzåq* "strong *dågeš*." Consonants are long:

1. as a result of the juncture of two identical consonants, the

first of which ends its syllable; the two are fused into one long consonant: *נָתַנְנוּ > נָתַנּוּ *nåṯannu* "we gave";

2. as a result of the assimilation of one consonant to another: מִן זֶה *min zɛ* "from this" combines as מִזֶּה *mizzɛ*, with *nun* having assimilated to *zayin*, and *zayin*, therefore, long;

3. as a characteristic of the form: the article הַ- *ha-* "the" requires that the following consonant be long: הַבֵּן *habben* "the son."

2.11 When *begaḏ kefaṯ* are long (i.e., bear within them a strong *dågeš*), they are pronounced as stops even though they follow a vowel (as in the case of הַבֵּן). The strong *dågeš* thus serves the function of the gentle *dågeš* when it appears in *begaḏ kefaṯ*.

Assignment

Learn the names of the vowels and other diacritical marks. Know their functions.

§ 3

THE NOUN SENTENCE

3.1 A sentence (or clause) in which the subject is a noun and the predicate is a noun or adjective is called a noun sentence (or clause). Its simplest form consists of two nouns, or a noun and an adjective, juxtaposed. The tense of a noun sentence is determined by its context; when there is no context, the present tense is understood.

Examples, using יוֹסֵף "Joseph," גָּדוֹל "big," נַ֫עַר "(a)[1] lad": יוֹסֵף גָּדוֹל "Joseph is big"; יוֹסֵף נַ֫עַר "Joseph is a lad."

3.2 The normal order is subject—predicate. If the predicate is to be emphasized, it is placed first; e.g., נַ֫עַר יוֹסֵף "Joseph is (only) a lad."

* * * * * * *

big	גָּדוֹל	Joseph	יוֹסֵף
small	קָטֹן	lad	נַ֫עַר
brother	אָח	Benjamin	בִּנְיָמִין

[1] Hebrew has no element equivalent to the English indefinite article ("a[n]").

what?	מַה[2]	Jacob	יַעֲקֹב
who?	מִי	man	אִישׁ

Read and translate:

1. יוֹסֵף נַעַר. 2. בִּנְיָמִין נַעַר. 3. יוֹסֵף גָּדוֹל. 4. בִּנְיָמִין קָטֹן.
5. בִּנְיָמִין אָח. 6. יוֹסֵף אָח. 7. יַעֲקֹב אִישׁ. 8. יַעֲקֹב גָּדוֹל.
9. קָטֹן בִּנְיָמִין. 10. אִישׁ יַעֲקֹב.

Render your translation back into Hebrew, without referring to the above. Answer in Hebrew:

1. מַה יוֹסֵף? 2. מַה בִּנְיָמִין? 3. מִי נַעַר? 4. מִי גָּדוֹל? 5. מִי קָטֹן? 6. מִי אָח? 7. מִי אִישׁ? 8. מַה יַעֲקֹב?

---

[2] See § 5.3 for vocalization of מה.

§ 4

ON THE STRUCTURE OF THE NOUN

4.1 Hebrew recognizes two genders: masculine and feminine, and all nouns are either the one or the other according to their form. The masculine has no distinguishing sign; the feminine is distinguished by the ending ־ָה or ־ת. Thus נַ֫עַר "lad," אָח "brother," and אִישׁ "man" are masculine; פָּרָה "cow," אִשָּׁה "woman," כְּתֹ֫נֶת "tunic" are feminine.

Some nouns are feminine though they lack the characteristic feminine ending. Among these are אֶ֫רֶץ "land," עִיר "city," פַּ֫עַם "a time"; paired organs of the body, such as יָד "hand," עַ֫יִן "eye," אֹ֫זֶן "ear," רֶ֫גֶל "foot"; and words denoting females, such as אֵם "mother," אָתוֹן "she-donkey."

4.2 The regular plural ending of masculines is ־ִים; e.g., נְעָרִים "lads," אַחִים "brothers"

The regular plural ending of feminines is ־וֹת; e.g., פָּרוֹת "cows."

But the plural form is not always indicative of the gender of a word. The plural of אָב "father" is אָבוֹת, of אִשָּׁה "woman" is נָשִׁים. Hence the singular is a better guide to gender — but see §4.1. The only sure index of gender, when it is available, is the form of an associated adjective or verb, which must agree with the noun in gender.

4.3 Hebrew also has a dual number, indicated by the termination ַ֫יִם, which serves to indicate two-ness in certain nouns; e.g., expressions of time: פַּ֫עַם "one time," פַּעֲמַ֫יִם "twice." In objects that come normally in pairs, the dual termination is used for the plural: יָדַ֫יִם "hands," אָזְנַ֫יִם (*'ŏz-*) "ears," רַגְלַ֫יִם "feet," עֵינַ֫יִם "eyes."

Thus "seven eyes" is שֶׁ֫בַע עֵינַ֫יִם (this does *not* mean "seven pairs of eyes"). To say "two eyes," the word for "two" must be used: שְׁתֵּ֫י עֵינַ֫יִם.

4.4 The main stress generally falls on the final syllable; e.g., יוֹסֵף *Yosẹ́f*, נְעָרִ֫ים *ne'ārím.*

In certain vowel patterns, however, the stress always falls on the first of a pair of vowels, resulting in penultimate (next-to-last-syllable) stress. Such vowel patterns are ֶ ֶ (רֶ֫גֶל), ֶ ֹ (כְּתֹ֫נֶת, אֹ֫זֶן), ַ ַ (פַּ֫עַם, נַ֫עַר), ִ ַ (עַ֫יִן, and in the dual termination; e.g., יָדַ֫יִם). There are other exceptions to the rule of final stress; they will be marked with ֫ as they occur.

4.5 When a noun is inflected in the plural or dual, or an adjective receives the feminine ָה, these plural, dual, and feminine terminations attract the stress to themselves, away from the beginning of the word. Consequently, the beginning of the word is pronounced hurriedly, with the result that vowels there may be shortened or slurred, or such sequences as *-ayi-* contracted into single vowels. For example: the *ḥolɛm* of אֹ֫זֶן is shortened to *qåmeṣ ḥåṭuf* in the dual אָזְנַ֫יִם (*'ŏz-*); the *qåmeṣ* of גָּדוֹל is slurred to mobile *šewå* in the feminine גְּדוֹלָה and the plural גְּדוֹלִים, גְּדוֹלוֹת; the sequence *-ayi-* in עַ֫יִן contracts to *e* in the dual עֵינַ֫יִם.

These vowel changes due to the shift in the place of the stress follow regular rules, but discussion of them must be deferred till later. For the present it is enough to note that when in the course of inflection the stress of a word shifts forward (to the end), vowel changes — shortening or slurring — may be expected to occur at the beginning of the word.

* * * * * * *

The words of the previous lesson are inflected thus:

big	גָּדוֹל, גְּדוֹלָה f, גְּדוֹלִים mpl, גְּדוֹלוֹת fpl		lad	נַעַר, נְעָרִים pl
small	קָטֹן, קְטַנָּה[1] f, קְטַנִּים mpl, קְטַנּוֹת fpl		brother	אָח, אַחִים pl
			man	אִישׁ, אֲנָשִׁים pl

New words:

Leah	לֵאָה		and (*see below for vocalization*)	וְ־
to, for (*see below for vocalization*)	לְ־		Reuben	רְאוּבֵן
hand	יָד f(du יָדַיִם)		Rachel	רָחֵל
eye	עַיִן f(du עֵינַיִם)		woman, wife	אִשָּׁה (pl נָשִׁים)

Vocalization of ו : Normally וְ; וּ before labials (ב, מ, פ) and *šewå* (e.g., וּרְאוּבֵן, וּבִנְיָמִין); before *ḥaṭåfs*, vocalized with the vowel component of the *ḥaṭåf* (e.g., וַאֲנָשִׁים).

Vocalization of ל : Normally לְ; לִ before *šewå* (e.g., לִרְאוּבֵן); before *ḥaṭåfs*, vocalized with the vowel component of the *ḥaṭåf* (e.g., לַאֲנָשִׁים).

"Have" is expressed thus: לְיוֹסֵף אָח "Joseph has a brother" (lit., "to Joseph [is] a brother"). (אָח לְיוֹסֵף can mean the same, but when the phrase is in the predicate it means only "a brother to/of Joseph"; e.g., בִּנְיָמִין אָח לְיוֹסֵף "Benjamin is a brother to/of Joseph)."

---

1 This and the following forms are based on an alternative base קָטָן

Read and translate:

1. בִּנְיָמִין וְיוֹסֵף נְעָרִים. 2. יוֹסֵף וּבִנְיָמִין קְטַנִּים. 3. רְאוּבֵן אָח.
4. יוֹסֵף וּבִנְיָמִין וּרְאוּבֵן אַחִים. 5. יוֹסֵף וּבִנְיָמִין קְטַנִּים וּרְאוּבֵן גָּדוֹל.
6. רְאוּבֵן אִישׁ וְיַעֲקֹב אִישׁ. 7. יַעֲקֹב וּרְאוּבֵן אֲנָשִׁים. 8. יַעֲקֹב וּרְאוּבֵן
גְּדוֹלִים. 9. רָחֵל אִשָּׁה וְלֵאָה אִשָּׁה. 10. רָחֵל וְלֵאָה נָשִׁים. 11. רָחֵל
גְּדוֹלָה וְלֵאָה גְּדוֹלָה. 12. רָחֵל וְלֵאָה גְּדוֹלוֹת. 13. לְיַעֲקֹב נָשִׁים.
14. רָחֵל וְלֵאָה נָשִׁים לְיַעֲקֹב. 15. יָד גְּדוֹלָה. 16. יָדַיִם גְּדוֹלוֹת. 17. עַיִן
קְטַנָּה. 18. עֵינַיִם קְטַנּוֹת. 19. לַאֲנָשִׁים יָדַיִם וְעֵינַיִם. 20. לְמִי עֵינַיִם?
לְאִישׁ עֵינַיִם. 21. לְמִי יָד? לְאִשָּׁה יָד. 22. לַאֲנָשִׁים וּלְנָשִׁים יָדַיִם
וְעֵינַיִם.

Answer in Hebrew:

1. מִי נְעָרִים? 2. מִי קְטַנִּים? 3. מִי גְּדוֹלִים? 4. מִי אַחִים? 5. מִי אֲנָשִׁים?
6. מִי אִשָּׁה? 7. מִי נָשִׁים? 8. מִי גְּדוֹלָה? 9. מִי גְּדוֹלוֹת? 10. לְמִי נָשִׁים?
11. מִי נָשִׁים לְיַעֲקֹב? 12. לְמִי יָדַיִם? 13. לְמִי עֵינַיִם? 14. מַה קְּטַנָּה?

§ 5

THE ARTICLE AND THE ADJECTIVE

The article

5.1 The article is ·־הַ; i.e., prepositive הַ followed by a long consonant (one bearing within it a strong *dågeš*): הַנַּעַר "the lad."

5.2 Laryngals (א, ה, ח, ע) and ר are not normally susceptible to lengthening and hence do not normally bear strong *dågeš* in them. When the article is prefixed to a word beginning with a laryngal it is vocalized thus:

(a) If the initial consonant is א or ר, the ַ of the article is lengthened to ָ (§ 2.6) by way of compensation: הָאִישׁ "the man," הָרֶגֶל "the foot." This usually occurs with initial ע as well: הָעַיִן "the eye."

(b) If the initial consonant is ה or ח, the article remains הַ, though the laryngal does not take *dågeš*: thus הַחַיָּה "the animal."

(c) But if the initial consonant is חָ or unstressed הָ or עָ, the article is vocalized הֶ : הֶעָרִים "the cities," הֶחָכָם "the wise man."

5.3 The vocalization of מה "what?" is similar. Generally מה is closely attached to the following word and is vocalized ·מַה; e.g., מַה זֹּאת "What is this (f)?" (In the biblical text a hyphen connects מַה with the next word, making the two words a single grammatical unit.)

When the initial consonant of the following word is a laryngal or ר:

(a) If it is א or ר, the *páṯaḥ* of מה is lengthened to *qâmeṣ*; e.g., מָה רָאָה "what did he see?"

(b) If it is עָ, חָ, הָ, the vocalization is מֶה; e.g., מֶה הָיָה "what was...?"

(c) If it is ע, ח, ה with other vowels, the vocalization varies, except that before the article it is regularly מָה.

5.4 When the article is preceded by the prepositions לְ־ "to, for," בְּ־ "in," כְּ־ "like," the ה is elided and its vowel is thrown back to the preposition; thus לַנַּעַר (<לְ+הַנַּעַר) "to the lad," כָּאִישׁ (<כְּ+הָאִישׁ) "like the man," בֶּעָרִים (<בְּ+הֶעָרִים) "in the cities."

The adjective

5.5 In Hebrew, attributive adjectives follow their noun and agree with it in number and gender; moreover, if the noun has the article, the attributive must have it too.

An attributive adjective is one that, in English, stands before the noun it qualifies to denote the qualification as assumed rather than predicated. In *the big man* the adjective *big* is an attributive, as distinguished from *the man is big*, where it is a predicate adjective.

Examples of the attributive:

"a big woman"	אִשָּׁה גְּדוֹלָה	"a big man"	אִישׁ גָּדוֹל
"the big woman"	הָאִשָּׁה הַגְּדוֹלָה	"the big man"	הָאִישׁ הַגָּדוֹל
"big women"	נָשִׁים גְּדוֹלוֹת	"big men"	אֲנָשִׁים גְּדוֹלִים
"the big women"	הַנָּשִׁים הַגְּדוֹלוֹת	"the big men"	הָאֲנָשִׁים הַגְּדוֹלִים

The explanation for this thoroughgoing agreement is that the attributive adjective is really in apposition to its noun. The adjective is actually a substantive (a noun equivalent), and the phrase אִישׁ גָּדוֹל is thus literally "a man, a big one," while הָאִישׁ הַגָּדוֹל is literally "the man, the big one."

5.6 Predicate adjectives also agree with their nouns in number and gender, but they do not take the article (except where they would in English).

Examples of the predicate adjective:

"the woman is big"	הָאִשָּׁה גְּדוֹלָה	"the man is big"	הָאִישׁ גָּדוֹל
"the women are big"	הַנָּשִׁים גְּדוֹלוֹת	"the men are big"	הָאֲנָשִׁים גְּדוֹלִים

[but רְאוּבֵן הַגָּדוֹל "(it is) Reuben (who) is the big one"]

Ambiguities do remain. By itself אִישׁ גָּדוֹל can mean both "a big man" and "a man is big"; and while הָאִישׁ הַגָּדוֹל would normally be taken as "the big man," it may also mean "(it is) the man (who) is the big one." Such theoretical ambiguities are almost always resolved by the context.

* * * * * * *

house(hold)	m (pl בָּתִּים) בַּיִת	cow	(pl פָּרוֹת) פָּרָה
field	m (pl שָׂדוֹת) שָׂדֶה	good	טוֹב
father	אָב	shepherd	(pl רוֹעִים) רוֹעֶה
is not	m אֵינֶנּוּ	beau-tiful, handsome	(fpl יָפוֹת ,mpl יָפִים ,f יָפָה) יָפֶה
where?	אֵיפֹה		

in   ־בְּ

Read and translate:

1. הָאָח קָטֹן. 2. הָאַחִים הַקְּטַנִּים. 3. הַפָּרָה טוֹבָה. 4. הָרוֹעֶה טוֹב. 5. הָאִשָּׁה יָפָה. 6. הַנָּשִׁים הַיָּפוֹת בַּבַּיִת. 7. הַשָּׂדֶה הַגָּדוֹל יָפֶה. 8. הַפָּרָה בַּשָּׂדֶה. 9. הָאָב הַטּוֹב בַּבַּיִת. 10. הַשָּׂדֶה הַיָּפֶה לְיַעֲקֹב. 11. לָרוֹעִים בָּתִּים. 12. יַעֲקֹב הָאָב. 13. יַעֲקֹב אָב טוֹב. 14. הָאַחִים רוֹעִים. 15. הָרוֹעִים הַטּוֹבִים בַּשָּׂדֶה. 16. הַפָּרוֹת בַּשָּׂדֶה. 17. בִּנְיָמִין נַעַר קָטֹן וְיוֹסֵף נַעַר גָּדוֹל. 18. בִּנְיָמִין אֵינֶנּוּ בַּשָּׂדֶה וְיַעֲקֹב אֵינֶנּוּ בַּשָּׂדֶה.

19. בִּנְיָמִין וְיַעֲקֹב וְהַנָּשִׁים בַּבַּיִת. 20. הָאַחִים הַגְּדוֹלִים רוֹעִים בַּשָּׂדֶה הַיָּפֶה. 21. הָאָב יַעֲקֹב אֵינֶנּוּ רוֹעֶה.

Answer in Hebrew :

1. מִי רוֹעִים? 2. מִי אֵינֶנּוּ רוֹעֶה? 3. מִי בַּשָּׂדֶה? 4. מִי בַּבַּיִת? 5. מִי גָּדוֹל וּמִי קָטֹן? 6. אֵיפֹה הַנָּשִׁים? 7. לְמִי הַנָּשִׁים? 8. אֵיפֹה יַעֲקֹב? 9. אֵיפֹה יוֹסֵף? 10. אֵיפֹה בִּנְיָמִין? 11. מָה הָאַחִים? 12. לְמִי הַבַּיִת? 13. לְמִי בָּתִּים? 14. לְמִי הַשָּׂדֶה?

Translate :

1. The good shepherd is in a field. 2. Jacob has a beautiful house. 3. In the big house are a man and a woman. 4. The wife is good to Jacob. 5. The big man is a shepherd. 6. The small brother is good. 7. The handsome lad is in the house. 8. The shepherd has a beautiful wife.

Rewrite the preceding exercise, pluralizing all nouns and adjectives.

§ 6

THE CONSTRUCT STATE

6.1 Two nouns may be combined so that the second defines or otherwise particularizes the first (e.g., through indicating its possessor). Thus יָד "hand" may be defined by הַנַּעַר "the lad" in the combination יַד הַנַּעַר "the lad's hand." The first noun, יַד, is said to govern the second, and to be in *construction* (i.e., combination; Lat. *construere* "bring together") with it. Phonetically the two are considered one word: the first, or governing, noun loses its main stress (retaining, at best, a secondary stress), which now falls on the second, or governed, noun. Consequently, the governing noun often undergoes vowel reduction or loss. Note how the *qåmeṣ* of יָד shortens to *pataḥ* in construction. Again, when בַּיִת is in construction with, say, הָאִישׁ, as in בֵּית הָאִישׁ "the man's house," the sequence *ayi* contracts to *e* due to the shift of stress.

6.2 The governing noun, which often undergoes change, is said to be in the *construct state*; the governed noun, unchanged, is said to be in the *absolute state*. The various internal vowel changes that nouns in the construct state undergo will be treated later; here we shall note certain regular changes that occur at the end of such nouns.

(a) The feminine termination ָה becomes ַת. Example: פָּרָה "cow," פָּרַת יַעֲקֹב "Jacob's cow."

The explanation of this change is as follows: The feminine termination was originally *-aṯ*. When in final position, the *ṯ* dropped off, and the vowel was compensatorily lengthened to *å*. This final, long *å* was represented by the vowel-letter ה, later by the preceding *qåmeṣ*. Thus פָּרָה < **pårаṯ*. Now, the condition of the loss of the *ṯ* was that it be the final consonant. When *pårаṯ* was in the construct state, it was the first part of a compound word; the *ṯ*, now internal, was not dropped, and thus the original *-aṯ* termination reappears in the feminine singular construct state.

(b) The dual ַ֫יִם and the — usually masculine — plural ִים terminations become ֵי. Examples: עֵינַ֫יִם "eyes," עֵינֵי הָאִישׁ "the man's eyes"; אַחִים "brothers," אֲחֵי יוֹסֵף "Joseph's brothers."

No change occurs in the termination of masculine singular and the— usually feminine — plural termination וֹת.

6.3 A noun in the construct state does not take the definite article, because it is already defined by the noun it governs. The governed noun, on the other hand, may take the article. These, then, are the possibilities: בֵּית אִישׁ "a man's house"; בֵּית הָאִישׁ "the man's house" ("the house of the man," but also "a house of the man").

* * * * * * *

Henceforth, for nouns in which there is some irregularity, the following data will be given in parentheses and in this order: singular construct state, plural, plural construct state. Construct state forms will be followed by a hyphen.

Irregular forms of some nouns so far met with:

man	אִישׁ (אִישׁ־, אֲנָשִׁים, אַנְשֵׁי־)	father	אָב (אֲבִי־, אָבוֹת, אֲבוֹת־)
woman	אִשָּׁה (אֵשֶׁת־, נָשִׁים, נְשֵׁי־)	brother	אָח (אֲחִי־, אַחִים, אֲחֵי־)

house(hold) בַּיִת (בֵּית־, בָּתִּים, בָּתֵּי־)

New words

land	f (w art הָאָרֶץ) אֶרֶץ	these	אֵלֶּה
Canaan	כְּנַעַן	son	בֵּן (בֶּן־, בָּנִים, בְּנֵי־)
Judah	יְהוּדָה	he	הוּא
sheep (more exactly: small cattle — sheep, goats)	f צֹאן	they	m הֵם

The 3 pers pronoun is frequently used as a binder between the subject and predicate of a noun sentence; e.g., יַעֲקֹב הוּא אִישׁ "Jacob is a man."

Read and translate:

1. יַעֲקֹב הוּא אֲבִי יוֹסֵף וַאֲבִי רְאוּבֵן. 2. אֵלֶּה בְּנֵי יַעֲקֹב: רְאוּבֵן וִיהוּדָה[1] וְיוֹסֵף וּבִנְיָמִין. 3. בְּנֵי יַעֲקֹב הֵם אֲחֵי יוֹסֵף. 4. רְאוּבֵן הוּא בֶּן יַעֲקֹב. 5. הוּא רוֹעֵה צֹאן.[2] 6. בְּנֵי יַעֲקֹב הֵם רוֹעֵי צֹאן. 7. רָחֵל אֵשֶׁת יַעֲקֹב. 8. עֵינֵי רָחֵל יָפוֹת. 9. נְשֵׁי יַעֲקֹב טוֹבוֹת. 10. נְשֵׁי יַעֲקֹב בְּבֵית יַעֲקֹב. 11. בֵּית יַעֲקֹב בְּאֶרֶץ כְּנַעַן. 12. הָאָרֶץ אֶרֶץ יָפָה. 13. אֲחֵי יוֹסֵף רוֹעֵי צֹאן בְּאֶרֶץ כְּנַעַן הַיָּפָה. 14. בִּנְיָמִין אֲחִי יוֹסֵף הַקָּטֹן אֵינֶנּוּ רוֹעֶה. 15. בִּנְיָמִין הַקָּטֹן וּנְשֵׁי יַעֲקֹב בַּבַּיִת. 16. לַאֲחֵי יוֹסֵף בָּתִּים. 17. בְּבָתֵּי הָאַחִים נָשִׁים. 18. אֵשֶׁת רְאוּבֵן טוֹבָה. 19. אֵלֶּה נְשֵׁי יַעֲקֹב: רָחֵל וְלֵאָה. 20. פָּרַת אֵשֶׁת יַעֲקֹב גְּדוֹלָה. 21. פָּרוֹת הַנָּשִׁים בַּשָּׂדֶה. 22. הַצֹּאן בַּשָּׂדֶה וְהַשָּׂדֶה בָּאָרֶץ.

---

1 Note that וִי־ > וְיְ־.

2 Not a tautology. רוֹעֶה (cs רוֹעֵה) means "one who pastures" ("pastor" in the original sense); standing alone it is understood to refer to צֹאן, but the full expression is רוֹעֵה צֹאן.

Answer in Hebrew :

1. אֲבִי מִי יַעֲקֹב? 2. מִי בְּנֵי יַעֲקֹב? 3. מִי אֲחֵי יוֹסֵף? 4. מִי רוֹעֵי צֹאן?
5. מִי נְשֵׁי יַעֲקֹב? 6. לְמִי עֵינַיִם יָפוֹת? 7. אֵיפֹה נְשֵׁי יַעֲקֹב? 8. אֵיפֹה
בֵּית יַעֲקֹב? 9. אֵיפֹה רוֹעֵי הַצֹּאן? 10. מִי אֵינֶנּוּ רוֹעֶה? 11. מִי בַּבַּיִת?
12. מִי בְּבָתֵּי הָאַחִים? 13. אֵיפֹה פָּרוֹת הַנָּשִׁים? 14. אֵיפֹה הַצֹּאן?
15. אֵיפֹה הַשָּׂדֶה?

Translate :

1. Who is he? He is Joseph's father. 2. Who are they? They are Joseph's big brothers. 3. The beautiful land is the land of Canaan. 4. Judah's wife has small sons. 5. These are men of Canaan. 6. Jacob's wives have sheep. 7. The sheep of Judah's son are in the field. 8. Jacob's sons have good wives.

§ 7

PRONOUNS AND DEMONSTRATIVES

7.1 The independent personal pronouns are:

	plural			*singular*	
we	אֲנַחְנוּ, נַחְנוּ (אָנוּ)	1c	I	אֲנִי, אָנֹכִי	1c
you	אַתֶּם	2m	thou	אַתָּה	2m
you	אַתֵּן (אַתֶּן), אַתֵּנָה	2f	thou	אַתְּ	2f
they	הֵם, הֵמָּה	3m	he	הוּא	3m
they	הֵנָּה (הֵן)	3f	she	הִיא	3f

הִיא is written הִוא throughout the Pentateuch in all but eleven occurrences; the reason for this is uncertain.

Forms in parentheses are found in Postbiblical Hebrew.

The independent pronouns may be used only as subjects (or in agreement with subjects); they cannot be used as objects or with prepositions.

7.2 In addition to the independent pronouns there are pronominal suffixes, which may be attached to nouns to indicate possession or to prepositions or verbs to indicate their object. For example, the 3ms suffix וֹ־ may be attached to nouns, as in צֹאנוֹ "his sheep"; to prepositions, as in לוֹ "to him," or to verbs, as in שְׁמָרוֹ "he guarded (שָׁמַר) him."

The pronominal suffixes will be set forth in detail later.

7.3 The demonstratives are:

	plural		*singular*
these	אֵלֶּה c	this	זֶה m
			זֹאת f

The demonstratives for far objects — "that," "those" — are the 3 pers independent pronouns: הוּא, הִיא, הֵם, הֵנָּה.

The demonstratives may be used as pronouns or as adjectives.

(a) As pronouns: זֶה אִישׁ "this is a man," זֹאת אִשָּׁה "this is a woman," אֵלֶּה אֲנָשִׁים "these are men," הוּא הָאִישׁ "that is the man."

(b) As adjectives: הָאִישׁ הַזֶּה "this man," הָאִישׁ הַהוּא "that man," הָאֲנָשִׁים הָהֵם "those men" (note the *qâmeṣ* of הָהֵם). The demonstrative, as well as the noun, takes the article.

7.4 When a noun is qualified both by an attributive and a demonstrative adjective, the order is attributive–demonstrative; e.g., הָאִישׁ הַגָּדוֹל הַזֶּה "this great man."

* * * * * * *

Read and translate:

1. מִי אַתָּה? אֲנִי יַעֲקֹב אֲבִי יוֹסֵף. 2. מִי אַתֶּם? אֲנַחְנוּ בְּנֵי יַעֲקֹב. 3. מִי אַתְּ? אֲנִי אֵשֶׁת יַעֲקֹב. 4. וּמִי אַתֶּן? אֲנַחְנוּ נְשֵׁי רְאוּבֵן. 5. מִי זֶה? זֶה בִּנְיָמִין אֲחִי יוֹסֵף הַקָּטֹן. 6. מִי זֹאת? זֹאת אֵשֶׁת רְאוּבֵן הַטּוֹבָה. 7. מִי

אֵלֶּה? אֵלֶּה צֹאן יַעֲקֹב. 8. הַבָּנִים הָאֵלֶּה בְּנֵי יַעֲקֹב הֵם. 9. מִי הַנְּעָרִים
הַקְּטַנִּים הָהֵם? הֵם רוֹעֵי צֹאן יַעֲקֹב. 10. הַבָּתִּים הָאֵלֶּה וְהַשָּׂדֶה הַהוּא
לִרְאוּבֵן. 11. לְמִי הַפָּרָה הַהִיא? הִיא לִבְנֵי יַעֲקֹב. 12. אַנְשֵׁי הַבַּיִת
הַזֶּה גְּדוֹלִים הֵם וְטוֹבִים. 13. הָאָרֶץ הַיָּפָה הַזֹּאת אֶרֶץ כְּנַעַן הִיא.

Translate :

1. What are you? I am a shepherd. 2. Whose son is that? That is Jacob's son. 3. Reuben's beautiful wife is in this house. 4. The houses of the sons are in this land. 5. Those are the hands of a man, and these are the eyes of a woman. 6. Reuben has a large hand. 7. This house is not small. 8. Those sheep belong to those men. 9. That field is good for the cows. 10. Those cows have big eyes. 11. Whose cow is this? She belongs to Jacob's men.

§ 8

THE VERB

Roots

8.1 One of the chief characteristics of the Semitic languages is that roots of three consonants, expressing some general idea, are the basis of most words. By means of fixed vowel patterns and formative elements the root is embodied in words particularizing aspects and nuances of the root idea. (In the language itself of course we meet only the words from which the root is a grammatical abstraction.)

Thus the root פתח "opening" is embodied in the words פָּתַח "he opened," נִפְתַּח "he (it) was opened," פֶּתַח "doorway."

The root שקל "weight" is embodied in the words שָׁקַל "he weighed," נִשְׁקַל "he was weighed," שֶׁקֶל "a *shekel* weight," מִשְׁקָל "weight."

The root שמר "guarding" is embodied in the words שָׁמַר "he guarded," נִשְׁמַר "he was guarded, he guarded himself," מִשְׁמָר "guardhouse, jail."

8.2 There is also a large number of biconsonantal roots, from which are derived the "hollow" verbs (§ 17) — verbs having a long vowel between their two root consonants. These roots exhibit the same patterning; e.g., from קוּם "standing, arising" are derived קָם "he stood, arose," מָקוֹם "place" (lit., "where one stands"); from בּוֹא "coming" are derived בָּא "he came," מָבוֹא "entrance."

Verb patterns

8.3 The first word of each series in § 8.1 — פָּתַח, שָׁקַל, שָׁמַר — illustrates one verb pattern, active in meaning. The second word of each series — נִפְתַּח, נִשְׁקַל, נִשְׁמַר — illustrates another, passive (and, in the case of נִשְׁמַר, reflexive) in meaning. Note that besides the internal vowel difference the passive pattern augments the root with a preformative נ.

Other verb patterns are seen in סִפֵּר "he recounted, told" and its passive סֻפַּר "(it) was recounted." These patterns have an internal augment in the lengthening of the middle root consonant (indicated by the *dåḡeš*). The pattern of הִתְאַפֵּק "he restrained himself" — reflexive in meaning — shows the same internal augment and a preformative הִתְ besides. The patterns of הִזְכִּיר "he reminded" and its passive הָזְכַּר (*hŏzkar*) "he was reminded" have a preformative ה as an augment.

These patterns may be grouped according to their form and interrelationship thus:

III	II	I	
הִזְכִּיר	סִפֵּר	שָׁמַר	active
הָזְכַּר	סֻפַּר	נִשְׁמַר	passive
	הִתְאַפֵּק	נִשְׁמַר	reflexive

For convenience the patterns have been given names: The שָׁמַר pattern, since it is wholly unaugmented, is called קַל *qal* "light" (i.e., "unencumbered"). For the rest, the model root פעל ("acting") is articulated with the vowels and augments of each pattern, the resulting forms being the names of the patterns. Thus נִשְׁמַר belongs to the נִפְעַל

nif'al pattern, סִפֵּר to the פִּעֵל *pi'el*,[1] הִזְכִּיר to the הִפְעִיל *hif'il*, and so on. The system of Hebrew verb patterns is, then, as follows:

hif'il group	*pi'el* group	*qal* group	
הִפְעִיל (הִזְכִּיר)	פִּעֵל (סִפֵּר)	קַל (שָׁמַר)	active
הָפְעַל (הָזְכַּר)	פֻּעַל (סֻפַּר)	נִפְעַל[2] (נִשְׁמַר)	passive
	הִתְפַּעֵל (הִתְאַפֵּק)	נִפְעַל (נִשְׁמַר)	reflexive

Very few verbal roots actually appear in all patterns.

The interrelation of members within each group is clear; it remains only to indicate the relation of *pi'el* and *hif'il* to *qal*.

8.4 Roughly speaking the relation is this: In the *pi'el*, the verbal idea of the *qal* is made more complex or given a special nuance; *qal* סָפַר "he counted," *pi'el* סִפֵּר "he recounted, told" [compare early English "tell" = count (as in "teller"), modern English "tell" = recount].

The *hif'il* is commonly causative: the subject makes the object do the action or be in the state expressed by the *qal* verb; *qal* זָכַר "he remembered," *hif'il* הִזְכִּיר "he reminded" (lit., "made remember").

Comparable in English are "lie" (שָׁכַב), "lay" (הִשְׁכִּיב); "fall" (נָפַל), "fell" (הִפִּיל < הִנְפִּיל*).

8.5 Other, less common, patterns exist, of which the by-forms of the *pi'el* group appearing with biconsonantal and otherwise irregular roots are the most important. כִּלְכֵּל "he sustained" (root כול) illustrates the *pilpel* pattern, a by-form of *pi'el* found with some hollow verbs. הִתְגּוֹלֵל "he found a pretext" (root גלל) illustrates the *hiṯpolel* pattern, a by-form of *hiṯpa'el* found with some geminate (§30) and hollow verbs.

---

1 Since the laryngal ע is not susceptible to lengthening (cf. § 5.2), the lengthened middle root consonant of *pi'el* cannot be indicated in the name.

2 Originally the passive of *qal* was expressed by a *pu'al* form (presumably distinguished from the *pu'al* passive of *pi'el* by its short middle consonant); thus שֻׁמַר* "he was guarded," נִשְׁמַר "he guarded himself." This *qal* passive survives only rudimentarily in Biblical Hebrew, and in most cases is vocalized as the passive of *pi'el*.

* * * * * * *

Identify the root and verb pattern of the following verbs:

1. הָלַךְ 2. נִבְהַל 3. הִשְׁלִיךְ 4. חִפֵּשׂ 5. נִכְמַר 6. גֻּנַּב 7. בִּקֵּשׁ 8. אָהַב
9. הִפְשִׁיט 10. סִפֵּר 11. יָדַע 12. הִתְחַנֵּן 13. הִרְחִיק 14. דִּבֵּר
15. הִתְאַבֵּל 16. לָקַח 17. נִשְׁאַר 18. מִלֵּא 19. הִתְנַפֵּל 20. הִשְׁבִּיר.

In the following verbs there are some irregularities, owing to the presence of a laryngal or a weak consonant (א, ה) *; identify the verb pattern:*

1. מָצָא 2. נִמְצָא 3. נִחֵשׁ 4. שִׁלַּח 5. נֶאֱמַן 6. הֶאֱמִין 7. הֶחֱיָה 8. עָלָה
9. כִּלָּה 10. הִתְנַחֵם 11. מֵאֵן 12. הִתְרָאָה 13. נֶאֱסַר 14. חָטָא
15. עָשָׂה 16. הִתְוַדַּע.

Supply the meaning:

________	נִשְׁמַע	:	he heard	שָׁמַע
________	הִשְׁמִיעַ	:	he heard	"
________	הִפְשִׁיט	:	he undressed (intr.)	פָּשַׁט
________	נִמְכַּר	:	he sold	מָכַר
________	הִמְלִיךְ	:	he was king	מָלַךְ
________	בֻּקַּשׁ	:	he sought	בִּקֵּשׁ
________	(*hif'il*)הוֹרִיד	:	he went down	יָרַד
________	נִבְחַן	:	he tested	בָּחַן
________	הָשְׁלַךְ	:	he threw	הִשְׁלִיךְ
________	סֻפַּר	:	he narrated	סִפֵּר
________	הִתְנַחֵם	:	he consoled	נִחַם
________	הִתְמַלֵּא	:	he filled	מִלֵּא
________	(*hif'il*) הֵבִיא	:	he came	(*qal*) בָּא[3]
________	(*hif'il*) הֵמִית	:	he died	(*qal*) מֵת
________	(*hif'il*) הֵשִׁיב	:	he came back	(*qal*)שָׁב

(*To be followed by Reading 1, p. 139.*)

---

3 This and the following two verbs derive from hollow roots (§ 8.2).

§ 9

QAL PERFECT

Active and stative roots

9.1 The *qal* expresses the verbal idea of the root in its simplest sense; thus from ישׁב "sitting," יָשַׁב "he sat"; from אהב "loving," אָהַב "he loved"; and from שׁמר "guarding," שָׁמַר "he guarded."

9.2 These roots all convey the idea of some activity. There are, however, roots denoting quality or state. Verbs derived from such roots are *stative*, as opposed to *active* verbs derived from active roots. So, for example, from זקן "agedness," זָקֵן "he was/became aged"; from כבד "heaviness," כָּבֵד "he was/became heavy"; from קטן "smallness," קָטֹן "he was/became small." Stative verbs are in reality nothing but adjectives inflected verbally.

The perfect

9.3 Each verb pattern has two aspects: a *perfect* and an *imperfect.*[1] The perfect (used in the sense of Lat. *perfectus*, "carried through to the

[1] These are commonly called "tenses"; but "tense" is here a misnomer, since the perfect and imperfect do not denote *time* of action or state so much as *type* of action or state. See ahead in the text and §10.1.

end, finished") denotes action that is completed and over with, or a state achieved and complete. It generally corresponds to English past tenses and is conventionally rendered by the English past, though the precise nuance depends on the context.

Often, especially with statives, the perfect denotes the English present perfect or the present; i.e., it is expressive of an accomplished act or state whose effect is presently felt or apparent. Thus כָּבֵד may also be rendered "he has become/is heavy."

9.4 The *qal* perfect has an active form — שָׁמַר "he guarded," with *páṯaḥ* as the second vowel — and two stative forms — כָּבֵד "he was heavy" and קָטֹן "he was small," with *ṣére* and *ḥólɛm*, respectively, as second vowel. This, the 3ms, is called the *groundform*. The inflectional elements are affixed to the end of the groundform; they are *afformatives*.

The *qal* perfect:

singular

1c	שָׁמַרְתִּי	כָּבַדְתִּי	קָטֹנְתִּי
2m	שָׁמַרְתָּ	כָּבַדְתָּ	קָטֹנְתָּ
2f	שָׁמַרְתְּ	כָּבַדְתְּ	קָטֹנְתְּ
3m	שָׁמַר	כָּבֵד	קָטֹן
3f	שָׁמְרָה	כָּבְדָה	קָטְנָה

plural

1c	שָׁמַרְנוּ	כָּבַדְנוּ	קָטֹנּוּ (=*קָטֹנְנוּ)
2m	שְׁמַרְתֶּם	כְּבַדְתֶּם	קְטָנְתֶּם (-ṭŏn-)
2f	שְׁמַרְתֶּן	כְּבַדְתֶּן	קְטָנְתֶּן (-ṭŏn-)
3c	שָׁמְרוּ	כָּבְדוּ	קָטְנוּ

(a) Note that the *ṣére*-stative is identical with the active except in the groundform. The *ḥólɛm*-stative, on the other hand, retains its characteristic vowel throughout the 1 and 2 pers.

(b) Afformatives made up of one consonant are not stressed; the stress remains on the second syllable, as in the groundform. But the "heavy," biconsonantal afformatives of 2mpl and 2fpl (־תֶּם, ־תֶּן) are stressed. Consequently, in these forms the *qâmeṣ* of the first syllable is slurred to mobile *šewâ*. Moreover, in the *ḥólɛm*-stative, the now unstressed *ḥólɛm* is shortened to *qâmeṣ ḥâṭuf*.

(c) The afformatives of the 1cpl ־נוּ, 2ms ־תָּ, 2fs ־תְּ, 2mpl ־תֶּם, and 2fpl ־תֶּן are identical with the terminations of the corresponding independent pronouns. The afformative of the 1cs ־תִּי may be derived from the *-ki* of אָנֹכִי with $k > t$ under the influence of the 2 pers afformatives. The 3 pers afformatives are noun terminations: ־ָה for fs, and ־וּ for the pl (an old plural termination of nouns).

* * * * * * *

Conjugate:

יָשַׁב, זָקֵן, יָכֹל "be able."

Complete with the correct perfect form of the indicated verb:

שָׁמַר: 1. אַתֶּם ____ אֶת הַצֹּאן. 2. רָחֵל וְלֵאָה ____ אֶת הַנְּעָרִים. 3. אֲנַחְנוּ ____ אֹתוֹ.
יָשַׁב: 4. אַתְּ ____ בַּבַּיִת. 5. רָחֵל ____ בְּבֵית יַעֲקֹב. 6. יַעֲקֹב וּבִנְיָמִין ____ בַּבַּיִת.
אָהַב: 7. אֲנִי ____ אֶת הַבֵּן. 8. אַתָּה ____ אֶת הַדָּבָר. 9. אֲנַחְנוּ ____ אֶת הָאָרֶץ.
שָׂנֵא: 10. הִיא ____ כָּל רָע. 11. אֲחֵי יוֹסֵף ____ אֹתוֹ.
זָקֵן: 12. אַתֶּם ____. 13. לֵאָה ____. 14. אֲנַחְנוּ ____.
כָּבֵד: 15. הָאִישׁ ____ מִן הָאִשָּׁה. 16. הַנָּשִׁים ____. 17. יַד הָאָב ____ עַל הַבֵּן.

Change the number of the subjects in the preceding exercise and complete again.

Vocalize and translate:

1. הנשים ישבו בבית כי זקנו. 2. שמרתם את הצאן מכל רע.
3. אהבנו את הארץ. 4. ידי האיש כבדו כי זקן. 5. הדבר קטן בעיני

האיש. 6. לאה, עם מי ישבת? 7. ישבה אשת הרועה ושמרה את
כל בניו. 8. שנאו את הדבר הרע ההוא. 9. לא הגיד לו איפה ישב
כי שנא אתו.

(*To be followed by Reading 3, p. 141.*)

§ 10

QAL IMPERFECT AND RELATED FORMS

10.1 The imperfect aspect expresses action or state as unaccomplished, continuing, or customary. It corresponds generally to English present and future: יִשְׁמֹר "he guards, will guard." When expressing continuity or custom (e.g., Genesis 44:5 זֶה אֲשֶׁר יִשְׁתֶּה אֲדֹנִי בּוֹ "this is (the very one) from which my lord *always drinks*"), it may refer to the past as well (e.g., Judges 21:25 אִישׁ הַיָּשָׁר בְּעֵינָיו יַעֲשֶׂה "every man *used to do* as he pleased").

10.2 Occasionally (especially in poetry) the imperfect is used as a simple past tense, like the perfect. In all likelihood this is due to the coalescence with the imperfect of a distinct preterit form found in Akkadian. A far more important survival of this preterit is the so-called *imperfect consecutive* (see §16).

10.3 The imperfect also expresses that which may, could, should, is wished, or is supposed to be. For example: Genesis 37:8 הֲ... תִּמְלֹךְ עָלֵינוּ "Do... *you mean to be king* over us?"; 37:10 הֲ... נָבוֹא "*Are...*

we supposed to come?"; 43:7 הֲ... נֵדַע כִּי יֹאמַר "*Could... we have known* that he would say"; 44:8 וְאֵיךְ נִגְנֹב "How, then, *could we steal?*"

10.4 The inflectional elements of the imperfect are attached to the beginning (*preformatives*) and the end (*afformatives*) of the verb form.

The imperfect of active verbs has *ḥólɛm* as its second, thematic vowel (יִשְׁמֹר "he will guard"). The thematic vowel of both statives is *páṯaḥ* (יִכְבַּד "he will be heavy," יִקְטַן "he will be small").

The *qal* imperfect:

plural				singular			
נִקְטַן	נִכְבַּד	נִשְׁמֹר	1c	אֶקְטַן	אֶכְבַּד	אֶשְׁמֹר	1c
תִּקְטְנוּ	תִּכְבְּדוּ	תִּשְׁמְרוּ	2m	תִּקְטַן	תִּכְבַּד	תִּשְׁמֹר	2m
(=תִּקְטַנְּנָה)[1] תִּקְטַנָּה	תִּכְבַּדְנָה	תִּשְׁמֹרְנָה	2f	תִּקְטְנִי	תִּכְבְּדִי	תִּשְׁמְרִי	2f
יִקְטְנוּ	יִכְבְּדוּ	יִשְׁמְרוּ	3m	יִקְטַן	יִכְבַּד	יִשְׁמֹר	3m
תִּקְטַנָּה	תִּכְבַּדְנָה	תִּשְׁמֹרְנָה	3f	תִּקְטַן	תִּכְבַּד	תִּשְׁמֹר	3f

(a) The preformatives of the 1 and 2 pers are either the initial (א־) or characteristic consonant (נ־, ת־) of the corresponding independent pronouns. The preformative of 3m (י־) is of uncertain origin. That of 3f is probably the same as the *t* of the original feminine noun termination [§ 6.2(a)].

(b) To distinguish 2fs from 2ms, an old feminine termination ־ִי [which appeared also in the original form of the 2fs independent pronoun אתי* (*'atti*) as in the written text of II Kings 4:16, 23] is employed. The 2 and 3mpl are distinguished from their respective singulars by the old plural noun termination ־וּ, which also appears in the pf 3cpl. The 2 and 3fpl are distinguished from their respective singulars by the afformative ־נָה, found also in the corresponding independent pronouns אַתֵּנָה, הֵנָּה.

---

1 Cf. § 2.10(b)1.

The cohortative, the jussive, and negative commands

10.5 The *cohortative* expresses volition on the part of the 1 pers: אֶשְׁמְרָה "let me guard!" "I would (fain) guard," נִשְׁמְרָה "let's guard!" Its form is the impf 1 pers with *paragogic* (i.e., protracting) ־ָה.

Thus:

plural				*singular*		
נִקְטְנָה	נִכְבְּדָה	נִשְׁמְרָה		אֶקְטְנָה	אֶכְבְּדָה	אֶשְׁמְרָה

10.6 The *jussive* expresses volition concerning the 2 or 3 pers: תִּשְׁמֹר "may you (ms) guard!" יִשְׁמֹר "may he (let him) guard." In *qal* of the regular verb the jussive forms are identical with the impf 2 and 3 pers.

10.7 Negative commands are expressed by אַל with the jussive: אַל תִּשְׁמֹר "don't guard!" אַל יִשְׁמֹר "may he (let him) not guard!"

The imperative

10.8 Positive commands are expressed by the imperative. The imv ms is generally identical with the base to which the preformatives of the imperfect are attached, and may be derived by removing the ־תּ preformative of the 2ms, thus (תִּ)שְׁמֹר. The rest of the forms follow closely the impf 2 pers.

plural				*singular*		
כִּבְדוּ	שִׁמְרוּ	m		כְּבַד	שְׁמֹר	m
כְּבַדְנָה	שְׁמֹרְנָה	f		כִּבְדִי	שִׁמְרִי	f

Imperatives do not occur for קָטֹן-type statives.

10.9 The imv ms is often found with paragogic ־ָה; e.g., שִׁלְחָה, lengthened from שְׁלַח "send!" Originally the lengthened form expressed emphasis or urgency, but this is no longer evident in many cases.

* * * * * * *

Conjugate in the qal *imperfect and imperative:*

זָקֵן, מָלַךְ.

Complete with the imperfect of the indicated verbs:

שָׁמַר: 1. הַבֵּן ____ אֶת הָאֲלֻמּוֹת. 2. אַתָּה ____ אֶת הָאַחִים.
3. הָאִשָּׁה ____ אֶת הַדָּבָר.

מָלַךְ: 4. יוֹסֵף ____ עַל אֶחָיו. 5. אַל ____ אִשָּׁה עַל הָאָרֶץ!
6. אֲנִי ____ עַל כָּל הָאֲנָשִׁים.

זָקֵן: 7. הָאֵם ____. 8. הָאָב ____. 9. אַתְּ ____.

כָּבֵד: 10. יַד הַזָּקֵן ____. 11. הָאִישׁ ____ מִן הָאִשָּׁה.
12. אַתָּה ____.

Change subjects and verbs of the above to plural and complete again (pl of אֵם *is* אִמּוֹת*).*

Vocalize and translate:

1. חלמתי חלום על השמש. 2. אמך מלכה עלינו. 3. הנה הנער אשר שמר את הצאן. 4. אחיך שמרו את הבתים. 5. את שמרת את בניו מכל רע. 6. זקנו עוד. 7. יד האיש אשר מלך כבדה עלינו. 8. לא שמרתם את השדה.

Change above verbs to imperfect.

Change the following negative commands to positive ones (i.e., imperatives):

1. אַל תִּשְׁמֹר![2] 2. אַל תִּמְלְכִי! 3. אַל תִּכְבְּדוּ! 4. אַל תִּמְלֹךְ! 5. אַל

2 Hereafter in the Hebrew exercises imperatives (positive and negative) will be indicated by an exclamation mark.

תִּזְקַן! 6. אַל תִּזְקְנוּ! 7. אַל תִּשְׁמֹרְנָה! 8. אַל תִּשְׁמְרִי! 9. אַל
תִּכְבַּדְנָה! 10. אַל תִּכְבְּדִי! 11. אַל תִּמְלְכוּ! 12. אַל תִּשְׁמְרוּ!

(*To be followed by Reading 5, p. 144.*)

§ 11

QAL INFINITIVE AND PARTICIPLE

The infinitive absolute

11.1 There are two infinitives, an absolute and a construct. The infinitive absolute takes the form שָׁמוֹר[1]; it is commonly used to add some sort of emphasis to the finite verb, which immediately follows it. For example, in Genesis 37:8 הֲמָלֹךְ תִּמְלֹךְ עָלֵינוּ אִם מָשׁוֹל תִּמְשֹׁל בָּנוּ "Do you *really* mean to be king over us? Do you *really* mean to rule us?" The two infinitives absolute express the indignation of the brothers over Joseph's pretentious dreams. Similarly 37:10 הֲבוֹא נָבוֹא "Are we *actually* supposed to come?...." Other kinds of emphasis: 43:7 שָׁאוֹל שָׁאַל הָאִישׁ "The man inquired *closely*"; הֲיָדוֹעַ נֵדַע "Could we *possibly* have known"; 37:33 טָרֹף טֹרַף[2] יוֹסֵף "Joseph *must* have been torn to pieces."

---

1 Often written defectively (i.e., without the vowel letter, see § 2.3) as in some of the following examples. (The infinitive absolute of the biconsonantal roots is like בּוֹא.)

2 A rare example of old passive *qal* (§ 8.3, note 2).

The infinitive construct

11.2 Whereas the infinitive absolute is not inflected or commonly brought into grammatical construction with other words in the sentence,[3] the infinitive construct is. It is a verbal noun, the name of the action or state expressed by the verb, having the form שְׁמֹר "(the act of) guarding" in the *qal* regular verb. [Statives, too, generally have *ḥōlɛm* in the infinitive construct, notwithstanding their *a*-vowel in the imperfect; e.g., שְׂנֹא "(the state/act of) hating" from יִשְׂנָא—שָׂנֵא.] Like all nouns, the infinitive construct may govern another noun (שְׁמֹר הָאִישׁ "the man's guarding," בּוֹא יוֹסֵף "Joseph's coming") and take pronominal suffixes (שָׁמְרוֹ "his guarding," בּוֹאִי "my coming") and prepositions (כְּבוֹאִי "at my coming" = "when I come"). Most commonly it appears with לְ־ in the form לִשְׁמֹר, employed just like the English infinitive "to guard."

The participles

11.3 The active participle has the form שׁוֹמֵר "(one) guarding"; the statives, כָּבֵד "heavy" and יָכֹל "able." Stative participles are pure adjectives.

The participle inflects like any noun or adjective:

	singular			*plural*		
m	שׁוֹמֵר	כָּבֵד	יָכֹל[4]	שׁוֹמְרִים	כְּבֵדִים	יְכֹלִים
f	שׁוֹמֶרֶת (שׁוֹמְרָה)	כְּבֵדָה	יְכֹלָה	שׁוֹמְרוֹת	כְּבֵדוֹת	יְכֹלוֹת

---

[3] With some exceptions; e.g., when it is used as an imperative: שָׁמוֹר אֶת יוֹם הַשַּׁבָּת (Deuteronomy 5:12) "Keep the Sabbath day."

[4] Since קָטֹן does not inflect regularly it is here replaced by יָכֹל.

11.4 Being a verbal adjective, the active participle has the qualities both of a verb and of an adjective. Like an adjective, it may be used as an attributive or in the predicate; e.g., הָאִישׁ הַשּׁוֹמֵר "the guarding man" ("the man who is guarding"); הָאִישׁ שׁוֹמֵר "the man is guarding." And just as an adjective may be used substantivally (הַגָּדוֹל "the big one"), so may a participle: הַשּׁוֹמֵר "the guard" (lit., "the guarding one"). As a substantive, it may be in construct with a following noun, שׁוֹמֵר הָאִישׁ "the man's guard" ("the one guarding the man"), or take pronominal suffixes, שׁוֹמְרוֹ "his guard."

Like a verb, the participle may govern an object; e.g., יוֹסֵף שׁוֹמֵר אֶת הַצֹּאן "Joseph is guarding the sheep."

The use of רוֹעֶה illustrates the substantival and verbal sides of the participle: in יוֹסֵף רוֹעֶה "Joseph is a shepherd," the substantival; in יוֹסֵף רוֹעֶה אֶת הַצֹּאן "Joseph is tending the sheep," the verbal.

11.5 Active verbs have a passive participle, which inflects thus: ms שָׁמוּר "guarded," fs שְׁמוּרָה, mpl שְׁמוּרִים, fpl שְׁמוּרוֹת.

* * * * * * *

Complete with active or stative participle of indicated verb:

מָצָא: 1. יוֹסֵף ______ אֶת אֶחָיו. 2. הָרוֹעִים ______ אֶת הַצֹּאן. 3. הַנָּשִׁים ______ אֶת בְּנוֹ.

הָלַךְ: 4. אֵשֶׁת יַעֲקֹב ______ אֶל הַבַּיִת. 5. הֵן ______ אֶל הַשָּׂדֶה. 6. בְּנֵי יַעֲקֹב ______ שְׁכֶמָה.

אָהֵב: 7. טוֹב הָאִישׁ הָ______ שָׁלוֹם. 8. טוֹבָה הָאִשָּׁה הָ______ אֶת הָאִישׁ הַהוּא.

זָקֵן: 9. הָאִשָּׁה ______. 10. הַנָּשִׁים הַ______ בַּבַּיִת. 11. אַחַי ______.

מָלַךְ: 12. נְעָרִים ______ עָלֵינוּ. 13. הָאִשָּׁה הַ______ טוֹבָה. 14. רַע הָאִישׁ הַ______ עַל הָאָרֶץ.

Complete with passive participle of verb in the first clause:

1. הוּא שׂוֹנֵא[5] אֶת הָאִישׁ; הָאִישׁ ______. 2. לוֹקְחִים אֶת הָאִשָּׁה; הָאִשָּׁה
______. 3. שׁוֹמְרִים אֶת הַדָּבָר; הַדָּבָר ______. 4. הָאֵם שׁוֹמֶרֶת
אֶת בָּנָיו; בָּנָיו ______. 5. לוֹקְחִים אֶת הַפָּרוֹת; הַפָּרוֹת ______.

In the preceding exercise change the number of the object of the first clause and complete again.

Vocalize and translate:

1. אני הולך למצא את אחי. 2. אמרנו לך לשאל אתו. 3. שמענו
אתו אומר: אני הולך אל ביתו. 4. כאשר ראו היושבים את הזקן
בא, קמו מעל הארץ. 5. שומעים אנחנו כי (that) תמלך עלינו.
6. אני אוהבת לשאל. 7. החולם חלומות כל היום איננו אהוב.
8. תמצאו את בעל הבית בשדה עם אחיו. 9. האיש המבקש שלום
הוא המוצא אתו. 10. טוב לשנא את הרע. 11. אחד מבניו בקש
למלך. 12. הצאן הולכות משדה אל שדה. 13. הם לוקחים בית
בעמק היפה ההוא.

(*To be followed by Reading 7, p. 146.*)

5 Although שָׂנֵא—יִשְׂנָא is a stative, like other statives expressing a relational (transitive) state ("be hostile toward") it is often construed actively (הוּא שָׂנֵא אוֹתוֹ "he hated him"), and its participle takes the active form שׂוֹנֵא.

§ 12
THE PI'EL

12.1 The *pi'el* serves to modify the meaning of *qal* in a number of ways, the precise modification in any given case being unpredictable. The *pi'el* meaning may be more complex or somehow more intensive than that of *qal* (hence the usual styling of *pi'el* as the "intensive" stem); e.g., *qal* סָפַר "he counted," *pi'el* סִפֵּר "he recounted, narrated"; *qal* שָׁלַח "he sent," *pi'el* שִׁלַּח "he let go, released."

Frequently *pi'el* has a causative sense, especially with stative roots; e.g., *qal* מָלֵא "he was full," *pi'el* מִלֵּא "he filled"; *qal* כָּלָה "he came to an end," *pi'el* כִּלָּה "he finished, made an end of"; *qal* שָׁכֹל "he was bereaved," *pi'el* שִׁכֵּל "he bereaved."

Pi'el is the favored stem for denominative verbs (i.e., verbs made out of nouns); e.g., אִלֵּם "he made a sheaf" (אֲלֻמָּה); נִחֵשׁ "he practiced divination" (נַחַשׁ).

Some *pi'el* verbs have no *qal* to which they stand in relation; e.g., בִּקֵּשׁ "he sought," צִוָּה "he ordered."

12.2 The formal characteristic of the *pi'el* (and the rest of its group) is the lengthening of the second root consonant (indicated by strong *dågeš*).

The *piʿel* סִפֵּר "he recounted":

INFINITIVE ABSOLUTE

סַפֵּר, סַפֹּר

INFINITIVE CONSTRUCT

(לְ)סַפֵּר

PARTICIPLE

מְסַפֵּר	ms
מְסַפֶּרֶת	f
מְסַפְּרִים	mpl
מְסַפְּרוֹת	f

COHORTATIVE[1]

אֲסַפְּרָה	s
נְסַפְּרָה	pl

IMPERATIVE

סַפֵּר	ms
סַפְּרִי	f
סַפְּרוּ	mpl
סַפֵּרְנָה	f

IMPERFECT		PERFECT	
אֲסַפֵּר	1cs	סִפַּרְתִּי	1cs
תְּסַפֵּר	2m	סִפַּרְתָּ	2m
תְּסַפְּרִי	2f	סִפַּרְתְּ	2f
יְסַפֵּר	3m	סִפֵּר	3m
תְּסַפֵּר	3f	סִפְּרָה	3f
נְסַפֵּר	1cpl	סִפַּרְנוּ	1cpl
תְּסַפְּרוּ	2m	סִפַּרְתֶּם	2m
תְּסַפֵּרְנָה	2f	סִפַּרְתֶּן	2f
יְסַפְּרוּ	3m	סִפְּרוּ	3c
תְּסַפֵּרְנָה	3f		

The pf 3ms often has ַ for its second vowel, e.g., שִׁלַּם "he repaid," נִחַם "he consoled, comforted." The *sɛgol* of דִּבֶּר "he spoke" is anomalous [דִּבֵּר only in pause; see § 29.1(e)].

12.3 The passive of *piʿel* is *puʿal*, the skeleton paradigm of which is: pf 3ms סֻפַּר; impf 3ms יְסֻפַּר; pt ms מְסֻפָּר.

* * * * * * *

Conjugate:

נִחַם, בִּקֵּשׁ.

When the second root consonant is a laryngal it does not receive a *dågeš*. If it is ח, as in נִחַם, usually no change in the preceding vowel takes place. In forms in which the second consonant would normally take *šewå*, the laryngal takes *ḥaṭåf páṭaḥ*; e.g., pf 3cpl נִחֲמוּ, impf 3mpl יְנַחֲמוּ.

---

1 Jussive forms are the same as the impf 2 and 3 pers.

Fill in the perfect, imperfect, and participle of the indicated verbs:

סִפֵּר: 1. הַבָּנוֹת ______ לוֹ אֶת הַחֲלוֹם. 2. אַתֶּם ______ אֶת כָּל
אֲשֶׁר עָשָׂה.
בִּקֵּשׁ: 3. אֲנַחְנוּ ______ אֶת אָחִינוּ. 4. הֵם ______ לִמְכֹּר אֶת הַשָּׂעִיר.
נִחַם: 5. בְּנוֹת הַזָּקֵן ______ אֹתוֹ. 6. אַתֶּן ______ אֹתָהּ יָמִים רַבִּים.

Change verbs and subjects in the preceding exercise to singular.

Translate:

1. Seek (fs) the valley and you will find it. 2. If we relate the dream, will you (mpl) listen or not? 3. Don't sell a slaughtered he-goat. 4. Relate (fpl) to me what you heard when you sat inside the house. 5. If you love (pt ms) her, comfort her. 6. When you (mpl) asked her why she did not go, what did the daughter say?

Vocalize and translate:

1. כאשר לא היה מה לאכל נתנו את השעיר לשוחט לשחט. 2. יבקשו את הדם ולא ימצאו אתו. 3. אנשים רעים השליכו את הפרה בבור; אנשים טובים העלו אתה משם. 4. השוחט את פרתו לא ימכר אתה. 5. לא שמעתי מה שאל האיש. 6. באו ימים טובים והיה שלום לכל יושבי הארץ. 7. לא הכיר הזקן את בניו. 8. שאלנו את האב השבו בנותיו אם לא.

(*To be followed by Reading 9, p. 148.*)

§ 13
THE HIF'IL

13.1 The *hif'il* serves, in the first place, as the causative of *qal*. Thus: *qal* פָּשַׁט "he took off (his garment)," *hif'il* הִפְשִׁיט "he stripped (someone else of his garment)," lit., "made (him) take off"; מָלַךְ "he was king," הִמְלִיךְ "he made king"; בָּא "he came," הֵבִיא "he brought," lit., "made come"; שָׁב "he came back," הֵשִׁיב "he brought/gave back"; מֵת "he died," הֵמִית "he put to death."

Hif'il verbs derived from statives have an elative meaning: רָחַק "he went far," הִרְחִיק "he went very far."

Related to the causative meaning of *hif'il* is the estimative or declarative: אָמֵן "he was true, firm," הֶאֱמִין "he considered true, believed."

Some *hif'il* verbs have no *qal* to which they stand in relation; e.g., הִשְׁלִיךְ "he threw."

13.2 The prepositive ה, which is the characteristic of *hif'il*, appears in the perfect, imperative, and infinitives. In the imperfect and participle it is elided after the preformatives: יַשְׁלִיךְ < *יְהַשְׁלִיךְ; מַשְׁלִיךְ < *מְהַשְׁלִיךְ.

The *hif'il* הִשְׁלִיךְ "he threw":

INFINITIVE ABSOLUTE	COHORTATIVE	IMPERFECT	PERFECT
הַשְׁלֵךְ	אַשְׁלִיכָה s	אַשְׁלִיךְ 1cs	הִשְׁלַכְתִּי 1cs
	נַשְׁלִיכָה pl	תַּשְׁלִיךְ 2m	הִשְׁלַכְתָּ 2m
INFINITIVE CONSTRUCT		תַּשְׁלִיכִי 2f	הִשְׁלַכְתְּ 2f
(לְ)הַשְׁלִיךְ	JUSSIVE	יַשְׁלִיךְ 3m	הִשְׁלִיךְ 3m
	יַשְׁלֵךְ 3ms	תַּשְׁלִיךְ 3f	הִשְׁלִיכָה 3f
PARTICIPLE		נַשְׁלִיךְ 1cpl	הִשְׁלַכְנוּ 1cpl
מַשְׁלִיךְ ms	IMPERATIVE	תַּשְׁלִיכוּ 2m	הִשְׁלַכְתֶּם 2m
מַשְׁלֶכֶת f	הַשְׁלֵךְ ms	תַּשְׁלֵכְנָה 2f	הִשְׁלַכְתֶּן 2f
מַשְׁלִיכִים mpl	הַשְׁלִיכִי f	יַשְׁלִיכוּ 3m	הִשְׁלִיכוּ 3c
מַשְׁלִיכוֹת f	הַשְׁלִיכוּ mpl	תַּשְׁלֵכְנָה 3f	
	הַשְׁלֵכְנָה f		

13.3 The passive of *hif'il* is *hŏf'al* (*huf'al*), the skeleton paradigm of which is: pf 3ms הָשְׁלַךְ; impf 3ms יָשְׁלַךְ; pt מֻשְׁלָךְ.

The first vowel varies between (the original) *u* and its phonetic variant *ŏ*. In the participle it is usually *u*.

* * * * * * *

Conjugate:

הִכִּיר, הִגִּיד, הִפְשִׁיט.

The last two verbs are derived from נגד and נכר, respectively. In *hif'il* the נ assimilates to the following consonant, which is, consequently, lengthened [§2.10(b)2]. The vowel pattern remains unchanged.

Complete with perfect, imperfect, and participle of the indicated verbs:

הִמְלִיךְ: 1. הַמִּצְרִים ______ אֶת פַּרְעֹה. 2. אַתֶּם ______ אֶת הַשָּׂר.

הִכִּיר: 3. אֲנַחְנוּ ______ אֶת הַמָּקוֹם. 4. הֵנָּה ______ אֶת פְּנֵי הָעֶבֶד.

הִגִּיד: 5. הַבָּנוֹת ______ אֶת הַדָּבָר. 6. הַשָּׂרִים ______ לַמֶּלֶךְ.

Change verbs and subjects of the preceding exercise into the singular.

Translate:

1. Don't tell (ms) the king what you know (pt) about that place. 2. You (mpl) won't recognize him at night. 3. The wicked king will throw many officers into the pit. 4. Just as you (fs) told me, so it was. 5. In the morning you (fs) will recognize the face of the mother. 6. Tell (ms) me, what will you seek there? 7. I shall seek to become familiar with (recognize) the houses of the place. 8. We told them that we recognized the blood that was on the ground. 9. How did you (fpl) throw the lad into the pit?

Vocalize and translate:

1. אחר הלילה בא הבקר. 2. המלך השליך את השרים אשר חטאו לו אל הבור. 3. אין הרועים יודעים אנה הלכו הצאן. 4. לא ידעתי אם שב עוד אל מקומו. 5. הגִּידי לי, הישיב לי את הפרה ביום אם בלילה? 6. חרה אףּ המלך ברועה כי לא הביא לו שעיר טוב לאכל. 7. המלך ימִית את אשר לקח את ביתו.

(*To be followed by Reading 11, p. 151.*)

§ 14

PRONOMINAL SUFFIXES WITH MASCULINE NOUNS

14.1 Pronominal suffixes are attached to nouns to express possession: חֲמוֹר "donkey," חֲמוֹרִי "my donkey." Prolongation of the noun by the suffix causes the stress to move forward (as in the construct state, §6.1)

Hence it is that when the construct form of a noun differs from its absolute form, it is to the construct form (or a modification of it) that suffixes are attached; e.g., בַּ֫יִת, בֵּית־, with suffix בֵּיתִי; שָׁלוֹם, שְׁלוֹם־, with suffix שְׁלוֹמִי.

14.2 The pronominal suffixes, as attached to חֲמוֹר, are:

plural suffixes		*singular suffixes*		
our d.	חֲמוֹרֵ֫נוּ	my d.	חֲמוֹרִי	1c
your (m) d.	חֲמוֹרְכֶם	thy (m) d.	חֲמוֹרְךָ	2m
your (f) d.	חֲמוֹרְכֶן	thy (f) d.	חֲמוֹרֵךְ	2f
their (m) d.	חֲמוֹרָם	his d.	חֲמוֹרוֹ	3m
their (f) d.	חֲמוֹרָן	her d.	חֲמוֹרָהּ	3f

14.3 Attached to the plural — more exactly, to the construct plural חֲמוֹרֵי־ — the suffixes are:

plural suffixes		*singular suffixes*		
our dd.	חֲמוֹרֵינוּ	my dd.	חֲמוֹרַי	1c
your (m) dd.	חֲמוֹרֵיכֶם	thy (m) dd.	חֲמוֹרֶיךָ	2m
your (f) dd.	חֲמוֹרֵיכֶן	thy (f) dd.	חֲמוֹרַיִךְ	2f
their (m) dd.	חֲמוֹרֵיהֶם	his dd.	חֲמוֹרָיו	3m
their (f) dd.	חֲמוֹרֵיהֶן	her dd.	חֲמוֹרֶיהָ	3f

Note that the י is pronounced only in חֲמוֹרַי and חֲמוֹרַיִךְ. In the other forms it is written but not pronounced. It derives from *-ay*, the original dual and plural construct termination, which in most forms has contracted to ־ֵי or ־ֶי, the י quiescing.

Note also that the "heavy," biconsonantal suffixes ־כֶם, ־כֶן, ־הֶם, ־הֶן attract the stress to themselves.

14.4 The pronominal possessive suffixes as attached to regular nouns may be tabulated as follows:

plural suffixes		*singular suffixes*		
with pl nouns	*with s nouns*	*with pl nouns*	*with s nouns*	
־ֵינוּ	־ֵנוּ	־ַי	־ִי	1c
־ֵיכֶם	־ְכֶם	־ֶיךָ	־ְךָ	2m
־ֵיכֶן	־ְכֶן	־ַיִךְ	־ֵךְ	2f
־ֵיהֶם	־ָם	־ָיו	־וֹ	3m
־ֵיהֶן	־ָן	־ֶיהָ	־ָהּ	3f

(a) The 1 and 2 pers suffixes are like the endings of the corresponding independent pronouns — the ת element of the 2 pers being replaced throughout by כ.

(b) The 3m suffix was originally *hu* (still seen with certain noun forms ending in a vowel: אָבִיהוּ "his father," פִּיהוּ "his mouth," alternating with the commoner contracted forms אָבִיו, פִּיו). Affixed with a connecting vowel *a* to the singular (e.g., **ḥamor-a-hu*) it contracted to *aw* > *o*. Affixed to the plural (**ḥamoray-hu*) *ayhu* > *ayw*, and then, with the quiescing of the *yod̲*, ָיו.

(c) The 3f suffix was originally *ha* (appearing still in אָבִ֫יהָ "her father," פִּ֫יהָ "her mouth"). Affixed to the singular, *-a-ha* > ָהּ; to the plural, *-ay-ha* contracted to ֶיהָ.

14.5 Here are some irregular inflections:

"son"	"brother"	"father"
בֵּן, בֶּן־:	אָח, אֲחִי־:	אָב אֲבִי־:
בְּנִי	אָחִי	אָבִי
בִּנְךָ	אָחִ֫יךָ	אָבִ֫יךָ
בְּנֵךְ	אָחִיךְ	אָבִיךְ
בְּנוֹ	אָחִיו	אָבִיו
בְּנָהּ	אָחִ֫יהָ	אָבִ֫יהָ
בְּנֵ֫נוּ	אָחִ֫ינוּ	אָבִ֫ינוּ
בִּנְכֶם–ן	אֲחִיכֶם–ן	אֲבִיכֶם–ן
בְּנָם–ן	אֲחִיהֶם–ן	אֲבִיהֶם–ן
בָּנִים, בְּנֵי־:	אַחִים, אֲחֵי־:	אָבוֹת, אֲבוֹת־:
בָּנַי	אַחַי	אֲבוֹתַי...
בָּנֶ֫יךָ	אַחֶ֫יךָ	
בָּנַ֫יִךְ	אַחַ֫יִךְ	
בָּנָיו	אֶחָיו	
בָּנֶ֫יהָ	אַחֶ֫יהָ	
בָּנֵ֫ינוּ	אַחֵ֫ינוּ	
בְּנֵיכֶם–ן	אֲחֵיכֶם–ן	
בְּנֵיהֶם–ן	אֲחֵיהֶם–ן	

(similarly פָּנִים, נָשִׁים)

14.6 Some common prepositions and particles:

direct object sign	"to"	"in"
אֵת, אֶת־:	לְ:	בְּ:
אֹתִי	לִי	בִּי
אֹתְךָ	לְךָ	בְּךָ
אֹתָךְ	לָךְ	בָּךְ
אֹתוֹ	לוֹ	בּוֹ
אֹתָהּ	לָהּ	בָּהּ
אֹתָנוּ	לָנוּ	בָּנוּ
אֶתְכֶם–ן	לָכֶם–ן	בָּכֶם–ן
אֹתָם–ן	לָהֶם–ן	בָּהֶם/בָּם
		בָּהֶן

"with"	"with"
עִם:	אֵת, אֶת־:
עִמִּי	אִתִּי
עִמְּךָ	אִתְּךָ
עִמָּךְ	אִתָּךְ
עִמּוֹ	אִתּוֹ
עִמָּהּ	אִתָּהּ
עִמָּנוּ	אִתָּנוּ
עִמָּכֶם–ן	אִתְּכֶם–ן
עִמָּהֶם–ן	אִתָּם–ן

Note that in all the above forms the connecting vowel before the 2fs and 1cpl suffixes is ָ (לָךְ, אֹתָךְ; לָנוּ, אֹתָנוּ, etc.) instead of ֵ which is normal with nouns.

* * * * * * *

Inflect with pronominal suffixes:

פִּתְרוֹן, תּוֹךְ־, צֹאן, אִישׁ, אֱלֹהִים, פָּנִים, פִּתְרוֹנִים, שְׂעִירִים

Translate:

1. אָסַפְתָּ אֶת צֹאנְךָ מִן הַשָּׂדֶה. 2. אֵין נוֹתְנִים לָאֲסוּרִים אֹכֶל כִּי חָטְאוּ לַמֶּלֶךְ וְחָרָה אַפּוֹ בָּהֶם. 3. עִמְדוּ עִמָּהּ! 4. אִם יְכַלֶּה הָרָעָב אֶת כָּל הָאֹכֶל אֲשֶׁר בְּבָתֵּיהֶם יָמוּתוּ. 5. אֶרֶץ מִצְרַיִם קְרוֹבָה אֶל אַרְצֵנוּ. 6. חַכְמֵיהֶם פָּתְרוּ לוֹ אֶת חֲלוֹמוֹ. 7. חָטָא פַּרְעֹה לֵאלֹהִים כִּי הִשְׁלִיךְ אֶת בָּנֵינוּ לְתוֹךְ הַיְאוֹר. 8. יִתֵּן אֱלֹהִים שָׁלוֹם לְעַמּוֹ. 9. בָּנֶיהָ יָדְעוּ כִּי אָהֲבָה אֶת אִישָׁהּ. 10. אֵין עוֹד מָקוֹם בְּבֵיתְכֶם כִּי אֲסַפְתֶּם לְתוֹכוֹ אֹכֶל רַב. 11. חֲכָמָה הָאִשָּׁה כִּי רוּחַ אֱלֹהִים בָּהּ.

Translate:

1. Thy (m) son restored (returned) my spirit to me. 2. Your (m) wise brother knew (how) to speak with him. 3. Our God and the God of our fathers is king over us. 4. Her sons gave her food many days. 5. They will not recognize thy (f) son. 6. You (m) asked her and her brother where her father stood on that day, but they did not answer you. 7. We took their sons and went with them to their fathers' houses. 8. Their (m) house was in the valley in which their sheep pastured. 9. Your (m) son is a prisoner with us, and we will sell him as a slave if you tell the king.

(*To be followed by Reading 13, p. 153.*)

§ 15

PRONOMINAL SUFFIXES WITH FEMININE NOUNS AND WITH VERBS

15.1 Since suffixes are attached to the construct form of nouns (§14.1), feminine nouns ending in ־ָה recover their original ־ת ending [§6.2(a)] before suffixes: פָּרָה "cow," פָּרַת־, פָּרָתִי "my cow." The full inflection is:

plural suffixes		*singular suffixes*		
our c.	פָּרָתֵנוּ	my c.	פָּרָתִי	1c
your (m) c.	פָּרַתְכֶם	thy (m) c.	פָּרָתְךָ	2m
your (f) c.	פָּרַתְכֶן	thy (f) c.	פָּרָתֵךְ	2f
their (m) c.	פָּרָתָם	his c.	פָּרָתוֹ	3m
their (f) c.	פָּרָתָן	her c.	פָּרָתָהּ	3f

Note that the vowel preceding the ת is *qâmeṣ*, except with the heavy suffixes ־כֶם ־ן, where it is *pátaḥ* (as in the construct form).

15.2 The plural, פָּרוֹת "cows," inflects thus:

plural suffixes		*singular suffixes*		
our cc.	פָּרוֹתֵ֫ינוּ	my cc.	פָּרוֹתַי	1c
your (m) cc.	פָּרוֹתֵיכֶם	thy (m) cc.	פָּרוֹתֶ֫יךָ	2m
your (f) cc.	פָּרוֹתֵיכֶן	thy (f) cc.	פָּרוֹתַ֫יִךְ	2f
their (m) cc.	פָּרוֹתֵיהֶם	his cc.	פָּרוֹתָיו	3m
their (f) cc.	פָּרוֹתֵיהֶן	her cc.	פָּרוֹתֶ֫יהָ	3f

Note that the suffixes are the same as those attached to the plural masculine nouns: פָּרוֹתַי like חֲמוֹרַי, פָּרוֹתֶ֫יךָ like חֲמוֹרֶ֫יךָ, etc. The —י— element in ֶ֫יךָ, ַ֫יִךְ, ָיו, etc. — properly a plural termination of masculine nouns (§14.3) — has through analogy been retained with the feminine.

15.3 Some irregular feminines:

אִשָּׁה, אֵ֫שֶׁת־: אִשְׁתִּי...; נָשִׁים, נְשֵׁי... (like בָּנִים, §14.5) "woman"

בַּת, בַּת־: בִּתִּי...; בָּנוֹת, בְּנוֹת־: בְּנוֹתַי... "daughter"

15.4 אֶל "to" and עַל "on" inflect as masculine plurals:

אֶל:	עַל:
אֵלַי	עָלַי
אֵלֶ֫יךָ	עָלֶ֫יךָ
אֵלַ֫יִךְ	עָלַ֫יִךְ
אֵלָיו	עָלָיו
אֵלֶ֫יהָ	עָלֶ֫יהָ
אֵלֵ֫ינוּ	עָלֵ֫ינוּ
אֲלֵיכֶם־ן	עֲלֵיכֶם־ן
אֲלֵיהֶם־ן	עֲלֵיהֶם־ן

Verbal suffixes

15.5 The direct object pronoun is expressed either by inflected אֶת־ (§ 14.6) or by pronominal suffixes attached to the verb.[1]

Suffixes are attached to the perfect שָׁמַר "he guarded" thus:

he g. us	שְׁמָרָנוּ	he g. him	שְׁמָרוֹ	he g. me	שְׁמָרַנִי
he g. you	שְׁמַרְכֶם–ן	(it befell him	קָרָהוּ)	he g. thee (m)	שְׁמָרְךָ
he g. them	שְׁמָרָם–ן	he g. her	שְׁמָרָהּ	he g. thee (f)	שְׁמָרֵךְ

(a) Note that the connecting vowel between the pf 3ms and the suffix (when there is one) is *a*/*å* (ַ/ָ), except in שְׁמָרֵךְ.

(b) Contrast the verbal suffix for 1cs ־נִי with the nominal ִי.

(c) The 3ms suffix ־הוּ usually is attached to forms ending in a vowel. Exception: שְׁמָרַתְהוּ "she g. him."

15.6 Suffixes are attached to the imperfect יִשְׁמֹר "he will guard" thus:

he w.g. us	יִשְׁמְרֵנוּ	he w.g. him	יִשְׁמְרֶנּוּ	he w.g. me	יִשְׁמְרֵנִי
he w.g. you	יִשְׁמָרְכֶם–ן		יִשְׁמְרֵהוּ	he w.g. thee (m)	יִשְׁמָרְךָ
he w.g. them	יִשְׁמְרֵם–ן	he w.g. her	יִשְׁמְרֶנָּה		
			יִשְׁמְרֶהָ(־רָהּ)	he w.g. thee (f)	יִשְׁמְרֵךְ

(a) Note that the connecting vowel between the imperfect and the suffix (when there is one) is *ɛ*/*e* (ֶ/ֵ).

(b) The suffixes of the 3s have two forms: the primary m ֵהוּ, f ָהּ and one augmented with נ: m ֶנּוּ < הוּ + ֶנְ, f ֶנָּה < ָהּ + ֶנְ. The augmented forms occur with the ordinary imperfect; the primary, with the jussive and *wåw*-consecutive (§ 16).

(c) The imperfect theme vowel *o* becomes ְ before suffixes, but the *a* theme is retained as *qåmeṣ* before suffixes: יִשְׁלַח, יִשְׁלָחֵנִי "he will send me"; יִמְצָא, יִמְצָאֵם "he will find them."

---

1 Occasionally a verbal suffix stands for an indirect object.

15.7 Other verb forms also receive suffixes:

(a) the imperative שְׁמֹר : שָׁמְרֵהוּ (*šŏm-*) "guard him!"

(b) the infinitive לִשְׁמֹר : (לְ)שָׁמְרוֹ (*šŏm-*) "to guard him"

(c) the participle שׁוֹמֵר : שׁוֹמְרוֹ "his guard, the one guarding him."

15.8 The inflections of אֵין־, עוֹד, and מִן employ the verbal suffixes.

"from me," etc.	"I am still," etc.	"I am not," etc.
מִמֶּנִּי	עוֹדֶנִּי, עוֹדִי	אֵינֶנִּי
מִמְּךָ	עוֹדְךָ	אֵינְךָ
מִמֵּךְ	עוֹדָךְ	אֵינֵךְ
מִמֶּנּוּ	עוֹדֶנּוּ	אֵינֶנּוּ
מִמֶּנָּה	עוֹדֶנָּה	אֵינֶנָּה
מִמֶּנּוּ	עוֹדֵנוּ	אֵינֶנּוּ
מִכֶּם–ן	עוֹדְכֶם–ן	אֵינְכֶם–ן
מֵהֶם–ן	עוֹדָם–ן	אֵינָם–ן

* * * * * * *

Inflect with suffixes:

אָבוֹת, חֲלוֹמוֹת, חַיּוֹת, חַיָּה, אֲלֻמָּה.

Translate:

1. He is still gathering his sheaves. 2. She does not sit in her house during the day. 3. When Pharaoh's seven daughters came down to the river, his ten servants came up from it. 4. Do you (ms) remember if you sent him much food? 5. They said to her father: She is not coming today because her sons and daughters have not yet returned. 6. His wife recognized that he was wiser than she (from her). 7. How

can I remember which of you (who from you) spoke with me that day? 8. They did not speak the truth about you (fpl). 9. The land upon which we stand (pt) belongs to the Egyptians. 10. Send (mpl) twelve of them (from them) to seek the place in which the king is imprisoned.

Translate:

1. בִּתּוֹ יָרְדָה עִם פָּרוֹתָיו לְתוֹךְ שְׂדֵה הָעִיר וְעוֹדֶנָּה שָׁם. 2. הָעִיר הַהִיא אֵינֶנָּה קְרוֹבָה אֵלֵינוּ. 3. שָׁלַחְנוּ אֵלָיו שֶׁבַע פָּרוֹת. 4. נָשֵׁינוּ עָלוּ מִמִּצְרַיִם עִמָּנוּ. 5. שִׁלְחוּ מִכֶּם אֶחָד וִיבַקֵּשׁ אֹכֶל, וְלֹא תָמוּתוּ בָּרָעָב! 6. נַעַר חָכָם אֵינֶנּוּ מְדַבֵּר לִפְנֵי אִישׁ חָכָם מִמֶּנּוּ וְגָדוֹל מִמֶּנּוּ בַּשָּׁנִים. 7. בִּתָּהּ נָתְנָה לְפָנֶיהָ לֶחֶם.

Rewrite, replacing the verbal suffix with a corresponding form of אֶת־:

1. שְׁלָחַנִי אֱלֹהִים לִפְנֵיכֶם. 2. קָמוּ כָל בְּנוֹתָיו לְנַחֲמוֹ. 3. מִיָּדִי תְּבַקְשֶׁנּוּ. 4. חַיָּה רָעָה אֲכָלַתְהוּ. 5. הֵם לֹא הִכִּירוּהוּ. 6. אֶשְׁלָחֲךָ[2] אֶל אָחִיךָ. 7. נְתָנַנִי אֱלֹהִים אָדוֹן עַל כָּל אֶרֶץ מִצְרָיִם. 8. הַשְׁלִיכֵהוּ אֶל הַבּוֹר! 9. נִמְכְּרֶנּוּ לַיִּשְׁמְעֵאלִים. 10. רָאָם וְלֹא הִכִּירָם. 11. יִמְצָאֲכֶם בַּשָּׂדֶה. 12. לֹא יַכִּירוּךָ אוֹהֲבֶיךָ. 13. אֶזְכְּרֶנּוּ עוֹד. 14. לְקַחְתִּיהָ. 15. בִּקֵּשׁ לִרְאוֹתוֹ.

(*To be followed by Reading 15, p. 156.*)

---

[2] Cf. §15.6(c).

§ 16

WÅW-CONSECUTIVE

16.1 In the narratives, the two aspects of Biblical Hebrew are employed in the following sequence: If past events are being narrated, the first verb is normally in the perfect, but the consecutive verbs in the line of the narration — each standing at the head of a clause and linked by ו to the preceding clause — appear in the so-called *imperfect with wåw-consecutive*, or *imperfect consecutive*. For example, the report that Joseph's brothers made to Jacob upon their return from Egypt as it appears in Reading 16 runs:

דִּבֶּר הָאִישׁ... אִתָּנוּ קָשׁוֹת, וְנָתַן אֹתָנוּ כִּמְרַגְּלִים. אָמַרְנוּ אֵלָיו: לֹא הָיִינוּ מְרַגְּלִים... אָמַר אֵלֵינוּ הָאִישׁ...

But in the original of Genesis 42:30-33 the sequence of tenses is:

דִּבֶּר הָאִישׁ... אִתָּנוּ קָשׁוֹת, וַיִּתֵּן אֹתָנוּ כִּמְרַגְּלִים... וַנֹּאמֶר אֵלָיו: לֹא הָיִינוּ מְרַגְּלִים... וַיֹּאמֶר אֵלֵינוּ הָאִישׁ...

The first verb, דִּבֶּר, is in the perfect; the subsequent verbs in the line of the narrative (וַיֹּאמֶר, וַנֹּאמֶר, וַיִּתֵּן) each stand at the head of their clause and are in the imperfect consecutive (הָיִינוּ is in a quotation). The imperfect consecutive is rendered in English as a past.

This apparently inverted imperfect is in all likelihood a survival of an early preterit tense which later coalesced in form with the imperfect; see § 10.2.

16.2 A verb expressing an action or circumstance that is not consequent upon the preceding verb is thrown back into its normal aspect. The interruption of a line of imperfect consecutives by a perfect often indicates an action or circumstance simultaneous with, or prior to, what came before:

(a) Simultaneity: וַיִּפֹּל עַל צַוְּארֵי[1] בִנְיָמִן אָחִיו וַיֵּבְךְּ וּבִנְיָמִן בָּכָה עַל צַוָּארָיו[2] (45:14) "then he fell on his brother Benjamin's neck and wept, while Benjamin wept on his neck."

(b) Priority: וַיֵּבְךְּ אֹתוֹ אָבִיו. וְהַמְּדָנִים מָכְרוּ אֹתוֹ (37:35 f.) "...so his father bewailed him. Meanwhile, the Midianites had sold him..."

Note the distinctive, invariable word order of such nonconsecutive clauses: the subject precedes the verb.

16.3 *Wåw*-consecutive is vocalized. ·וַ; i.e., וַ followed by a long consonant (one bearing a strong *dågeš*; see the above examples). Before א it is וָ: וָאֶשְׁמֹר [ַ is lengthened to ָ because the laryngal א cannot be lengthened; cf. the vocalization of the article הַ, §5.1, 2(a)].

יְ following a *wåw*-consecutive is not lengthened; e.g., וַיְדַבֵּר.

16.4 When a shortening of the imperfect form is possible, *wåw*-consecutive is usually attached to the shortened form. In the sound (regular) verbs — verbs from triconsonantal roots in which there are no weak consonants (א, ה, ו, י) — the imperfect form is not susceptible to shortening. The one exception is the *hif'il* jussive יַשְׁלֵךְ (compare the imperfect יַשְׁלִיךְ); accordingly the imperfect consecutive is וַיַּשְׁלֵךְ.

---

1 Read *ṣawwere* (MH *ṣavvere*); the dot in the ו is a strong *dågeš*. Thus every וּ with a vowel sign is a long (doubled) *wåw*.

2 Read *ṣawwåråw* (MH *ṣavvåråv*).

But in "hollow" verbs (§8.2) such as שׁוּב, or in verbs one or more of whose consonants are weak, shortening of the imperfect form can occur. The more important cases are:

(a) When the imperfect has an open penult (next-to-last syllable). A syllable is open when it ends in a vowel; the penults of the following verbs are open: יֵשֵׁב, יֵלֵךְ, יָשׁוּב, יָשִׂים, יֹאמַר.

In the imperfect consecutive the stress recedes to the penult and the final vowel is, consequently, shortened: וַיֵּשֶׁב, וַיֵּלֶךְ, (*-šŏv*) וַיָּשָׁב, וַיָּשֶׂם, וַיֹּאמֶר.

There are many exceptions to this rule. It is not operative, for example, in 1cs; hence וָאֵלֵךְ, וָאָשׁוּב, וָאָשִׂים.

(b) When the imperfect ends in ־ֶה. The ־ֶה is dropped and the resultant short forms are variously vocalized; e.g.:

imperfect	*imperfect consecutive*	
יִהְיֶה	וַיְהִי	he/it was
יַעֲשֶׂה	וַיַּעַשׂ	he did, made
יִרְאֶה	וַיַּרְא	he saw
יְצַוֶּה	וַיְצַו	he ordered

16.5 Corresponding to the imperfect consecutive, which occurs in narration of past events, is the *perfect consecutive*, which occurs in narration of future events. The narration opens with a verb in the imperfect, imperative, or another form implying a future; it is then carried on by a chain of perfect consecutives.

For example, Genesis 45:9-11:

רְדָה אֵלַי אַל תַּעֲמֹד! וְיָשַׁבְתָּ בְאֶרֶץ גֹּשֶׁן[3] וְהָיִיתָ קָרוֹב אֵלַי...

[3] In most printings of vocalized Hebrew, when *ḥolɛm* precedes שׁ the characteristic dot over the right prong of the *šin* does duty for the *ḥolɛm* as well — as in גֹּשֶׁן.

וְכִלְכַּלְתִּי אֹתְךָ. "Come down to me without delay! You shall live in the land of Goshen and be near to me... and I shall sustain you."

16.6 *Wåw*-consecutive with the perfect is vocalized like the copula ו "and" (see p. 28). The stress moves forward to the end in the 1cs and 2ms forms of the perfect consecutive (וְכִלְכַּלְתִּי, וְיָשַׁבְתָּ); in 1cpl and many forms of final ה verbs (e.g., הָיָה) this stress shift does not occur (וְהָיִיתָ, וְשָׁמַרְנוּ).

* * * * * * *

Translate, then convert imperfect consecutives into perfects, perfect consecutives into imperfects; change object suffixes into אֶת־ *forms:*

1. וַיֵּשֶׁב יַעֲקֹב בְּאֶרֶץ כְּנָעַן. 2. וַיַּגֵּד לְאֶחָיו. 3. וַיֵּלְכוּ לִרְעוֹת אֶת הַצֹּאן. 4. וַיִּמְצָאֵהוּ אִישׁ בַּשָּׂדֶה. 5. וַיַּפְשִׁיטוּ אֶת יוֹסֵף אֶת כֻּתָּנְתּוֹ. 6. וַיְסַפֵּר אֶל אָבִיו. 7. וַיִּקָּחוּהוּ וַיַּשְׁלִיכוּהוּ הַבּוֹרָה. 8. וַיִּמְכְּרוּ אֶת יוֹסֵף. 9. וַיָּבוֹאוּ אֶל יוֹסֵף. 10. וַיָּשָׁב רְאוּבֵן אֶל הַבּוֹר. 11. וַיַּכִּירָהּ וַיֹּאמֶר: כְּתֹנֶת בְּנִי! 12. וַיְשַׁלְּחוּ אֶת כְּתֹנֶת הַפַּסִּים. 13. וַיֵּרֶד יְהוּדָה לִפְנֵיהֶם. 14. וַיָּבֹא אֲלֵיהֶם בַּבֹּקֶר וַיַּרְא אוֹתָם. 15. הִנֵּה שֶׁבַע שָׁנִים בָּאוֹת – שָׂבָע גָּדוֹל בְּכָל הָאָרֶץ; וְקָמוּ אַחֲרֵיהֶן שֶׁבַע שְׁנֵי רָעָב וְכִלָּה הָרָעָב אֶת הָאָרֶץ. 16. וַיַּכִּירֵם וַיְדַבֵּר אֲלֵיהֶם קָשׁוֹת. 17. וַיַּעַשׂ לָהֶם כֵּן. 18. וַיַּעַן רְאוּבֵן אֹתָם. 19. וַיִּקַּח מֵאִתָּם אֶת שִׁמְעוֹן וַיֶּאֱסֹר אוֹתוֹ. 20. וַנְּסַפֵּר לוֹ וַיִּפְתֹּר לָנוּ אֶת חֲלוֹמוֹתֵינוּ. 21. וַיְהִי יוֹסֵף אָדוֹן לְכָל אֶרֶץ מִצְרָיִם. 22. וַיִּקָּחֵהוּ וַיִּתְּנֵהוּ בְּבֵית הָאֲסוּרִים.

(*To be followed by Reading 17, p. 158.*)

§ 17

HOLLOW VERBS

17.1 Hollow verbs derive from biconsonantal roots. In many forms a characteristic long vowel appears between the two consonants, hence the term "hollow," adopted here from Arabic grammar. Examples: שׁוּב "return," שִׂים "put," בּוֹא "come," מוּת "die."[1]

These forms are infinitive construct, the form by which hollow verbs are referred to since their pf 3ms does not show the characteristic long vowel.

This long vowel appears in the *qal* imperfect and related forms and in the infinitive. In the perfect and participle, where it does not appear, hollow verbs all inflect alike (except insofar as statives differ from actives; see the paradigm).

---

[1] These verbs are commonly referred to as middle-*wåw* or middle-*yoḏ* verbs, reflecting the theory that the characteristic middle vowel was originally a consonantal *wåw* or *yoḏ*. Some evidence can be mustered for this view (e.g., the consonantal *wåw* in מָ֫וֶת "death" from the root מוּת); however the difficulties it puts in the way of deriving the verbal forms make it preferable to adopt the view set forth above and to assume that the consonantal *wåw* in such words as מָ֫וֶת arose secondarily.

17.2 The *qal*:

PERFECT

stative	*active*			
מַתִּי	בָּאתִי	שַׂמְתִּי	שַׁבְתִּי	1cs
מַתָּ	בָּאתָ	שַׂמְתָּ	שַׁבְתָּ	2m
מַתְּ	בָּאת	שַׂמְתְּ	שַׁבְתְּ	2f
מֵת	בָּא	שָׂם	שָׁב	3m
מֵתָה	בָּאָה	שָׂמָה	שָׁבָה	3f
מַתְנוּ	בָּאנוּ	שַׂמְנוּ	שַׁבְנוּ	1cpl
מַתֶּם	בָּאתֶם	שַׂמְתֶּם	שַׁבְתֶּם	2m
מַתֶּן	בָּאתֶן	שַׂמְתֶּן	שַׁבְתֶּן	2f
מֵתוּ	בָּאוּ	שָׂמוּ	שָׁבוּ	3c

IMPERFECT

אָמוּת	אָבוֹא	אָשִׂים	אָשׁוּב	1cs
תָּמוּת	תָּבוֹא	תָּשִׂים	תָּשׁוּב	2m
תָּמוּתִי	תָּבוֹאִי	תָּשִׂימִי	תָּשׁוּבִי	2f
יָמוּת	יָבוֹא	יָשִׂים	יָשׁוּב	3m
תָּמוּת	תָּבוֹא	תָּשִׂים	תָּשׁוּב	3f
נָמוּת	נָבוֹא	נָשִׂים	נָשׁוּב	1cpl
תָּמוּתוּ	תָּבוֹאוּ	תָּשִׂימוּ	תָּשׁוּבוּ	2m
תְּמוּתֶינָה	תְּבוֹאֶינָה	תְּשִׂימֶינָה	תְּשׁוּבֶינָה	2&3f
תָּמֹתְנָה	תָּבוֹאנָה	תָּשֵׂמְנָה	תָּשֹׁבְנָה	
יָמוּתוּ	יָבוֹאוּ	יָשִׂימוּ	יָשׁוּבוּ	3m

COHORTATIVE

אָמוּתָה	אָבוֹאָה	אָשִׂימָה	אָשׁוּבָה
נָמוּתָה	נָבוֹאָה	נָשִׂימָה	נָשׁוּבָה

JUSSIVE & IMPERFECT CONSECUTIVE

יָמֹת	יָבוֹא	יָשֵׂם	יָשֹׁב
וַיָּמָת	וַיָּבוֹא	וַיָּשֶׂם	וַיָּשָׁב

IMPERATIVE

מוּת	בּוֹא	שִׂים	שׁוּב	ms
מ֫וּתִי	בּ֫וֹאִי	שִׂ֫ימִי	שׁ֫וּבִי	f
מ֫וּתוּ	בּ֫וֹאוּ	שִׂ֫ימוּ	שׁ֫וּבוּ	mpl
מ֫תְנָה	בּ֫וֹאנָה	שֵׂ֫מְנָה	שׁ֫בְנָה	f

INFINITIVE ABSOLUTE & CONSTRUCT

מוֹת	בּוֹא	שׂוֹם	שׁוֹב
(לָ)מוּת	(לָ)בוֹא	(לָ)שִׂים	(לָ)שׁוּב
		(לָ)שׂוּם	

PARTICIPLE

מֵת	בָּא	שָׂם	שָׁב	ms
מֵתָה	בָּאָה	שָׂמָה	שָׁבָה	f
מֵתִים	בָּאִים	שָׂמִים	שָׁבִים	mpl
מֵתוֹת	בָּאוֹת	שָׂמוֹת	שָׁבוֹת	f

(a) In the perfect of בּוֹא the א quiesces and the preceding ַ > ָ by way of compensation (§21.1).

(b) The impf 2 and 3fpl have two forms: the longer, commoner one keeps the original long vowel and inserts a vowel ֶ before the נָה– termination; the spelling ֶי shows the influence of the final ה verb form תִּבְכֶּינָה (§19). In the shorter form וּ > ֹ, ִי > ֵ, as in the jussive. ֹ and ֵ are in turn shortened to ָ (ŏ) and ֶ, respectively, in the imperfect consecutive [see §16.4(a)]. The long וֹ of בּוֹא remains unchanged throughout.

(c) The pt ms is identical with the pf 3ms. The stress position of the pt fs (קָ֫מָה) distinguishes it from the pf 3fs (קָמָ֫ה).

17.3 The *hif'il*:

COHORTATIVE

אָשִׁיבָה
נָשִׁיבָה

JUSSIVE & IMPERFECT CONSECUTIVE

יָשֵׁב
וַיָּשֶׁב

IMPERATIVE

הָשֵׁב	ms
הָשִׁיבִי	f
הָשִׁיבוּ	mpl
הָשֵׁבְנָה	f

INFINITIVE ABSOLUTE & CONSTRUCT

הָשֵׁב
(לְ)הָשִׁיב

PARTICIPLE

מֵשִׁיב	ms
מְשִׁיבָה	f
מְשִׁיבִים	mpl
מְשִׁיבוֹת	f

PERFECT

	type a	*type b*	
1cs	הֲשִׁיבוֹתִי	הֵשַׁבְתִּי	הֵבֵאתִי
2m	הֲשִׁיבוֹתָ (הֱ- -שֵׁ-)	הֵשַׁבְתָּ	הֵבֵאתָ
2f	הֲשִׁיבוֹת	הֵשַׁבְתְּ	הֵבֵאת
3m	הֵשִׁיב	(*type a*)	הֵבִיא
3f	הֵשִׁיבָה	(*type a*)	הֵבִיאָה
1cpl	הֲשִׁיבוֹנוּ (הֱ-)	הֵשַׁבְנוּ	הֵבֵאנוּ
2m	הֲשִׁיבוֹתֶם (-שֵׁ-)	הֵשַׁבְתֶּם	הֲבֵאתֶם
2f	הֲשִׁיבוֹתֶן	הֵשַׁבְתֶּן	הֲבֵאתֶן
3c	הֵשִׁיבוּ	(*type a*)	הֵבִיאוּ

IMPERFECT

1cs	אָשִׁיב
2m	תָּשִׁיב
2f	תָּשִׁיבִי
3m	יָשִׁיב
3f	תָּשִׁיב
1cpl	נָשִׁיב
2m	תָּשִׁיבוּ
2f	תָּשֵׁבְנָה
3m	יָשִׁיבוּ
3f	תָּשֵׁבְנָה

(a) Perfect *type a* is the more common in Biblical Hebrew; *type b* (closer to the pattern of the sound verb, cf. הִשְׁלַכְתִּי) more common in Post-biblical. The paradigm shows the dominant pattern; the parentheses give divergences in attested forms of הֵשִׁיב.

17.4 The *hŏf'al*: pf 3ms הוּשַׁב, impf 3ms יוּשַׁב, pt ms מוּשָׁב.[2]

* * * * * * *

Conjugate in qal:

קום.

Conjugate in hif'il :

כון.

Supply correct form of indicated verb in perfect, imperfect, participle :

1. שָׂם: הָאִשָּׁה ______ אֶת הָאֹכֶל לִפְנֵי אִישָׁהּ. 2. בָּא: אֲנִי ______ עִמְּךָ. 3. הֵשִׁיב: אַתְּ ______ לִי אֶת חֲמוֹרִי. 4. הֵבִיא: אַתָּה ______ מַיִם.

Change the subjects and verbs of the preceding exercise to the plural.

Vocalize and translate :

1. הכן את הלחם והמים כי באים השרים לאכל אתנו! 2. אם תשובו, תשיבו לו את הכסף. 3. המיתו את העבד כי בקש להמית את המלך. 4. צרות גדולות תבואנה עליכם אם לא תכינו אכל לדרך. 5. זכרנו את רחמיך הרבים. 6. המים משיבים את הנפש. 7. באמת הדרך קשה, והיא תביא אתכם אל עירכם. 8. בתחלה ישימו מים לפניו, ואחר יביאו את הלחם. 9. אני מביאה את הילד אל אמו.

Translate :

1. Let him come (juss) into your (ms) house. 2. They will put the rations on their donkeys. 3. At noon she gave them money and

2 In Genesis 43:12 הַמּוּשָׁב occurs in close connection with the following word — a quasi-construct form.

returned them by the way in which they came. 4. They did not find the present that they had brought for the king. 5. Many men have feared to bring blood upon their hands. 6. Ten donkeys carrying food are coming down into the valley. 7. Who will tell us a good way to go back to our house? 8. Put (mpl) the sheaves there! 9. According to (עַל פִּי) the woman's words, she got up and returned to her father's house because her husband spoke to her harshly.

(*To be followed by Reading 19, p. 162.*)

§ 18

THE NIF‘AL AND HIṮPA‘EL

The nif‘al

18.1 The *nif‘al* is primarily the reflexive of *qal*, but serves often as its passive as well: נִשְׁמַר "he guarded himself," but also "he was guarded"; נִבְחַן "he was tested"; נִמְצָא "he was found."

Nif‘al verbs frequently express a state or feeling that comes or acts upon the subject: נִכְמַר "he grew hot," נֶעֱצַב "he was grieved," נִבְהַל "he became terrified."

Sometimes *nif‘al* is used as the passive of patterns other than *qal*; e.g., נֶאֱמַן "he was confirmed, verified, held true" (passive of *hif‘il* הֶאֱמִין "hold true, believe").

18.2 The characteristic נ augment appears in the perfect, participle, and one form of the infinitive absolute. In the imperfect and related forms and in other forms of the infinitive — where it is preceded by preformatives — the נ is assimilated to the first root consonant, which is therefore lengthened: *יִנְשָׁמֵר > יִשָּׁמֵר.

The *nif'al* נִשְׁמַר "he guarded himself/was guarded":

INFINITIVE ABSOLUTE	COHORTATIVE	IMPERFECT	PERFECT
נִשְׁמֹר, הִשָּׁמֵר	אִשָּׁמְרָה s	אֶשָּׁמֵר 1cs	נִשְׁמַרְתִּי 1cs
	נִשָּׁמְרָה pl	תִּשָּׁמֵר 2m	נִשְׁמַרְתָּ 2m
INFINITIVE CONSTRUCT		תִּשָּׁמְרִי 2f	נִשְׁמַרְתְּ 2f
(לְ)הִשָּׁמֵר	IMPERATIVE	יִשָּׁמֵר 3m	נִשְׁמַר 3m
	הִשָּׁמֵר ms	תִּשָּׁמֵר 3f	נִשְׁמְרָה 3f
	הִשָּׁמְרִי f	נִשָּׁמֵר 1cpl	נִשְׁמַרְנוּ 1cpl
PARTICIPLE	הִשָּׁמְרוּ mpl	תִּשָּׁמְרוּ 2m	נִשְׁמַרְתֶּם 2m
נִשְׁמָר ms	הִשָּׁמַרְנָה f	תִּשָּׁמַרְנָה 2f	נִשְׁמַרְתֶּן 2f
נִשְׁמֶרֶת f		יִשָּׁמְרוּ 3m	נִשְׁמְרוּ 3c
נִשְׁמָרִים mpl		תִּשָּׁמַרְנָה 3f	
נִשְׁמָרוֹת f			

(a) The pf 3ms and the pt ms are alike save for the second vowel: in the perfect it is ◌ַ; in the participle, which is a noun form, it is ◌ָ [see §§ 11.3 and 25.8(a)].

(b) When the first root consonant is a laryngal or ר, in the imperfect, imperative, and infinitive construct the preformative vowel is always lengthened to ◌ֵ in order to compensate for the lack of lengthening of the laryngal; e.g., יֵאָסֵר "he will be imprisoned"; יֵעָצֵב "he will be grieved."

The hitpa'el

18.3 The *hitpa'el* serves as the reflexive, less often as the passive, of *pi'el*: הִתְנַחֵם "he consoled himself, was consoled," הִתְוַדַּע "he made himself known." Frequently, however, no corresponding *pi'el* is attested, as in the case of הִתְאַפֵּק "he restrained himself," הִתְנַפֵּל "he fell upon, attacked."

In the plural, *hitpa'el* may have a reciprocal sense: הִתְרָאוּ "they stared at one another."

Sometimes it has the sense "to act as, play the part of": הִתְנַכֵּר "he acted as a stranger."

18.4 Like *pi'el, hitpa'el* has a long (*dågeš*-bearing) middle root consonant. The prepositive הִתְ־ appears in the perfect, imperative, and infinitives; elsewhere the ה is elided after the preformatives.

The *hitpa'el* הִתְאַפֵּק "he restrained himself":

INFINITIVE ABSOLUTE	
הִתְאַפֵּק	

INFINITIVE CONSTRUCT	
(לְ)הִתְאַפֵּק	

PARTICIPLE	
מִתְאַפֵּק	ms
מִתְאַפֶּקֶת	f
מִתְאַפְּקִים	mpl
מִתְאַפְּקוֹת	f

COHORTATIVE	
אֶתְאַפְּקָה	s
נִתְאַפְּקָה	pl

IMPERATIVE	
הִתְאַפֵּק	ms
הִתְאַפְּקִי	f
הִתְאַפְּקוּ	mpl
הִתְאַפֵּקְנָה	f

IMPERFECT		PERFECT	
אֶתְאַפֵּק	1cs	הִתְאַפַּקְתִּי	1cs
תִּתְאַפֵּק	2m	הִתְאַפַּקְתָּ	2m
תִּתְאַפְּקִי	2f	הִתְאַפַּקְתְּ	2f
יִתְאַפֵּק	3m	הִתְאַפֵּק	3m
תִּתְאַפֵּק	3f	הִתְאַפְּקָה	3f
נִתְאַפֵּק	1cpl	הִתְאַפַּקְנוּ	1cpl
תִּתְאַפְּקוּ	2m	הִתְאַפַּקְתֶּם	2m
תִּתְאַפֵּקְנָה	2f	הִתְאַפַּקְתֶּן	2f
יִתְאַפְּקוּ	3m	הִתְאַפְּקוּ	3cpl
תִּתְאַפֵּקְנָה	3f		

18.5 When the first root consonant is a sibilant (a consonant pronounced with a hissing sound: ז, ס, צ, ש), in order to avoid the juncture of the sibilant and the ת of the prepositive הִתְ־, the two exchange places. Thus the *hitpa'el* of שמר is הִשְׁתַּמֵּר; the *hitpa'el* of שחוה is הִשְׁתַּחֲוָה (but see note, p. 141). This exchange is called metathesis.

When the sibilant is צ, after metathesis the ת becomes ט: the *hitpa'el* of צדק is הִצְטַדֵּק. The ת has been partially assimilated to the צ by being pronounced, like it, as an emphatic (see §1.4).

* * * * * * *

Conjugate in nif'al:

נִגְנַב, נִמְכַּר.

Conjugate in hitpa'el:

הִתְחַנֵּן, הִתְאַבֵּל.

Translate :

1. הַחֲמוֹרִים אֲשֶׁר נִגְנְבוּ נִמְצְאוּ בְּבֵית הָעֶבֶד. 2. נִשְׁלַחְתֶּם לִרְדֹּף אַחַר
הָעֶבֶד אֲשֶׁר יָצָא מִבֵּית אֲדוֹנָיו בַּלַּיְלָה וְלֹא הִשַּׂגְתֶּם אֹתוֹ. 3. הָאֲנָשִׁים
יֵאָסְרוּ כִּי אֲשֵׁמִים הֵם. 4. הַשַּׂקִּים נִפְתְּחוּ, וְהַכֶּסֶף הַנִּמְצָא בְּתוֹכָם
נִגְנַב. 5. בָּכוּ וְהִתְאַבְּלוּ וְלֹא הִתְנַחֲמוּ. 6. הַיּוֹם תֵּאָסַפְנָה הָאֲלֻמּוֹת
הָעוֹמְדוֹת בַּשָּׂדֶה. 7. יִבָּחֲנוּ דְּבָרָיו וְיִמָּצְאוּ אֱמֶת. 8. אִם לֹא יִנָּתֵן
לָאֲסוּרִים לֶחֶם לֶאֱכֹל וּמַיִם לִשְׁתּוֹת יָמוּתוּ בָּרָעָב. 9. הָאֲשֵׁמִים נִלְקְחוּ
לְהִמָּכֵר לַעֲבָדִים. 10. גַּם אִם תִּתְחַנְּנוּ אֵלָיו לֹא יִשְׁמַע אֲלֵיכֶם.

Translate :

1. I was asked whether I recognized her face; after these many years I could not. 2. Bring her back to the land from which (that from there) she and her daughter were taken. 3. Ten men from your (mpl) midst will be taken and sent; they shall not return. 4. The words that come out of the mouth of the wise man are listened to (heard). 5. Will you (ms) mourn (over) your son all your days? 6. The slave came out of the city this morning, has been pursued all day, but they still haven't overtaken him. 7. We were consoled because we were not alone in our distress. 8. Don't (fs) plead with me; you will be put in prison today! 9. Will she be remembered when she is gone (is not)?

(*To be followed by Reading 21, p. 164.*)

§ 19

FINAL ה VERBS

19.1 The third root consonant of such verbs as בָּכָה "he wept," עָשָׂה "he made, did," עָלָה "he went up" was in most cases originally י. Except in the *qal* passive participle (e.g., עָשׂוּי "made, done"), this י has as a rule quiesced.

(a) When in final position, the quiescent י is replaced in writing by the vowel letter ה, which stands for the following vowels:

ָ in the pf 3ms: *qal* בָּכָה "he wept," *pi'el* צִוָּה "he ordered," *hif'il* הִרְבָּה "he did/made much."

ֶ in the impf and pt ms: יִבְכֶּה, בּוֹכֶה; יְצַוֶּה, מְצַוֶּה; יַרְבֶּה, מַרְבֶּה

ֵ in the imv: בְּכֵה, צַוֵּה, הַרְבֵּה

(b) Before consonantal afformatives the י is written as part of a long vowel, which is:

ֶי in the impf (and imv): תִּבְכֶּינָה, תְּצַוֶּינָה, תַּרְבֶּינָה

ִי or ֵי in the pf: בָּכִיתִי, צִוִּיתִי (צִוֵּיתִי), הִרְבֵּיתִי

ֶי/ה and ֵי/ה have contracted from an original *ay*: יִבְכֶּה from **yibkay* (after the stative pattern of יִכְבַּד), תִּבְכֶּינָה from **tibkayna*, הִרְבֵּיתִי from **hirbayti* (cf. the sound הִשְׁלַכְתִּי). [Compare the analogous contraction of the original plural construct termination *ay* in חֲמוֹרֵי־ (< **ḥamoray*), with suffix חֲמוֹרֶיךָ (< **ḥamorayka*), §14.3.] ִי is contracted from *iy*: בָּכִיתִי from **bakiyti* (after the stative pattern **kabidti* > כָּבַדְתִּי).

(c) Before vowel afformatives the י is dropped, hence תִּבְכִּי, בָּכוּ, בּוֹכָה. It is likewise dropped before the infinitive construct ending, which is uniformly וֹת־: (לְ)בְכּוֹת, (לְ)צַוּוֹת, (לְ)הַרְבּוֹת.

(d) The pf 3fs, בָּכְתָה, has a double feminine termination: **baka+t+å(h)*, bringing it into conformity with the pattern of the sound verb: שָׁמְרָה.

19.2 An apocopated ("clipped") form, in which the ֶה termination of the imperfect is dropped, serves for the jussive and imperfect consecutive; e.g., יֵבְךְּ (<יִבְכֶּה), יְצַו. In *qal* (and *hif'il*) apocopation results in the formation of a consonant cluster; e.g., **tirb* < תִּרְבֶּה (from רבה "be great"); **yiḥr* < יֶחֱרֶה (from חרה "burn"); **ya'n* < יַעֲנֶה (from ענה "answer"). The cluster is then often broken by the insertion of a helping vowel: ֶ as in תֶּרֶב, or, after laryngals, ַ as in יַחַר, יַעַן. For more apocopated forms see §16.4(b).

19.3 In the *qal* imperfect of verbs that have both final ה and initial ע (such as עָנָה, עָלָה, עָשָׂה) the preformative ִ vowel is replaced by ַ, in accordance with the tendency of laryngals to demand homorganic vowels before them: thus יַעֲלֶה (but אֶעֱלֶה). The apocopated form is יַעַל; the inf cs לַעֲלוֹת.

19.4 Exceptions to the rule that laryngals demand homorganic vowels before them are the verbs הָיָה and חָיָה. These inflect alike, except in the pt, which is rare for הָיָה.

impf: אֶהְיֶה, תִּהְיֶה, תִּהְיִי, יִהְיֶה, תִּהְיֶה, נִהְיֶה, תִּהְיוּ, תִּהְיֶינָה, יִהְיוּ, תִּהְיֶינָה

apoc: יְהִי

imv: הֱיֵה, הֲיִי, הֱיוּ, הֱיֶינָה

inf cs: הֱיוֹת, לִהְיוֹת

pt: (חָיָה): חַי, חַיָּה, חַיִּים, חַיּוֹת

19.5 Final ה verbs:

HIF'IL	PI'EL	QAL	
הִרְבֵּיתִי (־בִּ־)	צִוִּיתִי (־וֵּ־)	בָּכִיתִי	1cs pf
הִרְבִּיתָ (־בֵּ־)	צִוִּיתָ	בָּכִיתָ	2m
הִרְבִּית (־בֵּ־)	צִוִּית	בָּכִית	2f
הִרְבָּה	צִוָּה	בָּכָה	3m
הִרְבְּתָה	צִוְּתָה	בָּכְתָה	3f
הִרְבִּינוּ	צִוִּינוּ	בָּכִינוּ	1cpl
הִרְבֵּיתֶם—ן (־בִּ־)	צִוִּיתֶם—ן	בְּכִיתֶם—ן	2m&f
הִרְבּוּ	צִוּוּ	בָּכוּ	3c
אַרְבֶּה	אֲצַוֶּה	אֶבְכֶּה	1cs impf
תַּרְבֶּה	תְּצַוֶּה	תִּבְכֶּה	2m
תַּרְבִּי	תְּצַוִּי	תִּבְכִּי	2f
יַרְבֶּה	יְצַוֶּה	יִבְכֶּה	3m
תַּרְבֶּה	תְּצַוֶּה	תִּבְכֶּה	3f
נַרְבֶּה	נְצַוֶּה	נִבְכֶּה	1cpl
תַּרְבּוּ	תְּצַוּוּ	תִּבְכּוּ	2m
תַּרְבֶּינָה	תְּצַוֶּינָה	תִּבְכֶּינָה	2f
יַרְבּוּ	יְצַוּוּ	יִבְכּוּ	3m
תַּרְבֶּינָה	תְּצַוֶּינָה	תִּבְכֶּינָה	3f
יֶרֶב	יְצַו	יֵבְךְּ	apoc
הַרְבֵּה	צַוֵּה	בְּכֵה	ms imv
הַרְבִּי	צַוִּי	בְּכִי	f
הַרְבּוּ	צַוּוּ	בְּכוּ	mpl
הַרְבֶּינָה	צַוֶּינָה	בְּכֶינָה	f
הַרְבֵּה (הַרְבָּה)	צַוֹּה, צַוֵּה	בָּכֹה	inf abs
(לְ)הַרְבּוֹת	(לְ)צַוּוֹת	בְּכוֹת, לִבְכּוֹת	inf cs
מַרְבֶּה	מְצַוֶּה	בּוֹכֶה	ms pt
מַרְבָּה	מְצַוָּה	בּוֹכָה	f

	QAL	PI'EL	HIF'IL
mpl pt	בּוֹכִים	מְצַוִּים	מַרְבִּים
f	בּוֹכוֹת	מְצַוּוֹת	מַרְבּוֹת
pass pt	עָשׂוּי		

* * * * * * *

Conjugate in qal:

חיה, עשה, שתה.

Conjugate in pi'el:

כלה.

Conjugate in hif'il:

בכה.

Vocalize and translate:

1. עלינו למקומנו. 2. צוו להראות להם את הדם. 3. איפה רעית את צאנך בצהרים? 4. השיבותם לי רעה תחת הטובה אשר עשיתי לכם. 5. ראו כי נקרעו שמלותיו. 6. בכתה והתחננה אל המלך כי לא ימית אתה. 7. חפשו מים לשתות ולא מצאו בכל המקום ההוא. 8. הרעב כלה את הארץ. 9. כאשר עלתה השמש היינו בדרך. 10. השתחוו ארצה ובקשו רחמים לפני המלך. 11. ראיתם את אשר עשיתי. 12. שתית את כל המים אשר היו בבור. 13. כאשר כלתה לדבר איש לא ענה אתה.

Change above verbs to imperfects.

Replace the following imperfect consecutives with perfects:

1. וַיַּעַן אֹתָם רְאוּבֵן. 2. וַיֵּבְךְּ אֹתוֹ אָבִיו. 3. וַיִּחַר אַף הַמֶּלֶךְ. 4. וַתְּחִי רוּחַ יַעֲקֹב. 5. וַיְכַל אֶת הָאֹכֶל. 6. וַיְצַו יוֹסֵף אֶת אֲשֶׁר עַל בֵּיתוֹ. 7. וַתֹּאכַל וַתֵּשְׁתְּ וַתָּקָם וַתֵּלֶךְ. 8. וַתְּמַהֵר וַתַּעַשׂ אֶת דְּבַר הַמֶּלֶךְ.

Translate:

1. Drink (mpl) from this water but don't finish it. 2. We shall see what will come of (be) his dreams. 3. You (fs) shall yet see what will befall them. 4. Pharaoh's cows will go up from the river after (that) they finish drinking (to drink). 5. They (fpl) are doing that which she ordered them to do. 6. He who orders the old man to return alone has no compassion. 7. Better to die in well-being than to live in misery (evil). 8. What shall I do if he does not answer? 9. She had not yet finished speaking (to speak) when (and) her young son came into the room crying.

(*To be followed by Reading 23, p. 167.*)

§ 20

INITIAL י VERBS

20.1 Initial י verbs comprise two classes: verbs originally initial ו and a much smaller number of verbs originally initial י.

20.2 Original ו > י wherever it was initial. Thus from ולד* "give birth" are derived *qal* יָלַד, *pi'el* יִלֵּד, *pu'al* יֻלַּד and, by analogy, *hitpa'el* הִתְיַלֵּד. The inflection of the entire *pi'el* group is regular, since the secondary י is maintained even after preformatives (e.g., *pi'el* impf יְיַלֵּד, pt מְיַלֵּד). In *qal* impf, etc., the initial root-consonant drops, as described below.

Original ו was maintained when preceded by the נ augment of *nif'al* (נוֹלַד, יִוָּלֵד) and the ה augment of *hif/hŏf'al* (הוֹלִיד, יוֹלִיד; הוּלַד).

(a) Maintained ו is consonantal when it begins the syllable: יִוָּלֵד < **yinwaled*.[1] At the syllable end, ו and the preceding vowel contract to וֹ, וּ: **hawlid* > הוֹלִיד, **huwlad* > הוּלַד

(b) Initial ו > י in nouns too: **wald* > **yald* > יֶלֶד "child"; but **mawladt* > מוֹלֶדֶת "family."

20.3 In *qal* impf, etc., initial ו verbs fall into two inflectional patterns, according as they are active or stative.

---

1 Cf. הִתְוַדַּע; הִתְיַלֵּד, cited above, follows the analogy of *pi'el*.

The actives — including the common verbs יָשַׁב, יָרַד, יָצָא, יָלַד — build their imperfect and imperative on a biconsonantal base consisting of only the last two root consonants vocalized with ◌ֵ◌ֵ; the preformatives of the imperfect are also vocalized with ◌ֵ: יֵשֵׁב, יֵרֵד, יֵצֵא, יֵלֵד; לֵד! שֵׁב! רֵד! צֵא! But יֵדַע! דַּע, the ◌ַ due to the laryngal (§ 23.2).

The infinitive construct adds the feminine ת ending to this biconsonantal base: (לָ)שֶׁבֶת, (לָ)רֶדֶת, (לָ)צֵאת[1], (לָ)לֶדֶת, (לָ)דַעַת.

20.4 The imperfect and related forms and the infinitive construct of הָלַךְ inflect in the same pattern: יֵלֵךְ, לֵךְ! (לְכָה!), (לָ)לֶכֶת.

20.5 The stative initial ו verbs inflect after the pattern of יִכְבַּד. Thus יָרֵא "he was afraid": יִירָא, יְרָא!, לִירֹא.

In the imperfect and imperative of יָרֵא, ◌ֵ is lengthened to ◌ָ to compensate for the quiescence of the א.

20.6 The verb יָכֹל has an anomalous imperfect, יוּכַל, which appears to be inflected according to the *hŏf'al* pattern.

20.7 Initial ו verbs:

QAL

stative		*active*		
אוּכַל	אִירָא	אֵדַע	אֵלֵד	1cs impf
תּוּכַל	תִּירָא	תֵּדַע	תֵּלֵד	2m
תּוּכְלִי	תִּירְאִי	תֵּדְעִי	תֵּלְדִי	2f
יוּכַל	יִירָא	יֵדַע	יֵלֵד	3m
תּוּכַל	תִּירָא	תֵּדַע	תֵּלֵד	3f
נוּכַל	נִירָא	נֵדַע	נֵלֵד	1cpl
תּוּכְלוּ	תִּירְאוּ	תֵּדְעוּ	תֵּלְדוּ	2m
תּוּכַלְנָה	תִּירֶאנָה	תֵּדַעְנָה	תֵּלַדְנָה	2&3f
			תֵּצֶאנָה	
יוּכְלוּ	יִירְאוּ	יֵדְעוּ	יֵלְדוּ	3m

1 צֵאת is contracted from צֶאֶת*.

QAL

stative	*active*		
		יֵלֵד (וַיֵּלֶד)	juss
יְרָא	דַּע	לֵד, רְדָה	ms imv
יְרְאִי	דְּעִי	לְדִי	f
יְרְאוּ	דְּעוּ	לְדוּ	mpl
יְרֶאנָה	דַּעְנָה	לֵדְנָה	f
		צֵאנָה	
(לְ)ירֹא	(לָ)דַעַת	(לָ)לֶדֶת	inf cs
		(לָ)צֵאת	

HIF'IL	NIF'AL	
הוֹלַדְתִּי	נוֹלַדְתִּי	1cs pf
הוֹלַדְתָּ–תְּ	נוֹלַדְתָּ–תְּ	2m&f
הוֹלִיד	נוֹלַד	3m
הוֹלִידָה	נוֹלְדָה	3f
הוֹלַדְנוּ	נוֹלַדְנוּ	1cpl
הוֹלַדְתֶּם–ן	נוֹלַדְתֶּם–ן	2m&f
הוֹלִידוּ	נוֹלְדוּ	3c
אוֹלִיד	אִוָּלֵד	1cs impf
תּוֹלִיד	תִּוָּלֵד	2m
תּוֹלִידִי	תִּוָּלְדִי	2f
יוֹלִיד	יִוָּלֵד	3m
תּוֹלִיד	תִּוָּלֵד	3f
נוֹלִיד	נִוָּלֵד	1cpl
תּוֹלִידוּ	תִּוָּלְדוּ	2m
תּוֹלֵדְנָה	תִּוָּלַדְנָה	2&3f
יוֹלִידוּ	יִוָּלְדוּ	3m
יוֹלֵד (וַיּוֹלֶד)	יִוָּלֵד	juss
הוֹלֵד	הִוָּלֵד	imv
(לְ)הוֹלִיד	(לְ)הִוָּלֵד	inf cs
מוֹלִיד	נוֹלָד	pt

20.8 The few originally initial י verbs inflect as statives; e.g., יטב "be good, pleasing," which occurs only in *qal* impf יִיטַב, וַיִּיטַב and *hif'il* pf הֵיטִיב, impf יֵיטִיב, pt מֵיטִיב.

* * * * * * *

Conjugate in qal *and* hif'il:

ישב, ירד.

Conjugate in nif'al:

יתר "be left, remaining."

Give corresponding forms :

in hif'il : יָדַעְתִּי, יָדְעוּ, תֵּדְעִי, יוֹדְעִים, לָדַעַת,
יָצְאָה, אֵצֵא, תֵּצְאוּ, צֵא! צְאֶנָה! לָצֵאת.

in nif'al : יָדְעָה, יְדַעְתֶּם, תֵּדְעִי, דְּעוּ! יוֹדְעוֹת,
יָשְׁבוּ, אֵשֵׁב, תֵּשַׁבְנָה, לָשֶׁבֶת.

Vocalize and translate :

1. מכל בניו נותרו לו שנים. 2. לא תלכו עמנו. 3. אם ישימו לפניהם אכל רב לא יוכלו לאכל אתו כי קטנים הם. 4. בבקר הורדנו את הצאן אל העמק. 5. אחר אשר התודעו אלי הכרתי אתם. 6. לא נירא למות. 7. הם הולידו בנים רבים לפני שני הרעב. 8. טוב כי תצאו מן העיר בטרם יוציאו אתכם השומרים. 9. דעו לפני מי אתם עומדים! 10. אל תיראו לרדת מצרימה! 11. האנשים אוהבים כי נשיהם תלדנה בנים.

Change verbs of above paragraph to singular.

Convert imperfect consecutives to perfects:

1. וַיִּוָּתֵר יַעֲקֹב לְבַדּוֹ. 2. וַיִּוָּלְדוּ לוֹ בָּנִים בְּחֶבְרוֹן. 3. וַתָּשָׁב אֶל אָבִיהָ וַתֵּשֶׁב לְפָנָיו וַתֵּבְךְּ. 4. וַיּוֹלֶד בָּנִים וּבָנוֹת. 5. וַיֹּאכַל וַיֵּשְׁתְּ וַיָּקָם וַיֵּלֶךְ. 6. וַנֵּרֶד מִצְרַיְמָה וַנֵּשֶׁב שָׁם.

Translate:

1. When they come down, we shall be able to go. 2. Can she rule this great land? 3. When they informed (caused to know) him that his brother reigned instead of his father, he raised his voice and wept. 4. How will one man be able to do that which many are not able to do? 5. If it pleases you, give him five wagons. 6. We shall prepare food for you (mpl) before the day is done (goes out). 7. His feelings were stirred toward the donkey, so he hastily took (down) the heavy saddlebag from off him. 8. May God take out his hard heart and put a good heart in its place. 9. Of all the goats that went out into the field not one remained, for the wild animals ate them.

(*To be followed by Genesis 37:1–8, 9–17.*)

§ 21

FINAL א AND INITIAL א VERBS

Final א *verbs*

21.1 When א stands at the end of a word and usually, also, when at the end of a syllable, it quiesces, and the preceding vowel is lengthened by way of compensation. Hence **måṣa'* > *måṣå* (מָצָא), **yimṣa'* > *yimṣå* (יִמְצָא).

21.2 This process results in some forms of final א verbs sounding like corresponding forms of final ה verbs; e.g., מָצָא like בָּכָה. Consequently a certain mixture of final א and final ה forms takes place, with final ה forms more often imposing themselves on the final א paradigm than vice versa, owing to their greater frequency. Thus the impf 2 and 3fpl are תִּמְצֶאנָה, like תִּבְכֶּינָה; and outside of *qal* the perfect inflects throughout with ◌ֵ before consonantal afformatives: מִלֵּאתִי like צִוֵּיתִי ; הִמְצֵאתִי like הִרְבֵּיתִי.

In Rabbinic Hebrew final א verbs assimilated to the final ה pattern prevailingly.

21.3 Final א verbs:

HIF'IL	PI'EL	NIF'AL	QAL *stative*	QAL *active*	
הִמְצֵאתִי	מִלֵּאתִי	נִמְצֵאתִי	שָׂנֵאתִי	מָצָאתִי	1cs pf
הִמְצֵאתָ־ת	מִלֵּאתָ־ת	נִמְצֵאתָ־ת	שָׂנֵאתָ־ת	מָצָאתָ־ת	2m&f
הִמְצִיא־צִיאָה	מִלֵּא־לְאָה[1]	נִמְצָא־צְאָה	שָׂנֵא־נְאָה	מָצָא־צְאָה	3m&f
הִמְצֵאנוּ	מִלֵּאנוּ	נִמְצֵאנוּ	שָׂנֵאנוּ	מָצָאנוּ	1cpl
הִמְצֵאתֶם־ן	מִלֵּאתֶם־ן	נִמְצֵאתֶם־ן	שְׂנֵאתֶם־ן	מְצָאתֶם־ן	2m&f
הִמְצִיאוּ	מִלְאוּ[1]	נִמְצְאוּ	שָׂנְאוּ	מָצְאוּ	3c
אַמְצִיא	אֲמַלֵּא	אֶמָּצֵא		אֶמְצָא	1cs impf
etc.	etc.	etc.		תִּמְצָא־צְאִי	2m&f
				יִמְצָא, תִּ־	3m&f
				נִמְצָא	1cpl
				תִּמְצְאוּ	2m
תַּמְצֶאנָה	תְּמַלֶּאנָה	תִּמָּצֶאנָה		תִּמְצֶאנָה	2&3f
				יִמְצְאוּ	3m
הַמְצֶאנָה	מַלֶּאנָה	הִמָּצֶאנָה fpl		מְצָא fpl מְצֶאנָה	ms imv
				(לִ)מְצֹא	inf cs
מַמְצִיא	מְמַלֵּא	נִמְצָא		מוֹצֵא	ms pt
מַמְצֵאת	מְמַלֵּאת	נִמְצֵאת		מוֹצֵאת	f
מַמְצִיאִים־אוֹת	מְמַלְאִים־אוֹת[1]	נִמְצָאִים־אוֹת		מוֹצְאִים־אוֹת	m&fpl

(a) Note that in *qal* stative the ֵ is retained throughout the perfect (contrast כָּבַדְתִּי, etc.).

(b) *Qal* imperfect inflects always on the יִכְבַּד pattern.

(c) Note that the pt fs replaces ֶ ֶת with ֵאת (שׁוֹמֶרֶת but מוֹצֵאת).

---

1 On the unlengthened לְ see p. 105, note 1.

Initial א *verbs*

21.4 In the *qal* imperfect, initial א verbs fall into two inflectional patterns:

(a) When the א does not quiesce, as in אָסַף "he gathered," the inflection is:

אֶאֱסֹף, תֶּאֱסֹף, תַּאַסְפִי, יֶאֱסֹף, תֶּאֱסֹף, נֶאֱסֹף, תַּאַסְפוּ, תֶּאֱסֹפְנָה, יַאַסְפוּ, תֶּאֱסֹפְנָה.

The preformative vowel is ֶ, except in forms having vowel affirmatives, in which case it is ַ. In the latter case the vowel under the א is a full vowel, no longer a *ḥaṭåf*.

The imperative: אֱסֹף, אִסְפִי, אִסְפוּ, אֱסֹפְנָה. The infinitive construct: (לֶ)אֱסֹף.

(b) In five verbs (אָכַל "eat," אָמַר "say," אָבַד "perish," אָבָה "be willing," אָפָה "bake") the א quiesces, entailing vowel changes thus:

אֹכַל, תֹּאכַל, תֹּאכְלִי, יֹאכַל, תֹּאכַל, נֹאכַל, תֹּאכְלוּ, תֹּאכַלְנָה, יֹאכְלוּ, תֹּאכַלְנָה.

The imperfect consecutive: וַיֹּאכַל, but וַיֹּאמֶר [in pause (§29) וַיֹּאמַר].
The imperative: אֱכֹל, אִכְלִי, אִכְלוּ, אֱכֹלְנָה.
The infinitive construct: (לֶ)אֱכֹל, but לֵאמֹר.
In all else initial א verbs inflect as other initial laryngals (§23).

* * * * * * *

Conjugate in qal *and* nif'al:

יָרֵא, קָרָא

Conjugate in pi'el:

קִנֵּא

Conjugate in hif'il:

יָצָא, קָרָא

Fill in perfect, imperfect, and participle of indicated verbs:

שָׂנֵא: 1. הָאִשָּׁה ______ אֶת הַחַיָּה. 2. אַתְּ ______ כָּל עוֹשֶׂה רָע.
קִנֵּא: 3. אֲנִי ______ בְּךָ. 4. הָאִישׁ ______ בְּאָחִיו.
הֵבִיא: 5. הָרוֹעֶה ______ אֶת צֹאנוֹ אֶל הַשָּׂדֶה. 6. אַתְּ ______ אֶת בְּנֵךְ אֶל הַחֶדֶר.

Change subjects and verbs of the preceding exercise to plural.

Vocalize and translate:

1. אל תאמר לי מה לעשות! 2. אלהים צוה את בני ישראל כי לא ישתחוו לאלהים אחרים. 3. אחי יוסף היו מקנאים בו וכאשר שמעו את דבריו הוסיפו עוד לקנא בו. 4. אם יאמר השר לאסר אתכם, קראו אלי בקול גדול ואבוא אליכם! 5. אם השתחוית לשמש ולירח חטאת לאלהים. 6. אל תשנא את אחיך! 7. מלאו את שקיהם שבר כאשר דבר המושל. 8. תוציאו כל איש מהחדר. 9. הוספתי לקרא אליו והוא לא שמע. 10. יצאתם מן העמק הזה ובאתם אל עמק אחר. 11. רחל היתה מקנאת בלאה. 12. אם נבקש ארץ אחרת טובה מזאת לא נמצא. 13. פרותיכם נמצאו בתוך שדנו.

Translate:

1. The shepherds took (out) bread from their sacks and sought a place in which they could sit and eat. 2. Don't (ms) fear to say to her that she sinned. 3. You (mpl) were jealous of your brother because your father loved him more than all his sons. 4. Fill (fs) our sack with provisions for the way. 5. If we sit in the field we shall see

the sun coming up (out) in the morning. 6. Now we can prepare the food, for we know who will eat with us. 7. I cannot say whether she will come down or go up. 8. They will take out all the other prisoners, will put you there alone, and no man will know this. 9. Gather (ms) all the wise men of the city and let them say who will be king over them. 10. She is called Rachel.

(To be followed by Genesis 37:18–27, 28–36.)

§ 22

INITIAL נ VERBS

22.1 When נ occurs at the end of a syllable within a word it usually assimilates to the following consonant, if that consonant is not a laryngal (cf. *nif'al* imperfect *יִנְשָׁמֵר > יִשָּׁמֵר; שָׁם + מִן = מִשָּׁם).

Such assimilation occurs regularly in initial נ verbs; e.g., *qal* imperfect *יִנְפֹּל > יִפֹּל "he will fall," *nif'al* perfect *נִנְגַּשׁ > נִגַּשׁ "he drew near," throughout *hif'il* *הִנְכִּיר > הִכִּיר "he recognized," and *hŏf'al* *הֻנְכַּר > הֻכַּר "he was recognized."

22.2 Initial נ verbs:

HIF'IL		NIF'AL		QAL a *impf*	QAL o *impf*	
הִכַּרְתִּי	1cs pf	נִגַּשְׁתִּי	1cs pf	אֶגַּשׁ	אֶפֹּל	1cs
הִכַּרְתָּ–תְּ	2m&f	נִגַּשְׁתָּ–תְּ	2m&f	תִּגַּשׁ–גְּשִׁי	תִּפֹּל–פְּלִי	2m&f
הִכִּיר, הִכִּירָה	3m&f	נִגַּשׁ–גְּשָׁה	3m&f	יִגַּשׁ, תִּ־	יִפֹּל, תִּ־	3m&f
הִכַּרְנוּ	1cpl	נִגַּשְׁנוּ	1cpl	נִגַּשׁ	נִפֹּל	1cpl
הִכַּרְתֶּם–ן	2m&f	נִגַּשְׁתֶּם–ן	2m&f	תִּגְּשׁוּ	תִּפְּלוּ	2m
הִכִּירוּ	3c	נִגְּשׁוּ	3c	תִּגַּשְׁנָה	תִּפֹּלְנָה	2&3f
				יִגְּשׁוּ	יִפְּלוּ	3m

HIF'IL		NIF'AL		QAL		
				a *impf*	o *impf*	
אַכִּיר	1cs impf	נִגָּשׁ	ms pt	גַּשׁ	נְפֹל	ms imv
תַּכִּיר, תַּכִּירִי	2m&f	נִגֶּשֶׁת	f	גְּשִׁי	נִפְלִי	f
יַכִּיר, תַּ־	3m&f	נִגָּשִׁים	mpl	גְּשׁוּ	נִפְלוּ	mpl
נַכִּיר	1cpl	נִגָּשׁוֹת	f	גַּשְׁנָה	נְפֹלְנָה	f
תַּכִּירוּ	2m					
תַּכֵּרְנָה	2&3f			גֶּשֶׁת,לָגֶשֶׁת	נְפֹל,לִנְפֹּל	inf cs
יַכִּירוּ	3m					
הַכֵּר, הַכִּירִי	m&fs imv					
הַכִּירוּ, הַכֵּרְנָה	m&fpl					
(לְ)הַכִּיר	inf cs					
מַכִּיר	ms pt					

(a) Note that in the *qal a* imperfect נ is dropped in the imperative and infinitive construct. The latter is filled out with the feminine ת termination; cf. the infinitive construct of initial י/ו verbs (לָ)לֶדֶת (§ 20.3).

(b) The verb נִגַּשׁ inflects its perfect and participle in *nif'al*, but its imperfect and related forms and infinitive construct in *qal*, as in the above paradigm.

The verbs הִכָּה ,נָשָׂא ,לָקַח ,נָתַן

22.3 The verb נָתַן "he gave" inflects thus:

pf: נָתַתִּי, נָתַתָּ, נָתַתְּ, נָתַן, נָתְנָה, נָתַנּוּ, נְתַתֶּם־ן, נָתְנוּ

impf: אֶתֵּן, תִּתֵּן, תִּתְּנִי, יִתֵּן, תִּתֵּן, נִתֵּן, תִּתְּנוּ, תִּתֵּנָּה, יִתְּנוּ, תִּתֵּנָּה

imv: תֵּן (תְּנָה), תְּנִי, תְּנוּ, תֵּנָּה inf cs: תֵּת, לָתֵת, w suf תִּתִּי

With the ֵ of the imperfect compare יֵלֵד. The infinitive construct is formed thus: *tin-t>תֵּת, hence with suffix *tinti>תִּתִּי.

22.4 The verb לָקַח "he took" inflects its imperfect, imperative, and infinitive construct as though it were an initial נ verb; this is apparently owing to an analogy with its antonym נָתַן. Its theme vowel is ַ because of the laryngal.

:impf אֶקַּח, תִּקַּח, תִּקְחִי[1], יִקַּח, תִּקַּח, נִקַּח, תִּקְחוּ[1], תִּקַּחְנָה, יִקְחוּ[1], תִּקַּחְנָה

:imv קַח, קְחִי, קְחוּ, קַחְנָה :inf cs (לָ)קַחַת

22.5 The verb נָשָׂא "he carried" inflects with the peculiarities of both initial נ and final א verbs:

:impf אֶשָּׂא, תִּשָּׂא, תִּשְּׂאִי[1], יִשָּׂא, תִּשָּׂא, נִשָּׂא, תִּשְּׂאוּ[1], תִּשֶּׂאנָה, יִשְּׂאוּ[1], תִּשֶּׂאנָה.

:imv שָׂא, שְׂאִי, שְׂאוּ, שֶׂאנָה :inf cs (לָ)שֵׂאת

22.6 The verb נכה, common in *hif'il* הִכָּה "he smote, struck," inflects with the peculiarities of both initial נ and final ה verbs:

:pf הִכֵּיתִי, הִכִּיתָ, הִכִּית, הִכָּה, הִכְּתָה, הִכִּינוּ, הִכִּיתֶם־ן, הִכּוּ

:impf אַכֶּה, תַּכֶּה, תַּכִּי, יַכֶּה, תַּכֶּה, נַכֶּה, תַּכּוּ, תַּכֶּינָה, יַכּוּ, תַּכֶּינָה

:apoc יַךְ :imv הַכֵּה, הַכִּי, הַכּוּ, הַכֶּינָה :inf cs (לְ)הַכּוֹת

:pt מַכֶּה, מַכָּה, מַכִּים, מַכּוֹת

Conjugate in qal:

נשק (*a* impf).

Conjugate in nif'al:

נצל ("be saved" in *nif'al*).

---

1 Lengthening is often given up in sibilants (ז, ס, צ, ש), liquids (ל, מ, נ), and ק when they take mobile *šewå*.

Conjugate in hif'il:

נשׂג, נגד

Fill in perfect, imperfect, and participle of indicated verbs:

נָשָׂא: 1. הָאֵם ______ אֶת בְּנָהּ הַקָּטֹן. 2. הַחֲמוֹרִים ______ אֶת הַשַּׂקִּים.

נָגַשׁ: 3. אֲנִי ______ אֶל הַפֶּתַח. 4. אַתֶּם ______ אֵלָיו.

הִצִּיל: 5. אַתָּה ______ אֶת הַצֹּאן מִפִּי הַחַיָּה. 6. אֲנַחְנוּ ______ אֹתוֹ מִן הַבּוֹר.

הִכָּה: 7. אֲנַחְנוּ ______ אֶת הַחֲמוֹר. 8. הַנָּשִׁים ______ אֶת בְּנוֹתֵיהֶן.

Vocalize and translate:

1. שא עֵינֶיךָ אל אלהים! 2. אם תלך במדבר בלילה תפל בבורות אשר בו. 3. אל תסעו ביום פן תכה אתכם השמש! 4. מי יציל את שעיר העזים מן החיה הטורפת? 5. כאשר יפל הבן בדרך ולא יוכל ללכת עוד ישא אתו אביו. 6. משכו את החמור והכו אתו ולא קם מעל הארץ. 7. אֵין איש יכל לגשת אל המלך כי שומריו נצבים עליו. 8. הצלנו את העזים מחיות השדה. 9. תנו לי לחם לאכל! 10. עברו על פתח ביתם וקראו להם! 11. יסעו בעוד שנים עשר יום. 12. אל תשא את העז לבדך כי כבדה היא! 13. מי זה נצב שם בפתח?

Translate:

1. They told us that they would give much money to the man who

would rescue them from prison. 2. Tell (fs) me to whom I should give the garment. 3. Many days passed and they still could not overtake him. 4. It is better to give than to take. 5. He will not eat flesh even if you (fs) do not give him another thing. 6. Give well-being to the land and rescue us from all who hate us. 7. She came up to the weeping child and struck him on his face. 8. If you (ms) know who the owner (master) of this tunic is, take it and carry it off from before my house. 9. Many will fall before (that) they come out of the wilderness.

(*To be followed by Genesis 42:1–11, 12–20*).

§ 23

INITIAL LARYNGAL VERBS

The peculiarities of laryngals

23.1 Laryngals (א, ה, ח, ע) and ר are not normally lengthened. In positions where lengthening is called for, laryngals and ר remain short (i.e., do not take strong *dåḡeš*). By way of compensation, the preceding vowel may be lengthened: ◌ַ > ◌ָ, ◌ִ > ◌ֵ, ◌ֻ > ◌ֹ. Compensatory vowel lengthening occurs:

(a) always in *nif'al* imperfect (and related forms): יֵעָצֵב "he will be grieved" ||[1] יִשָּׁמֵר;

(b) almost always with א and ר in other forms as well: מֵאֵן "he refused" || סִפֵּר, יְמָאֵן || יְסַפֵּר, בֹּרַךְ "he was blessed" || סֻפַּר;

(c) only sporadically in other forms with ע, ח, ה: examples of nonoccurrence are מִהַר "he hastened," נִחֵשׁ "he divined."

---

[1] Read: "corresponding to."

23.2 Laryngals in what would normally be syllable-end position prefer to be preceded by ◌ַ. If in a stressed or a final syllable, they *must* be preceded by ◌ַ (or ◌ָ). If the preceding vowel according to the regular pattern is not ◌ַ:

(a) it is replaced by ◌ַ : סִפֵּר || שִׁלַּח, יִשְׁמֹר || יִשְׁלַח, תִּשְׁלֵ֫כְנָה || תִּשְׁמַ֫עְנָה;

(b) between it and a final laryngal, furtive *pa̍ṯaḥ* insinuates itself; this always occurs when the vowel in question is the naturally long וֹ, וּ, ◌ֵי, ◌ִי : הִשְׁלִיךְ || הִשְׁמִיעַ, לִשְׁמֹר || לִשְׁלֹחַ, שׁוֹמֵר || שׁוֹלֵחַ, שָׁמוּר || שָׁלוּחַ, שָׁמוֹר || שָׁלוֹחַ.

23.3 Laryngals often take *ḥaṭåf* in preference to simple *šewå*:

(a) Mobile *šewå* [§ 2.7(b)] is always replaced by *ḥaṭåf*, usually *ḥaṭåf pa̍ṯaḥ* : שָׁמְרוּ || שָׁאֲלוּ, שְׁמֹר || עֲמֹד;

(b) Quiescent *šewå* [§ 2.7(a)] in a stressed syllable never becomes *ḥaṭåf*: תִּשְׁלַ֫חְנָה, שָׁלַ֫חְנוּ;

(c) In an unstressed syllable quiescent *šewå* may or may not become *ḥaṭåf*. When it does, the *ḥaṭåf* is colored by the preceding vowel, resulting in the patterns ◌ַ ◌ֲ (יַעֲמֹד), ◌ֶ ◌ֱ (אֶעֱמֹד), ◌ָ ◌ֳ (יָעֳמַד);

(d) When in the course of inflection the vowel following the *ḥaṭåf* is reduced to *šewå*, the *ḥaṭåf* becomes a full vowel: יַעַמְדוּ, נֶעֶצְבוּ, יָעָמְדוּ (*yŏʿŏmedu*).

23.4 In certain forms, ◌ִ before a syllable-ending laryngal is changed to ◌ֶ (נִשְׁמַר || נֶעֱצַב, הִשְׁלִיךְ || הֶאֱמִין, יִכְבַּד || יֶחֱרַד) and ◌ֻ to *qåmeṣ ḥåṭuf* (מֻשְׁלָךְ || מָעֳמָד).

23.5 See paradigms of initial laryngal verbs. *Note*: Initial א verbs that depart from the regular laryngal pattern have been treated above (§21).

Remarks on the paradigm. The different preformative vowels of the two *qal* imperfects (active יַעֲמֹד, stative יֶחֱרַד) reflect original distinctions that have been lost in the sound verb. The original preformatives were active *ya-* stative *yi-*. The tendency of *a* to become *i* in closed, unstressed syllables caused the two to merge in the sound verb (יִכְבַּד, יִשְׁמֹר). But *ya-* still appears in the hollow verbs (יָשׁוּב) and with initial laryngals (in accordance with §23.2). Original *yi-* became *ye-* before laryngals (in accordance with §23.4).

Initial laryngal verbs עָמַד "he stood," חָרַד "he trembled," נֶעֱצַב "he was grieved," הֶאֱמִין "he believed":

HIF'IL	NIF'AL	QAL stative	QAL active	
הֶאֱמַנְתִּי	נֶעֱצַבְתִּי	חָרַדְתִּי	עָמַדְתִּי	1cs pf
הֶאֱמַנְתָּ–תְּ	נֶעֱצַבְתָּ–תְּ	חָרַדְתָּ–תְּ	עָמַדְתָּ–תְּ	2m&f
הֶאֱמִין	נֶעֱצַב	חָרַד	עָמַד	3m
הֶאֱמִינָה	נֶעֶצְבָה	חָרְדָה	עָמְדָה	3f
הֶאֱמַנּוּ	נֶעֱצַבְנוּ	חָרַדְנוּ	עָמַדְנוּ	1cpl
הֶאֱמַנְתֶּם–ן	נֶעֱצַבְתֶּם–ן	חֲרַדְתֶּם–ן	עֲמַדְתֶּם–ן	2m&f
הֶאֱמִינוּ	נֶעֶצְבוּ	חָרְדוּ	עָמְדוּ	3c
אַאֲמִין	אֵעָצֵב	אֶחֱרַד	אֶעֱמֹד	1cs impf
תַּאֲמִין	תֵּעָצֵב	תֶּחֱרַד	תַּעֲמֹד	2m
תַּאֲמִינִי	תֵּעָצְבִי	תֶּחֶרְדִי	תַּעַמְדִי	2f
יַאֲמִין	יֵעָצֵב	יֶחֱרַד	יַעֲמֹד	3m
תַּאֲמִין	תֵּעָצֵב	תֶּחֱרַד	תַּעֲמֹד	3f
נַאֲמִין	נֵעָצֵב	נֶחֱרַד	נַעֲמֹד	1cpl
תַּאֲמִינוּ	תֵּעָצְבוּ	תֶּחֶרְדוּ	תַּעַמְדוּ	2m

HIF'IL	NIF'AL	QAL *stative*	QAL *active*	
תַּאֲמֵנָּה	תֵּעָצַבְנָה	תֶּחֱרַדְנָה	תַּעֲמֹדְנָה	2&3fpl impf
יַאֲמִינוּ	יֵעָצְבוּ	יֶחֶרְדוּ	יַעַמְדוּ	3m
הַאֲמֵן	הֵעָצֵב	חֲרַד	עֲמֹד	ms imv
הַאֲמִינִי	הֵעָצְבִי	חִרְדִי	עִמְדִי	f
הַאֲמִינוּ	הֵעָצְבוּ	חִרְדוּ	עִמְדוּ	mpl
הַאֲמֵנָּה	הֵעָצַבְנָה	חֲרַדְנָה	עֲמֹדְנָה	f
(לְ)הַאֲמִין	(לְ)הֵעָצֵב	(לַ)חֲרֹד	(לַ)עֲמֹד	inf cs
מַאֲמִין	נֶעֱצָב	חָרֵד	עוֹמֵד	ms pt
מַאֲמֶנֶת	נֶעֱצֶבֶת	חֲרֵדָה	עוֹמֶדֶת	f
מַאֲמִינִים–נוֹת	נֶעֱצָבִים–בוֹת	חֲרֵדִים–דוֹת	עוֹמְדִים–דוֹת	m&fpl
			"killed" הָרוּג	ms pt pass
			הֲרוּגָה	f
			הֲרוּגִים–גוֹת	m&fpl

* * * * * * *

Give corresponding forms of verbs as indicated:

Of עָשָׂה, אָשֵׁם, עָבַר corresponding to: שְׁמֹר!, שִׁמְרוּ!, לִשְׁמֹר, שְׁמַרְתֶּם, אֶשְׁמֹר, תִּשְׁמְרִי, יִשְׁמֹר, יִשְׁמְרוּ

Of הָרַג corresponding to: אֶשָּׁמֵר, יִשָּׁמְרוּ, נִשְׁמֶרֶת, לְהִשָּׁמֵר, נִשְׁמַר, נִשְׁמְרָה

Of עָלָה, חָטָא, עָבַר corresponding to: מַשְׁלִיכִים, לְהַשְׁלִיךְ, הִשְׁלַכְתִּי, הִשְׁלִיךְ, הַשְׁלִיכָה, יַשְׁלִיךְ, תַּשְׁלֵכְנָה, הַשְׁלֵךְ!

Vocalize and translate:

1. ארץ! אל תכסי את דם הנהרגים אשר נשפך עליך! 2. האיש

אחד יחטא ובכל העם יחרה אפך? 3. אנשי העיר מנער עד זקן נאספו מרחוק ומקרוב לראות בבוא המלך. 4. תעברנה הפרות לפנינו ונראה מי הטובות בהן. 5. כאשר תעברו את הבית ראו היש בו איש אם ריק הוא? 6. חטאתם והחטאתם את הרבים. 7. אם יהרגו את הילד יחטאו לאלהים ויאשמו. 8. תוכל להאמין לדבריו כי איש אמת הוא. 9. החכם ידע לפתר כל חלום אשר יחלמו. 10. אחר אשר תהרג החיה הרעה לא נירא לצאת אל השדה. 11. נאסרנו ולא עשיתם דבר להציל אתנו. 12. תקחו את הילד ותשאו אתו אל אמו.

Translate:

1. We shall sin if we kill them. 2. Won't he answer if you talk to him? 3. She saw that they would pass the empty house. 4. The three who were imprisoned will come and stand before him. 5. The garment will be made as you requested. 6. The slain covered the face of the earth. 7. You (mpl) may not eat the flesh that you find in the field. 8. We didn't believe that he could bring the cow up from the pit. 9. Why do they tremble? Because they are guilty in the eyes of God. 10. We are bringing into the house all the sheaves that were not yet gathered from the midst of the field. 11. Put your (ms) hand in mine and we shall carry this old man.

(*To be followed by Genesis 42:21–28, 29–38.*)

§ 24

MIDDLE AND FINAL LARYNGAL VERBS

24.1 Middle laryngal verbs שָׁאַל "he asked," מֵאֵן "he refused," מִהַר "he hurried":

PI'EL			NIF'AL	QAL	
מִהַ֫רְתִּי	מֵאַ֫נְתִּי	1cs pf	נִשְׁאֲלָה	שָׁאֲלָה	3fs pf
מִהַ֫רְתָּ־תְּ	מֵאַ֫נְתָּ־תְּ	2m&f	נִשְׁאֲלוּ	שָׁאֲלוּ	3cpl
מִהַר	מֵאֵן	3m			
מִהֲרָה	מֵאֲנָה	3f		אֶשְׁאַל	1cs impf
מִהַ֫רְנוּ	מֵאַ֫נּוּ	1cpl		תִּשְׁאַל	2m
מִהַרְתֶּם־ן	מֵאַנְתֶּם־ן	2m&f	תִּשָּׁאֲלִי	תִּשְׁאֲלִי	2f
מִהֲרוּ	מֵאֲנוּ	3c		יִשְׁאַל	3m
				תִּשְׁאַל	3f
אֲמַהֵר	אֲמָאֵן	1cs impf		נִשְׁאַל	1cpl
תְּמַהֵר	תְּמָאֵן	2m	תִּשָּׁאֲלוּ	תִּשְׁאֲלוּ	2m
תְּמַהֲרִי	תְּמָאֲנִי	2f		תִּשְׁאַ֫לְנָה	2&3f
יְמַהֵר	יְמָאֵן	3m	יִשָּׁאֲלוּ	יִשְׁאֲלוּ	3m
תְּמַהֵר	תְּמָאֵן	3f			
נְמַהֵר	נְמָאֵן	1cpl		שְׁאַל	ms imv

PI'EL		
תְּמַהֲרוּ	תְּמָאֲנוּ	2mpl impf
תְּמַהֵרְנָה	תְּמָאֵנָּה	2&3f
יְמַהֲרוּ	יְמָאֲנוּ	3m
מַהֵר	מָאֵן	ms imv
מַהֲרִי	מָאֲנִי	f
מַהֲרוּ	מָאֲנוּ	mpl
מַהֵרְנָה	מָאֵנָּה	f
(לְ)מַהֵר	(לְ)מָאֵן	inf cs
מְמַהֵר	מְמָאֵן	ms pt
מְמַהֶרֶת	מְמָאֶנֶת	f
מְמַהֲרִים	מְמָאֲנִים	mpl
מְמַהֲרוֹת	מְמָאֲנוֹת	f

NIF'AL	QAL	
הִשָּׁאֲלִי	שַׁאֲלִי	fs imv
הִשָּׁאֲלוּ	שַׁאֲלוּ	mpl
	שְׁאַלְנָה	f
	(לִ)שְׁאֹל	inf cs
	שׁוֹאֲלִים	mpl pt
	שׁוֹאֲלוֹת	f

(a) In *qal* and *nif'al* the deviations from the normal pattern are those described in § 23.3. *Qal* imperfect usually has ◌ַ as its theme vowel.

(b) For the two inflectional patterns of *pi'el*, cf. § 23.1.

24.2 Final laryngal verbs שָׁלַח "he sent," שִׁלַּח "he released," הִשְׁמִיעַ "he caused to hear":

PI'EL	NIF'AL	QAL	
שִׁלַּחְתִּי	נִשְׁלַחְתִּי	שָׁלַחְתִּי	1cs pf
שִׁלַּחְתָּ, שִׁלַּחַתְּ	נִשְׁלַחְתָּ, נִשְׁלַחַתְּ	שָׁלַחְתָּ, שָׁלַחַתְּ	2m&f
שִׁלַּח־לְּחָה	נִשְׁלַח־לְחָה	שָׁלַח־לְחָה	3m&f
שִׁלַּחְנוּ	נִשְׁלַחְנוּ	שָׁלַחְנוּ	1cpl
שִׁלַּחְתֶּם־ן	נִשְׁלַחְתֶּם־ן	שְׁלַחְתֶּם־ן	2m&f
שִׁלְּחוּ	נִשְׁלְחוּ	שָׁלְחוּ	3c
אֲשַׁלַּח	אֶשָּׁלַח	אֶשְׁלַח	1cs impf
תְּשַׁלַּח־לְּחִי	תִּשָּׁלַח־לְחִי	תִּשְׁלַח־לְחִי	2m&f
יְשַׁלַּח, תְּ־	יִשָּׁלַח, תִּ־	יִשְׁלַח, תִּ־	3m&f

PI'EL	NIF'AL	QAL	
נְשַׁלַּח	נִשָּׁלַח	נִשְׁלַח	1cpl impf
תְּשַׁלְּחוּ	תִּשָּׁלְחוּ	תִּשְׁלְחוּ	2m
תְּשַׁלַּ֫חְנָה	תִּשָּׁלַ֫חְנָה	תִּשְׁלַ֫חְנָה	2&3f
יְשַׁלְּ֫חוּ	יִשָּׁלְחוּ	יִשְׁלְ֫חוּ	3m
שַׁלַּח, שַׁלְּחִי	הִשָּׁלַח, הִשָּׁלְחִי	שְׁלַח, שִׁלְחִי	m&f imv
שַׁלְּחוּ, שַׁלַּ֫חְנָה	הִשָּׁלְחוּ, הִשָּׁלַ֫חְנָה	שִׁלְחוּ, שְׁלַ֫חְנָה	m&fpl
שַׁלֵּחַ	נִשְׁלוֹחַ, הִשָּׁלֵחַ	שָׁלוֹחַ	inf abs
(לְ)שַׁלַּח,(לְשַׁלֵּחַ)	(לְ)הִשָּׁלַח	(לִ)שְׁלֹ֫חַ	inf cs
מְשַׁלֵּחַ, מְשַׁלַּ֫חַת	נִשְׁלָח, נִשְׁלַ֫חַת	שׁוֹלֵחַ, שׁוֹלַ֫חַת	m&fs pt
מְשַׁלְּחִים־וֹת	נִשְׁלָחִים־וֹת	שׁוֹלְחִים־וֹת	m&fpl
		שָׁלוּ֫חַ, שְׁלוּחָה	m&fs pt pass
		שְׁלוּחִים־וֹת	m&fpl

	HITPA'EL	
"he made himself known"	הִתְוַדַּע	3m pf
	יִתְוַדַּע	3m impf
	(לְ)הִתְוַדַּע	inf cs
	מִתְוַדֵּ֫עַ	ms pt

HIF'IL		HIF'IL	
תַּשְׁמִ֫יעוּ	2mpl impf	הִשְׁמַ֫עְתִּי	1cs pf
תַּשְׁמַ֫עְנָה	2&3f	הִשְׁמַ֫עְתָּ, הִשְׁמַ֫עַתְּ	2m&f
יַשְׁמִ֫יעוּ	3m	הִשְׁמִיעַ, הִשְׁמִ֫יעָה	3m&f
יַשְׁמַע	juss	הִשְׁמַ֫עְנוּ	1cpl
הַשְׁמַע, הַשְׁמִ֫יעִי	m&f imv	הִשְׁמַעְתֶּם־ן	2m&f
הַשְׁמִ֫יעוּ, הַשְׁמַ֫עְנָה	m&fpl	הִשְׁמִ֫יעוּ	3c
הַשְׁמֵעַ	inf abs		
(לְ)הַשְׁמִיעַ	inf cs	אַשְׁמִיעַ	1cs impf
		תַּשְׁמִיעַ, תַּשְׁמִ֫יעִי	2m&f
מַשְׁמִיעַ, מַשְׁמַ֫עַת	m&fs pt	יַשְׁמִיעַ, תַּ־	3m&f
מַשְׁמִיעִים־וֹת	m&fpl	נַשְׁמִיעַ	1cpl

(a) In the pf 2fs an auxiliary ◌ַ breaks the consonant cluster at the end of the form: *šalaḥt* > *šalа́ḥat* שָׁלַ֫חַתְּ. Because this vowel is secondary it does not cause spirantization of the ת.

(b) Owing to the laryngal the pt fs ends in ◌ַ֫◌ַת, in contrast to the ◌ֶ֫◌ֶת of the sound verb.

(c) Where the laryngal is at the end of the word, preceding vowels become ◌ַ except in the following cases: *hif'il* forms with long ◌ִי, infinitive absolute, *qal* (and an alternative *pi'el*) infinitive construct, participle masculine singular.

* * * * * * *

Give corresponding forms of verbs as indicated:

Of פָּתַח, נָסַע, שָׁחַט corresponding to: שָׁמַרְתְּ, שָׁמְרָה, יִשְׁמֹר, תִּשְׁמְרוּ, שְׁמֹר! שִׁמְרוּ! שׁוֹמֵר, שׁוֹמֶרֶת, שׁוֹמְרִים, לִשְׁמֹר

Of שָׁמַע, בָּחַן corresponding to: נִשְׁמַרְתְּ, נִשְׁמְרָה, יִשָּׁמֵר, יִשָּׁמְרוּ, הִשָּׁמֵר! הִשָּׁמְרִי! נִשְׁמֶרֶת, לְהִשָּׁמֵר

Of פִּתַּח ("loosen"), בֵּרַךְ ("bless"), נִחַם corresponding to: סִפַּרְתְּ, סִפֵּר, סִפְּרָה, יְסַפֵּר, מְסַפֵּר, תְּסַפְּרוּ, מְסַפֶּרֶת, לְסַפֵּר

Of תָּמַהּ, יָדַע corresponding to: הִשְׁלַכְתְּ, הִשְׁלִיךְ, הִשְׁלִיכָה, אַשְׁלִיךְ, תַּשְׁלֵכְנָה, מַשְׁלִיךְ, מַשְׁלֶכֶת

Vocalize and translate:

1. העבד ישא את צרורנו עד אשר נעבר את העמק. 2. לא תדע אם להאמין לה עד אשר יבחנו דבריה. 3. השליט ממאן לשלח את הסוחרים מבית האסורים. 4. ימיתו השומרים את אשר יבקש לשלח יד בנפש המלך. 5. אם תמשכי את שמלתי היא תקרע. 6. עוד לא

אדע מה לקחת עמי כאשר אצא לדרך. 7. פרתי תעתה בשדה.
8. הבנים יראו פן ילקח אביהם מאתם. 9. השמיעיני את קולך.

Translate:

1. He will answer if you (fpl) ask him. 2. Food is being collected to be sent to lands in which there is famine. 3. When the word that you brought back will be heard, the king will tear his clothes and weep. 4. You may tell the owner of that house that we refuse to sell our sheep to him. 5. Let her open her mouth and say what she fears. 6. You (ms) will be astonished to hear that I am taking them with me. 7. The man (who was) sent to me is not honest. 8. She ordered that I fill the vessel (with) water and carry it to her, that she might wash (רַחַץ) her face.

(*To be followed by Genesis 43:1–10, 11–23.*)

§ 25

VOWEL CHANGES IN NOUN INFLECTION

25.1 Vowel changes occur in a word owing to a shift in the position of the stress. The occasions of stress shifts in nouns are (a) the addition of the plural, dual, or feminine termination (§ 4.5); (b) entrance into the construct state (§ 6.1);[1] (c) the addition of possessive suffixes (§ 14.1). On these occasions the stress moves forward, and vowels that are subject to change will change, being either shortened or slurred to mobile *šewå*.

Unchangeable vowels

25.2 Not all vowels, however, are subject to change. The following classes of vowels are unchangeable:

(a) Naturally long vowels: namely, vowels written with a vowel letter in full writing (ֵי, ִי, וֹ, וּ) and certain others. Example:

---

1 The segolate nouns (e.g., כֶּ֫סֶף, עֶ֫בֶד, מֶ֫לֶךְ) are a notable exception: their penultimate stress is retained in the construct state; מֶ֫לֶךְ מִצְרַ֫יִם "king of Egypt." The peculiar inflection of segolates is treated in the next section.

the וֹ of חֲמוֹר does not change, regardless of the forward movement of the stress: חֲמוֹרִים, חֲמוֹרֵיהֶם.

(b) Vowels in closed, nonfinal syllables. Syllables are closed by a consonant with quiescent *šewå* (מִשְׁ–גֶּה, מַטְ–מוֹן, מִנְ–חָה) or by a long (i.e., doubled) consonant (טַבָּח = טַבְ–בָּח, תְּהִלָּה = תְּהִלְ–לָה). The first vowel of each of the above examples is unchangeable.

If in place of quiescent *šewå* a *ḥaṭåf* appears (under a laryngal), the preceding vowel is still unchangeable, though now no longer in a closed syllable: מַעֲשֶׂה || מִשְׁגֶּה. The basic form is that with quiescent *šewå*; the peculiar phonetics of laryngals are not enough to upset the stability of the vowel pattern.

(c) Vowels that have arisen by compensatory lengthening. The first *qåmeṣ* of פָּרָה is a compensatorily lengthened *páṯaḥ*, the basic form being **parrå* from the root פרר; hence it never changes, no matter how far ahead of it the stress falls: פָּרָתִי, פָּרוֹתֵיהֶם (contrast the first *qåmeṣ* of דָּבָר, which is changeable: דְּבָרִי).

Changeable vowels

25.3 Changeable vowels depend for their length and quality on the stress. Their primary form is short ◌ַ, ◌ֶ, ◌ֻ. In the stress or near it, these generally lengthen and undergo a qualitative change, becoming, respectively, ◌ָ, ◌ֵ, ◌ֹ. When removed from the stress, these stress-lengthened vowels revert to their original short form in closed syllables and may be slurred to mobile *šewå* in open syllables.

25.4 A closed syllable is one ending in a consonant, as defined above [§ 25.2(b)]. An open syllable is one ending in a vowel: מָ־קוֹם, שָׁ־נָה, דְּבָ־רִים.

25.5 The tables below give a simplified account of the changeable vowels in the regular noun (the noun stressed on the final syllable).

(a) Primary vowel ◌ַ

<table>
<tr><th colspan="3">SYLLABLE</th><th></th></tr>
<tr><th>stress</th><th>prestress</th><th>ante-prestress</th><th></th></tr>
<tr><td rowspan="2">◌ָ [1]</td><td>◌ָ</td><td>◌ְ</td><td>open</td></tr>
<tr><td colspan="2">◌ַ [2]</td><td>closed</td></tr>
</table>

1 Commonly ◌ַ in monosyllables whose final consonant is latently long (i.e., long, for etymological reasons, wherever it is nonfinal); e.g., רַב (but רַבִּים, from רבב); אַף (but אַפַּ֫יִם, from אנף).
2 Often becomes ◌ִ, as in בַּת (< *בנת) with suffix בִּתִּי.

Examples:

w suf	*s cs*	*s abs*	
דְּבָרִי	דְּבַר־	דָּבָר	**dabar* "thing"
שְׁנָתִי	שְׁנַת־	שָׁנָה	**šanat* "year"

(b) Primary vowel ◌ֵ

<table>
<tr><th colspan="3">SYLLABLE</th><th></th></tr>
<tr><th>stress</th><th>prestress</th><th>ante-prestress</th><th></th></tr>
<tr><td rowspan="2">◌ֵ</td><td>◌ֵ [1]</td><td>◌ְ</td><td>open</td></tr>
<tr><td colspan="2">◌ִ , ◌ֶ [2]</td><td>closed</td></tr>
</table>

1 Many exceptions, of which a common one is the final vowel of *qal* and *pi'el* active participles, which is slurred to ◌ְ in an open prestress: שׁוֹמְרִים (s שׁוֹמֵר); מְסַפְּרִים (s מְסַפֵּר). Contrast the behavior of the final vowel of the stative participle, s כָּבֵד, pl כְּבֵדִים.
2 Usually ◌ִ before a long consonant (אִתְּכֶם), ◌ֶ before a short (אֶתְכֶם).

Examples:

w suf	*s cs*	*s abs*	
שְׂעָרִי	שְׂעַר־	שֵׂעָר	**śiʿar* "hair"
לִבִּי	לֶב־	לֵב	**libb* "heart"

(c) Primary vowel ֻ

SYLLABLE

stress	*unstressed*	
ֹ	ְ	*open*
	ֻ , ָ[1] (*ŏ*)	*closed*

[1] Usually ֻ before a long consonant (כֻּלִּי), ָ before a short (כָּל־).

Examples:

w suf	*s cs*	*s abs*	
see § 25.6		שְׁמֹר	**šumur* "guarding" (inf)
כֻּלִּי	כָּל־	כֹּל	**kull* "all"

25.6 If in the course of inflection two consecutive vowels are reduced to ְ, the first is restored, though original ַ usually becomes ִ [§ 25.5(a), note 2], except when in contact with a larnygal.

Examples:

pl דְּבָרִים, pl cs (*דְּבְרֵי־ >) דִּבְרֵי־

pl חֲכָמִים, pl cs (*חֲכְמֵי־ >) חַכְמֵי־

**ṣadaqat* "righteousness": s צְדָקָה, s cs (*צְדְקַת־ >) צִדְקַת־

**ṣaʿaqat* "cry": s צְעָקָה, s cs (*צְעֲקַת־ >) צַעֲקַת־

**šumur* "guarding" (inf): שְׁמֹר, w suf (*שְׁמְרִי־ >) שָׁמְרִי־ (*šŏm-*)

25.7 *Paradigms* דָּבָר "thing," צְדָקָה "righteousness":

FEMININE pl	FEMININE s	MASCULINE pl	MASCULINE s	
צְדָקוֹת	צְדָקָה	דְּבָרִים	דָּבָר	abs
צִדְקוֹת־	צִדְקַת־	דִּבְרֵי־	דְּבַר	cs
צִדְקוֹתַי	צִדְקָתִי	דְּבָרַי	דְּבָרִי	1cs suf
צִדְקוֹתֶיךָ	צִדְקָתְךָ	דְּבָרֶיךָ	דְּבָרְךָ	2m
צִדְקוֹתַיִךְ	צִדְקָתֵךְ	דְּבָרַיִךְ	דְּבָרֵךְ	2f
צִדְקוֹתָיו	צִדְקָתוֹ	דְּבָרָיו	דְּבָרוֹ	3m
צִדְקוֹתֶיהָ	צִדְקָתָהּ	דְּבָרֶיהָ	דְּבָרָהּ	3f
צִדְקוֹתֵינוּ	צִדְקָתֵנוּ	דְּבָרֵינוּ	דְּבָרֵנוּ	1cpl
צִדְקוֹתֵיכֶם־ן	צִדְקַתְכֶם־ן	דִּבְרֵיכֶם־ן	דְּבַרְכֶם־ן	2m&f
צִדְקוֹתֵיהֶם־ן	צִדְקָתָם־ן	דִּבְרֵיהֶם־ן	דְּבָרָם־ן	3m&f

Note on דָּבָר: With heavy suffixes (הֶם־ן, כֶם־ן) the base is the construct form.

25.8 In the inflection of the verb the changeable vowels behave much as they do in nouns; cf. וַיֵּשֶׁב–יֵשֵׁב, תְּסֻבֶּינָה–תָּסֹב, קְטָנְתֶּם–קָטֹן, שְׁמַרְתֶּם–שָׁמַר. The chief differences are: (a) ◌ַ does not change to ◌ָ in a closed stressed syllable: שָׁמַר (contrast דָּבָר), יִכְבַּד (contrast מִדְבָּר)[1] (b) Vowels in an open prestress generally are slurred to ◌ְ: **yikbadu*> יִכְבְּדוּ (contrast מִדְבָּרוֹ), **liku*> לְכוּ (contrast **śiʿar* > שֵׂעָר), **šamarat*> שָׁמְרָה (contrast **ṣadaqat*> צְדָקָה).

* * * * * * *

Be able to account for every vowel change in the examples and the two paradigms.

---

[1] Hence the ◌ַ of *nifʿal* perfect נִשְׁמַר, a verb form, in contrast with the ◌ָ of the participle נִשְׁמָר, a noun form.

Inflect the following nouns in these forms: of the singular, the cs, and with suf 1cs, 2mpl; of the plural, the abs, cs, and with suf 1cs, 3mpl:

זָקֵן (זְקַן־), בָּשָׂר, גָּבִיעַ, שָׁלוֹם, אָדוֹן, רְעָבוֹן, כּוֹכָב, יָרֵחַ, מִדְבָּר,
תּוֹעֵבָה, שָׁנָה, עֵז (*‘inz*)

Translate:

1. We remained in our lodging place all (the) night. 2. Your (mpl) men will pass by before our men, and we shall see who are the more numerous (many). 3. She remembers how (what) hard the years of famine were, and she weeps. 4. Let us raise our hands to the king and plead with him in order to save our sons and daughters. 5. Their fathers scolded them, but they continued to do evil. 6. Shedders of blood will not be able to cover up the blood on their hands. 7. Do not tremble (fs), for your star is ascending (going up) and your year will be good. 8. Fearers of God, tremble before him. 9. His mother carried him by herself to her father's house and left him in charge of her brothers. 10. Your (fpl) gray hair testifies (answers) that you are among the old women of your people. 11. Her grief is bringing her down to Sheol. 12. Let them slaughter their goats as provisions for the way. 13. Inquire about their welfare and the welfare of their wives.

(*To be followed by Genesis 43:24–34, 44:1–10.*)

§ 26

SEGOLATE NOUNS

26.1 Masculine nouns stressed on their first syllable and having (normally) *sɛgol* as their second vowel are called segolates. There are three forms, exemplified by מֶ֫לֶךְ "king," סֵ֫פֶר "book," בֹּ֫קֶר "morning," evolved from the monosyllables **malk*, **sifr*, **buqr*, respectively.

The consonant cluster was broken by inserting ◌ֶ as a helping vowel before the last consonant (cf. § 19.2) — i.e., the monosyllable was *segolated*. Stressed *i* > ◌ֵ and stressed *u* > ◌ֹ [§ 25.5(b),(c)], yielding סֵ֫פֶר and בֹּ֫קֶר. The *a* of **malk* assimilated to the *sɛgol*, whence מֶ֫לֶךְ.

The segolated form is generally retained in the construct. Possessive suffixes are attached to the monosyllabic base thus:

26.2 *Singular segolates*:

בֹּ֫קֶר		סֵ֫פֶר		מֶ֫לֶךְ		abs & cs
pl suf	*s suf*	*pl suf*	*s suf*	*pl suf*	*s suf*	
בָּקְרֵ֫נוּ	בָּקְרִי	סִפְרֵ֫נוּ	סִפְרִי	מַלְכֵּ֫נוּ	מַלְכִּי	1c
בָּקְרְכֶם	בָּקְרְךָ	סִפְרְכֶם	סִפְרְךָ	מַלְכְּכֶם	מַלְכְּךָ	2m
בָּקְרְכֶן	בָּקְרֵךְ	סִפְרְכֶן	סִפְרֵךְ	מַלְכְּכֶן	מַלְכֵּךְ	2f
בָּקְרָם	בָּקְרוֹ	סִפְרָם	סִפְרוֹ	מַלְכָּם	מַלְכּוֹ	3m
בָּקְרָן	בָּקְרָהּ	סִפְרָן	סִפְרָהּ	מַלְכָּן	מַלְכָּהּ	3f

Qåmeṣ ḥåṭuf of בָּקְרִי is in accord with § 25.5(c) note 1.

26.3 *Plural segolates*. The absolute form of all three types has the pattern ־ְ־ָ־ִים; in the construct, the original vowel appears in the first syllable.

סְפָרִים	מְלָכִים	abs
סִפְרֵי־	מַלְכֵי־	cs

pl suf	*s suf*	*pl suf*	*s suf*	
סְפָרֵינוּ	סְפָרַי	מְלָכֵינוּ	מְלָכַי	1c
סִפְרֵיכֶם־ן	סְפָרֶיךָ־רַיִךְ	מַלְכֵיכֶם־ן	מְלָכֶיךָ־כַיִךְ	2m&f
סִפְרֵיהֶם־ן	סְפָרָיו־רֶיהָ	מַלְכֵיהֶם־ן	מְלָכָיו־כֶיהָ	3m&f

בְּקָרִים	abs
בָּקְרֵי־	cs

pl suf	*s suf*	
בְּקָרֵינוּ	בְּקָרַי	1c
בָּקְרֵיכֶם־ן	בְּקָרֶיךָ־רַיִךְ	2m&f
בָּקְרֵיהֶם־ן	בְּקָרָיו־רֶיהָ	3m&f

Note that the heavy suffixes are attached to the construct base.

26.4 Dual segolates keep their original first vowel in inflection: רֶגֶל (< **ragl*): רַגְלַיִם, רַגְלֵי־, רַגְלַי; אֹזֶן (< **'uzn*): אָזְנַיִם, אָזְנֵי־, אָזְנַי.

26.5 Corresponding to these masculines are three feminine forms: מַלְכָּה (< **malkat*) "queen," מִנְחָה (< **minḥat*) "present," טֻמְאָה (< **ṭum'at*) "impurity." They inflect normally in the singular (§15). In the plural they follow the segolate pattern: the absolute is ־ְ־ָ־וֹת for all three; in the construct and with suffixes the original vowel appears in the first syllable.

Skeleton paradigms:

s abs	מַלְכָּה	מִנְחָה	טֻמְאָה
s cs	מַלְכַּת־	מִנְחַת־	טֻמְאַת־
1cs suf	מַלְכָּתִי	מִנְחָתִי	טֻמְאָתִי
2mpl	מַלְכַּתְכֶם	מִנְחַתְכֶם	טֻמְאַתְכֶם
pl abs	מְלָכוֹת	מְנָחוֹת	טְמָאוֹת
pl cs	מַלְכוֹת־	מִנְחוֹת־	טֻמְאוֹת־
1cs suf	מַלְכוֹתַי	מִנְחוֹתַי	טֻמְאוֹתַי

26.6 Many segolates of the מֶלֶךְ-type inflect with *i* instead of the original *a* in the first syllable [cf. §25.5(a) note 2]: בֶּגֶד, בִּגְדִי; שֶׁבֶר, שִׁבְרִי.

26.7 Laryngals and weak consonants affect the segolate pattern as follows:

(a) initial laryngal:

סֵפֶר־type: חֵלֶב, חֶלְבִּי, חֲלָבִים, חֶלְבֵי־

בֹּקֶר־type: אֹכֶל אֳכָלִים

(b) middle laryngal:

מֶלֶךְ־type: בַּעַל, בַּעֲלִי, בַּעַלְךָ, בְּעָלִים, בַּעֲלֵי־;

פַּעַם, פַּעֲמַיִם (du); לֶחֶם, לַחְמִי

בֹּקֶר־type: צֹהַר, צָהֳרַיִם (du); אֹהֶל tent

(c) final laryngal:

מֶלֶךְ־type: פֶּתַח, פִּתְחֲךָ

(d) middle *wåw* and *yoḏ*:

מֶלֶךְ־type: תָּוֶךְ, תּוֹךְ־; עַיִן, עֵין־

* * * * * * *

Inflect the following nouns in these forms: of the singular, with suf 1cs, 2ms, 2mpl; of the plural, pl, cs, with suf 1cs, 2mpl.

שֶׁבֶר (שְׁ–), עֶבֶד, אֶרֶץ (pl ארצות), נַעַר, אֹזֶן (du.), חֶדֶר,
נֶפֶשׁ (pl נפשות), יַלְדָּה, שִׂמְלָה.

Vocalize and translate:

1. בגדו נקרע. 2. כאשר הגידו לעבדים כי יבוא מלכם בצהרי היום ההוא מהרו להכין לו את חדריו. 3. תן פיך אל אזני ולא ישמע איש מה תדבר אלי. 4. זה פעמים הציל מלכנו את ארצכם מיד השונא. 5. דרכי עוברת על פתחכם. 6. מתו כל מבקשי נפשך. 7. קשה להוציא מפיו דבר אמת על מקום כספו. 8. הוא נשא את רגליו והלך לדרכו. 9. לולא חפשו ילדינו ומצאו לנו מעט אכל כי עתה מתנו כלנו ברעב. 10. עבדי ישארו בעיר ואני אעבר את המדבר לבדי. 11. הוציאו את לחמכם לטף! 12. לולא נתתם לי את בגדיכם כי עתה לא היה לי במה לכסות את בשרי.

Translate:

1. What shall we do when we finish our bread? 2. Take (fs) your money with you and go down to Egypt to your husband. 3. Seven years they gathered grain; but after the famine passed through their land, nothing of it remained. 4. If you (ms) had not been afraid, you might have saved your master's life. 5. Let your (fs) ears hear what your mouth is speaking. 6. All his presents will not stand by (for) him if, indeed, the king has grown angry at him. 7. We answered her according to her words, but she continued to refuse to come out of her room. 8. They were astonished to find their money. 9. Said the youngest to the eldest, "Put a bit of water into my cup that I may drink." 10. Wash your (fs) face and prepare the presents that were given to you to give to our king. 11. May God repay you according to (as) the evil deed that you have done.

(*To be followed by Genesis 44:11–23, 24–34; 45:1–15, 16–28.*)

§ 27
WORD ORDER

27.1 There is a normal, expected word order associated with sentence types; when this order is departed from, a change in emphasis is expressed — the unusually placed element receiving the emphasis.

Noun sentences

27.2 The usual order in a noun sentence (or clause) is subject – predicate: וְהַבּוֹר רֵק (Genesis 37:24) "now the cistern was empty"; וְאָחִיו מֵת (44:20) "and his brother is dead"; אֲנִי יוֹסֵף (45:3) "I am Joseph."

27.3 When inversion occurs and the predicate is first, the predicate receives some emphasis: מְרַגְּלִים אַתֶּם (42:9) "you are spies," בְּנֵי אִישׁ אֶחָד נָחְנוּ כֵּנִים אֲנַחְנוּ (42:11) "we are sons of one man; we are honest men," אֲבָל אֲשֵׁמִים אֲנַחְנוּ (42:21) "ah, we are guilty."

(a) After אִם and כִּי there is normally an emphasis on the predicate, hence inversion usually occurs: כִּי אָחִינוּ בְשָׂרֵנוּ הוּא (37:27) "for he is our brother, our own flesh," כִּי שׁוֹמֵעַ יוֹסֵף (42:23) "that Joseph understood," אִם כֵּנִים אַתֶּם (42:19) "if you are (really) honest men."

If the emphasis remains on the subject, however, the normal order is retained: כִּי אָחִיו מֵת (42:38) "for his brother is dead."

(b) In questions, too, the emphasis is usually on the predicate; hence the interrogative order is usually inverted (cf. English "goest thou?"): הַכְּתֹנֶת בִּנְךָ הִוא (37:32) "is it your son's tunic?"

But when the emphasis is on the subject, or at least is not on the predicate, the normal order is retained: הֲזֶה אֲחִיכֶם הַקָּטֹן (43:29) "is this your youngest brother?" אָנָא אֲנִי בָא (37:30) "where am I to go?"

Verb sentences

27.4 Verbs with *wåw*-consecutive (§16) always stand at the head of their sentence or clause.

When *wåw* is separated from a verb to indicate the lack of consecution, the subject must precede the verb (see examples in §16.2).

27.5 Otherwise the order of subject and verb in a verb sentence is flexible:

(a) Normally the order is subject – verb: אֱלֹהֵיכֶם... נָתַן (43:23) "your God... has put," כַּסְפְּכֶם בָּא אֵלָי (*ibid.*) "your money came to me" (I received your money), אֲדֹנִי שָׁאַל אֶת עֲבָדָיו (44:19) "my lord asked his servants."

(b) But inversion is not uncommon, especially in animated or excited speech or with the report of news: וְהִנֵּה קָמָה אֲלֻמָּתִי, וְהִנֵּה תְסֻבֶּינָה... אֲלֻמֹּתֵיכֶם (37:7) "and lo! my sheaf stood up... then lo! your sheaves came around," טָרֹף טֹרַף יוֹסֵף (37:33) "Joseph must have been torn to pieces," הוּשַׁב כַּסְפִּי (42:28) "my money has been returned," דִּבֶּר הָאִישׁ...קָשׁוֹת (42:30) "the man spoke... harshly," בָּאוּ אֲחֵי יוֹסֵף (45:16) "Joseph's brothers have come."

(c) After כַּאֲשֶׁר ,אֲשֶׁר ,כֹּה ,לֹא ,אִם ,כִּי inversion usually occurs: כִּי נִכְמְרוּ רַחֲמָיו (43:30) "for his feelings were stirred," לֹא יֵרֵד בְּנִי (42:38) "my son shall not go down," כֹּה אָמַר בִּנְךָ יוֹסֵף (45:9) "thus said your son Joseph," אֲשֶׁר שָׁלַח יוֹסֵף (45:27) "that Joseph had sent," כַּאֲשֶׁר בָּא יוֹסֵף (37:23) "when Joseph came."

But when there is some emphasis on the subject the normal order is retained: לֹא אַתֶּם שְׁלַחְתֶּם אֹתִי (45:8) "it was not you who sent me," כִּי עַבְדְּךָ עָרַב אֶת הַנַּעַר (44:32) "now it was your servant who took the lad on pledge."

The position of objects

27.6 Normally the object follows the verb: הָאֱלֹהִים מָצָא אֶת עֲוֹן עֲבָדֶיךָ (44:16) "God has discovered the iniquity of your servants," אֲדֹנִי שָׁאַל אֶת עֲבָדָיו (44:19) "my lord asked his servants."

27.7 When the object precedes the verb it is emphatic: כִּי אֹתוֹ אָהַב אֲבִיהֶם (37:4) "that it was he whom their father loved," אֹתִי שִׁכַּלְתֶּם (42:36) "it is I whom you have bereaved," כִּי שְׁנַיִם יָלְדָה לִּי אִשְׁתִּי (44:27) "that my wife bore me only two sons," לֹא כִּי עֶרְוַת הָאָרֶץ בָּאתֶם לִרְאוֹת (42:12) "no, it's the secret parts of the land you've come to see" [contrast the place of the unemphasized object (42:9) לִרְאוֹת אֶת עֶרְוַת הָאָרֶץ בָּאתֶם].

27.8 Direct object nouns usually precede indirect object nouns: וַיִּמְכְּרוּ אֶת יוֹסֵף לַיִּשְׁמְעֵאלִים (37:28) "they sold Joseph to the Ishmaelites," וַיִּתֵּן מִסְפּוֹא לַחֲמֹרֵיהֶם (43:24) "he gave fodder to their donkeys."

(a) But if the indirect object noun is markedly shorter, it comes first: וְהִגַּדְתֶּם לְאָבִי אֶת כָּל כְּבוֹדִי בְּמִצְרַיִם (45:13) "tell my father all about my splendor in Egypt."

(b) Similarly, if either is represented by a pronoun, the pronoun comes first: וְעָשָׂה לוֹ כְּתֹנֶת פַּסִּים (37:3) "he had made for him an ornamented tunic," וַיְסַפֵּר אֹתוֹ לְאֶחָיו (37:9) "he told it to his brothers," לָתֵת לָהֶם צֵדָה (42:25) "to give them provisions."

§ 28

THE ACCENTS

28.1 In printed Hebrew Bibles an accent mark appears on every word that has a stress. Words not so marked are joined by a hyphen (מַקֵּף) to the stress word and are considered with it as one word for stress purposes. The accents appear, with a few exceptions, above or below the first letter of the stressed syllable. If that syllable has a vowel sign that would clash with the accent mark, the accent is placed to the left of the vowel sign. Note the position of the accent marks in the following verse (Genesis 37:15) וַיִּמְצָאֵ֣הוּ אִ֔ישׁ וְהִנֵּ֥ה תֹעֶ֖ה בַּשָּׂדֶ֑ה וַיִּשְׁאָלֵ֧הוּ הָאִ֛ישׁ לֵאמֹ֖ר מַה־תְּבַקֵּֽשׁ׃. The accents thus mark the stressed syllable(s) of a word, though this, indeed, is not their main purpose.

Certain of the accents are placed either at the extreme right (prepositives) or extreme left (postpositives) of the word, regardless of the stress position. In such cases, only knowledge of the form can indicate where the stress properly falls. In the case of the very common postpositive ֙ — פַּשְׁטָא, many printings repeat the mark over the stressed syllable in words not stressed on the final syllable (e.g., תְּסֻבֶּ֙ינָה֙ Genesis 37:7). (פַּשְׁטָא is to be distinguished from the similar קַדְמָא; the latter appears over the stressed syllable. In 37:2 שָׁנָה֙ הָיָ֨ה the accent of שָׁנָה֙ is פַּשְׁטָא, of הָיָ֨ה is קַדְמָא.)

28.2 The accents serve two main purposes: They are guides to the cantillation of the text and are accordingly called נְגִינוֹת "musical notes." At the same time they indicate the breaks and connections between the words of the sentence and are accordingly termed also טְעָמִים "senses."

The accentual system is very intricate. To describe it roughly, it may be said to operate on the "halving" principle: the verse is divided in two, then each part is subdivided until a unit too small for further subdivision is reached. For ordinary purposes of reading, it will be enough to recognize the accents that mark the main breaks in the sentence — the main *disjunctive* accents (distinguished from the *conjunctives*, which connect a word with what follows). In the prose books[1] the main disjunctives are:

(a) סִלּוּק ֽ ׃ (the final sublinear perpendicular bar in a verse[2]) followed by סוֹף פָּסוּק (the colon), marking the verse end.

(b) אֶתְנַחְתָּא ֑, marking the chief pause within the verse and dividing it into two (often unequal) parts.

(c) סְגוֹלְתָּא ֒ (postpositive), marking a lesser pause in the first part of the verse.

(d) זָקֵף קָטֹן ֔ and זָקֵף גָּדוֹל ֕, marking a lesser pause in either part of the verse (i.e., before or after the אֶתְנַחְתָּא).

---

1 The books of poetry — Psalms, Proverbs, and Job — have a different accentual system.

2 Distinct from מֶֽתֶג ("bit," "curb"), which is any but the last sublinear perpendicular bar in a verse. The *meteg* marks certain vowels — usually in open, nonfinal syllables — for care in pronunciation. Thus it distinguishes *qåmeṣ* from *qåmeṣ ḥåṭuf* in ambiguous positions: חָֽכְמָה (*ḥå-ḵᵉmå*) "she was wise"; חָכְמָה (*ḥŏḵ-må*) "wisdom" [*qåmeṣ ḥåṭuf*, being in a closed, unstressed syllable (§2.5)].

(e) טִפְחָא ֖, occuring before סִלּוּק or אֶתְנַחְתָּא; often the principal disjunctive in a verse too short to have אֶתְנַחְתָּא.

(f) רְבִיעַ ֗, marking a still slighter pause.

In reading the text aloud, the disjunctives ought carefully to be observed. They do not always accord with our notions of where pauses in the flow of thought or speech ought to come. Often, it seems, they indicate no more than a slight emphasis, a nuance suggested by vocal inflection. But the compactness of biblical narrative is so great that we must welcome every hint of significance that tradition offers. The delicate as well as the grosser meanings expressed by the accents make them indispensable aids to the fuller appreciation of this charged text.

§ 29

SOME EFFECTS OF THE STRESS

Pausal forms

29.1 The major disjunctive accents סִלּוּק (ֽ) and אֶתְנַחְתָּא (֑) regularly, the others sporadically, are accompanied by a particularly long stress that affects the forms of words in the following ways:

(a) ַ in the pausal stress becomes ָ: כְּנָֽעַן (Genesis 37:1), חָלָֽמְתִּי (37:6), אָֽרְצָה (37:10).

(b) The original *a* of מֶ֫לֶךְ-type segolates (< *\malk*) often reappears, stress-lengthened to ָ: נָֽפֶשׁ (37:21), כָּ֑סֶף (37:28), לַדָּ֑רֶךְ (42:25), לָֽחֶם (43:25).

(c) Vowels that were slurred before verbal afformatives reappear, bearing the pausal stress and hence stress-lengthened: נִצָּ֑בָה (37:7), תִּבָּחֵ֑נוּ (42:15), וָלֵֽכוּ (42:33), תִּסְחָֽרוּ (42:34), וְנֵלֵ֑כָה (43:8).

(d) The connecting vowel between the 2ms suf ךָ— and the singular noun, which is slurred in context, reappears in the pause as a stressed *sεgol*: בְּעַבְדֶּךָ (44:18). Note also its reappearance, as stress-lengthened ◌ָ, in the pausal form of לְךָ, which is לָךְ (45:11) (< **laka*).

(e) Other pausal forms: וַיֹּאמַר (37:30), וַיִּתְאַפָּק (43:31), נִּצְטַדָּק (44:16) (the latter two show that in *hitpa'el* impf cons, ◌ֵ becomes ◌ַ in a minor pause, ◌ָ in a major one); ◌ֹ > ◌ָ in שָׁכָלְתִּי (43:14) and קָטָן (44:20); ◌ֶ > ◌ֵ in דִּבֵּר (44:2).

Stress loss and recession

29.2 Hebrew rhythm dislikes the consecution of two main stresses that are not separated by some pause (i.e., a disjunctive accent). The close succession of a word with final stress by a monosyllable or by a word stressed on its first syllable is generally avoided, and that in two ways:

(a) The first word is joined by *maqqef* (§ 28.1) to the second, making one stress unit of the two and causing the first to lose its stress. Usually only the last word carries an accent mark:[1] וַיְקַנְאוּ־בוֹ, וַיִּגְעַר־בּוֹ (Genesis 37:10, 11), וַיַּעֲשׂוּ־כֵן (42:20); or, in a three-word series: אַל־תִּשְׁפְּכוּ־דָם (37:22).

Changeable vowels in the word before the *maqqef* shorten in accord with § 25.5: לֶךְ־נָא (37:14), לֶאֱכָל־לֶחֶם (37:25), הַכֶּר־נָא (37:32), יֶשׁ־שֶׁבֶר (42:1), לִשְׁבָּר־אֹכֶל (42:10).

(b) Alternatively, the stress of the first word may recede to the penult (this occurs as a rule only when the penult is an open syllable): וְעָשָׂה לוֹ (37:3), יֹאכְלוּ לָחֶם (43:25).

---

1 Occasionally a secondary stress on the word before the *maqqef* is indicated by an accent mark: וַיַּגֶּד־לוֹ (43:7).

§ 30

GEMINATE VERBS

30.1 Geminate ("doubled") verbs are so called because they repeat or lengthen their second root-consonant to fill out the triconsonantal pattern; e.g., סָבַב "he turned about."[1] Repeated (doubled) consonants appear usually in the *qal* active, perfect, 3 person forms and the participle (סָבַב, סָבְבָה; סוֹבֵב), and also in the *pi'el* group — which in geminates also takes the pattern of *polel* (below, §30.4). In the rest of the *qal* paradigm, and in *nif'al*, *hif'il*, and *hof'al* only two root-consonants appear, the second being long except when it is final (יָסֹב, יָסֹבּוּ; נָסַב, נָסַבּוּ; הֵסֵב, הֵסֵבּוּ).

30.2 See the paradigms of the geminate verb on p. 219; note the following in the inflection of the *qal*:

(a) The *o* connecting vowel before the pf afformatives [סַבּוֹתִי; cf. the similar case of הֲשִׁיבוֹתִי (§17.3)] may be derived from the *o* of אָנֹכִי; originally proper to the 1 pers only, it invaded the 2 pers forms as well.

(b) The alternative active impf, with a long first root-consonant (יִסֹּב), follows and probably is a reflex of the pattern of geminate verbs in Aramaic.

(c) In postbiblical Hebrew, geminates tend to assimilate their inflection to that of the sound verb: מָדַדְתִּי "I measured," יִמְדֹּד "he will measure."

1 Like hollow verbs, geminates are probably derived from biconsonantal roots.

30.3 The *hif'il* paradigm may be compared to the *hif'il* of hollow verbs, §17.3.

(a) Note that where the hollow verb shows long *i*, the geminate shows short *i* (followed by long consonant) in unstressed syllable, *e* (followed by simple consonant) in the stress:

hollow	*geminate*
הֲשִׁיבוֹתִי	הֲסִבּוֹתִי
הֵשִׁיב	הֵסֵב
יָשִׁיב	יָסֵב
מְשִׁיבָה	מְסִבָּה

(b) A simplified form of the pf (comparable to pf type-*b* of the hollow verb paradigm), הֵסַבְתִּי, is found rarely in biblical, more commonly in later Hebrew.

30.4 In the *pi'el* group geminates show two types of inflection: the regular (חִנֵּן, חֻנַּן, הִתְחַנֵּן) and the by-form *polel*, *polal*, and *hitpolel* (גּוֹלֵל, גּוֹלַל, הִתְגּוֹלֵל).

(a) The by-forms arose out of the regular form presumably by dissimilation (i.e., the development of dissimilarity between two identical sounds in a word); e.g., **gallel*[2] > *gālel*[3] > *gōlel*[4].

2 The groundform of *pi'el* is believed to have had *a* as its first vowel originally [cf. §25.5(a), note 2].

3 The first syllable *gal* became *gā* by dissimilation; the vowel lengthened compensatorily.

4 The shift of long *a* to long *o* in open, originally stressed syllables (as this was) is widely attested in Hebrew.

READINGS

Reading 1

his brothers	אֶחָיו	Bilhah	בִּלְהָה
no, not	לֹא	Zilpah	זִלְפָּה
he sat, stayed, dwelt	יָשַׁב	he was	הָיָה
he told	הִגִּיד (נגד *hif ʿil*)	they were	הָיוּ
they told	הִגִּידוּ	Simeon	שִׁמְעוֹן
his father	אָבִיו	shepherding	רוֹעֶה pt
he did, made	עָשָׂה	*sign of a definite direct object (e.g., one having the article, or a proper name); not translated*	אֶת־
they did, made	עָשׂוּ		
thing, matter	דָּבָר		
bad	רָע		
on, about, on account of	עַל	with	עִם

אֵלֶּה נְשֵׁי יַעֲקֹב: רָחֵל וְלֵאָה, בִּלְהָה וְזִלְפָּה. יוֹסֵף וּבִנְיָמִין הָיוּ בְּנֵי רָחֵל; רְאוּבֵן וְשִׁמְעוֹן וִיהוּדָה הָיוּ בְּנֵי לֵאָה.

הָאַחִים הָיוּ רוֹעֵי צֹאן. הַנַּעַר יוֹסֵף הָיָה רוֹעֶה אֶת הַצֹּאן בַּשָּׂדֶה עִם אֶחָיו בְּנֵי בִלְהָה וּבְנֵי זִלְפָּה.

יַעֲקֹב לֹא הָיָה בַּשָּׂדֶה; הוּא יָשַׁב בַּבַּיִת.

יוֹסֵף הִגִּיד לְאָבִיו מֶה עָשׂוּ אֶחָיו בַּשָּׂדֶה. עָשׂוּ אֶחָיו דָּבָר טוֹב, הִגִּיד יוֹסֵף אֶת הַדָּבָר הַטּוֹב לְאָבִיו. עָשׂוּ אֶחָיו דָּבָר רָע, הִגִּיד יוֹסֵף לְאָבִיו אֶת הַדָּבָר הָרָע. אֲחֵי יוֹסֵף לֹא הִגִּידוּ לְיַעֲקֹב דָּבָר עַל יוֹסֵף.

1. מִי נְשֵׁי יַעֲקֹב? 2. מִי בְּנֵי רָחֵל וּמִי בְּנֵי לֵאָה? 3. מֶה הָיוּ הָאַחִים? 4. אֵיפֹה הָיָה יוֹסֵף? 5. מֶה עָשָׂה עִם אֶחָיו? 6. אֵיפֹה יָשַׁב יַעֲקֹב? 7. מַה הִגִּיד יוֹסֵף לְאָבִיו עַל אֶחָיו? 8. מַה הִגִּידוּ הֵם עַל יוֹסֵף?

(*To be followed by Reading 2.*)

Reading 2

to him (3ms suf וֹ + ל)	לוֹ
ornamented tunic	כְּתֹנֶת פַּסִּים
meaning of פַּסִּים *here uncertain; traditional guesses:* varicolored strip(e)s, palm (*of hand*), sole (*of foot*), *hence* tunic reaching to extremities	
they hated (שָׂנֵא)	שָׂנְאוּ
because	כִּי
why? ("for what" מה + ל)	לָ֫מָּה
aged, old	זָקֵן
he loved	אָהַב
they loved	אָהֲבוּ
all (of) (*kŏl*)	כָּל־
his sons	בָּנָיו
him (3ms suf וֹ + את)	אֹתוֹ
son of old age (i.e., born to an aged parent)	בֶּן זְקֻנִים
from [§2.10(b)2]	מִן, מִ־
in comparisons: more than	

יַעֲקֹב הָיָה אִישׁ זָקֵן. הוּא אָהַב אֶת כָּל בָּנָיו. כָּל הַבָּנִים אָהֲבוּ אֶת יַעֲקֹב, וּנְשֵׁי יַעֲקֹב אָהֲבוּ אֹתוֹ.

יוֹסֵף הָיָה בֶּן זְקֻנִים לְיַעֲקֹב: אֶחָיו הָיוּ גְּדוֹלִים וְהוּא הָיָה נַעַר. יַעֲקֹב אָהַב אֶת יוֹסֵף מִכָּל בָּנָיו כִּי בֶן[1] זְקֻנִים הוּא לוֹ. יַעֲקֹב עָשָׂה לְיוֹסֵף כְּתֹנֶת פַּסִּים. הוּא לֹא עָשָׂה כְּתֹנֶת פַּסִּים לִרְאוּבֵן וְלֹא לִיהוּדָה וְלֹא לְכָל הָאַחִים. לְיוֹסֵף עָשָׂה יַעֲקֹב כְּתֹנֶת פַּסִּים כִּי אָהַב אֹתוֹ מִכָּל בָּנָיו.

אֲחֵי יוֹסֵף לֹא אָהֲבוּ אֶת יוֹסֵף. הֵם שָׂנְאוּ אֹתוֹ. שָׂנְאוּ אֹתוֹ כִּי הִגִּיד לְאָבִיו מֶה עָשׂוּ בַּשָּׂדֶה, וְשָׂנְאוּ אֹתוֹ עַל כְּתֹנֶת הַפַּסִּים.

1. מֶה הָיָה יַעֲקֹב? 2. אֶת מִי אָהַב יַעֲקֹב? 3. מִי אָהַב[2] אֹתוֹ? 4. מֶה הָיָה יוֹסֵף לְיַעֲקֹב? 5. אֶת מִי אָהַב יַעֲקֹב מִכָּל בָּנָיו? 6. לָ֫מָּה? 7. מֶה עָשָׂה יַעֲקֹב לְיוֹסֵף? 8. לָ֫מָּה? 9. עַל מָה שָׂנְאוּ אֲחֵי יוֹסֵף אֹתוֹ?

(*To be followed by* §*9, p. 45.*)

---

1 Note the spirantization of the בֶן, following so closely as it does upon כִּי, which ends in a vowel. In such situations, *b^{e}g̲ad k^{e}fat̲* (§1.5) are regularly spirantized.

2 מִי is construed as singular, though it may refer to plural subjects.

Reading 3

he dreamed	חָלַם
dream	חֲלוֹם
his dream	חֲלוֹמוֹ
my dream	חֲלוֹמִי
lo! behold!	הִנֵּה
binding (*pi'el*) pl מְאַלְּמִים, s	מְאַלֵּם
(*used only with* אֲלֻמָּה)	
sheaf	אֲלֻמָּה
my sheaf	אֲלֻמָּתִי
over us	עָלֵינוּ
your sheaves	אֲלֻמּוֹתֵיכֶם
he got up [קוּם (§ 8.2)] f קָמָה, m	קָם
(חוה[1] or שחוה) pl הִשְׁתַּחֲווּ, s	הִשְׁתַּחֲוָה
he prostrated himself	
he related (*pi'el*)	סִפֵּר
he said	אָמַר
interrogative particle; for vocalization, see below	ה
you (ms) will be king (מָלַךְ)	תִּמְלֹךְ

The normal vocalization of the interrogative particle is הֲ; before laryngals with *qåmeṣ* הֶ (e.g., הֶהָיָה "was he?"); before laryngals with other vowels and before *šᵉwå*, הַ [e.g., הַהִשְׁתַּחֲווּ "did they prostrate themselves?" הַשְׁמַרְתֶּם "did you (mpl) guard?"].

יוֹסֵף חָלַם חֲלוֹם.

בַּחֲלוֹמוֹ, הִנֵּה הוּא בַּשָּׂדֶה עִם אֶחָיו. הָאַחִים הָיוּ מְאַלְּמִים אֲלֻמּוֹת בַּשָּׂדֶה, וְיוֹסֵף הָיָה מְאַלֵּם אֲלֻמּוֹת. וְהִנֵּה קָמָה אֲלֻמַּת יוֹסֵף, וַאֲלֻמּוֹת הָאַחִים הִשְׁתַּחֲווּ לַאֲלֻמַּת יוֹסֵף.

סִפֵּר יוֹסֵף אֶת חֲלוֹמוֹ לְאֶחָיו. אָמַר יוֹסֵף: חָלַמְתִּי חֲלוֹם! בַּחֲלוֹמִי, הִנֵּה אֲנַחְנוּ מְאַלְּמִים אֲלֻמּוֹת בַּשָּׂדֶה. וְהִנֵּה קָמָה אֲלֻמָּתִי, וַאֲלֻמּוֹתֵיכֶם הִשְׁתַּחֲווּ לַאֲלֻמָּתִי!

אָמְרוּ לוֹ אֶחָיו: הֲתִמְלֹךְ עָלֵינוּ?!

אֲחֵי יוֹסֵף שָׂנְאוּ אֹתוֹ עַל הַחֲלוֹם הַזֶּה. שָׂנְאוּ אֹתוֹ כִּי הִגִּיד לְאָבִיו מֶה עָשׂוּ בַּשָּׂדֶה, שָׂנְאוּ אֹתוֹ עַל כְּתֹנֶת הַפַּסִּים וְעַל הַחֲלוֹם.

---

1 Traditionally derived from שָׁחָה (< *שחו) "bow," with doubling of the final root consonant (*שחוו > *שחוה); the verb pattern is הִתְפַּעֵל. Some now take it as a הִשְׁתַּפְעֵל (reflexive causative) of a root *חוה, meaning "coil" in Arabic.

1. אֵיפֹה הָיוּ הָאַחִים בַּחֲלוֹם יוֹסֵף? 2. מֶה הָיוּ עוֹשִׂים (doing)? 3. מֶה עָשׂוּ אֲלֻמּוֹת הָאַחִים? 4. מַה סִפֵּר יוֹסֵף לְאֶחָיו? 5. מָה אָמְרוּ לוֹ עַל חֲלוֹמוֹ? 6. עַל מָה שָׂנְאוּ אֲחֵי יוֹסֵף אֹתוֹ?

(*To be followed by Reading 4.*)

Reading 4

to you (ms) — לְךָ
that, which, who — אֲשֶׁר
we shall come — נָבוֹא (בּוֹא)
your (ms) mother — אִמְּךָ (אֵם)
your (ms) brothers — אַחֶיךָ
to prostrate oneself — לְהִשְׁתַּחֲווֹת
to the ground — אַרְצָה[1]
he watched, guarded, kept an eye on — שָׁמַר

still, yet, more; *before a noun,* another (besides the aforementioned) — עוֹד
sun — שֶׁמֶשׁ
moon — יָרֵחַ
eleven (lit., one-teen) m — אַחַד־עָשָׂר
star — כּוֹכָב
prostrating oneself — מִשְׁתַּחֲוֶה s, מִשְׁתַּחֲוִים pl
to me — לִי

יוֹסֵף חָלַם עוֹד חֲלוֹם.

בַּחֲלוֹמוֹ, וְהִנֵּה הַשֶּׁמֶשׁ וְהַיָּרֵחַ וְאַחַד־עָשָׂר כּוֹכָבִים מִשְׁתַּחֲוִים לוֹ.

סִפֵּר יוֹסֵף אֶת הַחֲלוֹם אֲשֶׁר חָלַם לְאֶחָיו. אָמַר: הִנֵּה חָלַמְתִּי עוֹד חֲלוֹם! בַּחֲלוֹמִי וְהִנֵּה הַשֶּׁמֶשׁ וְהַיָּרֵחַ וְאַחַד־עָשָׂר כּוֹכָבִים מִשְׁתַּחֲוִים לִי.

לֹא אָמְרוּ לוֹ אֶחָיו דָּבָר עַל חֲלוֹמוֹ.

סִפֵּר יוֹסֵף אֶת הַחֲלוֹם לְאָבִיו. אָמַר לוֹ יַעֲקֹב: מָה הַחֲלוֹם הַזֶּה אֲשֶׁר חָלָמְתָּ! הֲנָבוֹא אֲנִי וְאִמְּךָ וְאַחַד־עָשָׂר אַחֶיךָ לְהִשְׁתַּחֲווֹת לְךָ אַרְצָה!?

הָאַחִים שָׂנְאוּ אֶת יוֹסֵף עַל הַחֲלוֹמוֹת, וְאָבִיו שָׁמַר אֶת הַדָּבָר.

1. מִי הָיָה מִשְׁתַּחֲוֶה לְיוֹסֵף בַּחֲלוֹם הַזֶּה? 2. לְמִי סִפֵּר יוֹסֵף אֶת חֲלוֹמוֹ? 3. מָה אָמַר? 4. מָה אָמְרוּ לוֹ אֶחָיו? 5. לָמָּה סִפֵּר אֶת הַחֲלוֹם הַזֶּה לְאָבִיו? 6. מָה אָמַר לוֹ יַעֲקֹב? 7. מִי הֵם הַשֶּׁמֶשׁ, הַיָּרֵחַ, וְאַחַד־עָשָׂר הַכּוֹכָבִים?

(*To be followed by* §*10, p. 49.*)

---

1 A noun expressing the termination point of a motion often (though not necessarily) bears the *terminative* ָה ending. Note that it is *unstressed*, in contrast to the stressed feminine ָה ending.

Reading 5

עֵמֶק	valley
חֶבְרוֹן	Hebron
יוֹם	day
אֶחָד m	one
הָלַךְ	he went
לֵךְ!	go!
אֶל	to
בְּנוֹ	his son
שְׁכֶם	Shechem
שְׁכֶמָה (שְׁכֶם + ־ָה term)	to Shechem
הֲלֹא (הֲ + לֹא)	is/are not...? *invites an affirmative answer; used to call attention to a statement, like English "he's big,* isn't he?"
קוּם!	get up!
רָאָה	he saw
רְאֵה!	see!
לִרְאוֹת	to see
שָׁלוֹם (שְׁלוֹם־)	welfare, well-being
כַּאֲשֶׁר (כּ + אֲשֶׁר)	as
בָּא (בּוֹא)	he came
שָׁם	there
בִּקֵּשׁ (*pi'el*)	he sought
אָנָה (אָן + ־ָה term)	(to) where?

יַעֲקֹב וּבֵיתוֹ יָשְׁבוּ בְּעֵמֶק חֶבְרוֹן בְּאֶרֶץ כְּנַעַן. יוֹם אֶחָד קָמוּ אֲחֵי יוֹסֵף וְהָלְכוּ עִם הַצֹּאן שְׁכֶמָה. יוֹסֵף לֹא הָלַךְ עִם אֶחָיו; הוּא יָשַׁב עִם אָבִיו בְּעֵמֶק חֶבְרוֹן.

יוֹם אֶחָד אָמַר יַעֲקֹב אֶל בְּנוֹ יוֹסֵף: הֲלֹא אַחֶיךָ רוֹעִים בִּשְׁכֶם? קוּם לֵךְ שְׁכֶמָה וּרְאֵה אֶת שְׁלוֹם אַחֶיךָ וְאֶת שְׁלוֹם הַצֹּאן.

עָשָׂה יוֹסֵף כַּאֲשֶׁר אָמַר לוֹ אָבִיו. קָם וְהָלַךְ שְׁכֶמָה לִרְאוֹת אֶת שְׁלוֹם אֶחָיו וְאֶת שְׁלוֹם הַצֹּאן.

בָּא יוֹסֵף שְׁכֶמָה, וְהִנֵּה לֹא רָאָה אֶת אֶחָיו שָׁם. בִּקֵּשׁ יוֹסֵף אֶת אֶחָיו בַּשָּׂדֶה; הֵם לֹא הָיוּ שָׁם.

1. אֵיפֹה יָשְׁבוּ יַעֲקֹב וּבֵיתוֹ? 2. אָנָה הָלְכוּ אֲחֵי יוֹסֵף יוֹם אֶחָד?
3. מֶה עָשָׂה יוֹסֵף? 4. לָמָּה הָלַךְ יוֹסֵף שְׁכֶמָה? 5. אֵיפֹה בִּקֵּשׁ אֶת אֶחָיו?
6. הֶהָיוּ שָׁם?

(To be followed by Reading 6.)

Reading 6

let's go	(הָלַךְ) coh נֵלְכָה	he found	מָצָא
Dothan	דּוֹתָן	he asked	שָׁאַל
when	כַּאֲשֶׁר	you seek	(*pi'el*) impf תְּבַקֵּשׁ
coming	(בּוֹא) pt בָּא	my brothers	אַחַי
owner, master	בַּ֫עַל	seeking	(*pi'el*) pt מְבַקֵּשׁ
dreamer	בַּ֫עַל חֲלוֹמוֹת	pray tell!	הַגִּידָה־נָּא![1]
he took	לָקַח	he heard	שָׁמַע
pit, cistern	בּוֹר	saying	(אָמַר) pt pl אוֹמְרִים ,s אוֹמֵר

he threw (*hif'il* שלך) הִשְׁלִיךְ

אִישׁ אֶחָד מָצָא אֶת יוֹסֵף בַּשָּׂדֶה. שָׁאַל אֹתוֹ הָאִישׁ: מַה תְּבַקֵּשׁ? אָמַר לוֹ יוֹסֵף: אֶת אַחַי אָנֹכִי מְבַקֵּשׁ; הַגִּידָה־נָּא לִי אֵיפֹה הֵם רוֹעִים? אָמַר לוֹ הָאִישׁ: אַחֶיךָ הָלְכוּ מִזֶּה. שָׁמַעְתִּי אֶת אַחֶיךָ אוֹמְרִים: נֵלְכָה אֶל דּוֹתָן.

הָלַךְ יוֹסֵף אֶל דּוֹתָן. שָׁם מָצָא אֶת אֶחָיו.

כַּאֲשֶׁר רָאוּ הָאַחִים אֶת יוֹסֵף בָּא אָמְרוּ: הִנֵּה בַּעַל הַחֲלוֹמוֹת הַזֶּה בָּא!

כַּאֲשֶׁר בָּא יוֹסֵף לָקְחוּ הָאַחִים אֶת כְּתֹנֶת הַפַּסִּים אֲשֶׁר עָשָׂה לוֹ אָבִיו. רְאוּבֵן מָצָא בּוֹר; לָקְחוּ הָאַחִים אֶת יוֹסֵף וְהִשְׁלִיכוּ אֹתוֹ אֶל הַבּוֹר הַהוּא.

1. מִי מָצָא אֶת יוֹסֵף בַּשָּׂדֶה? 2. מַה שָּׁאַל אֹתוֹ הָאִישׁ? 3. מָה אָמַר לוֹ יוֹסֵף? 4. מַה שָּׁמַע הָאִישׁ אֶת הָאַחִים אוֹמְרִים? 5. אֵיפֹה מָצָא יוֹסֵף אֶת אֶחָיו? 6. מָה אָמְרוּ אֶחָיו כַּאֲשֶׁר רָאוּ אֹתוֹ בָּא? 7. מֶה עָשׂוּ לוֹ אֶחָיו כַּאֲשֶׁר בָּא? 8. מִי מָצָא אֶת הַבּוֹר?

(*To be followed by* §*11, p. 54.*)

---

[1] Two words connected by a hyphen (*maqqef*) are considered one, so far as stress is concerned; the main stress falls on נָּא, a secondary stress on הַגִּ֫ידָה. The *dåḡeš* in the נ is the *conjunctive dåḡeš*, which appears in monosyllables or words stressed on their first syllable when they follow closely upon a word ending in ָה or ֶה not stressed on its last syllable. Whether it signifies lengthening of the consonant (as is generally assumed) or merely that the preceding vowel is somewhat shortened is uncertain.

Reading 7

our hand	יָדֵנוּ	he ate	אָכַל
let (it) not be	אַל תְּהִי juss (הָיָה)	to eat	לֶאֱכֹל
in, on, upon him	בּוֹ	caravan	אֹרְחָה
our brother	אָחִינוּ	Ishmaelite	יִשְׁמְעֵאלִי
words of	דִּבְרֵי־ cs pl (דָּבָר)	to Egypt	מִצְרַיְמָה (מִצְרַיִם + ָ־ה term)
they brought up	הֶעֱלוּ (עָלָה *hif ʿil*)	go to! come!	לְכוּ! imv pl (הָלַךְ)
midst of, inside of	תּוֹךְ־ (תָּוֶךְ)	he sold	מָכַר
he came/went back	שָׁב (שׁוּב)	let's sell	נִמְכְּרָה (coh)

יָשְׁבוּ הָאַחִים לֶאֱכֹל וְיוֹסֵף בַּבּוֹר. הֵם הָיוּ אוֹכְלִים וְהִנֵּה אֹרְחַת יִשְׁמְעֵאלִים בָּאָה, הוֹלֶכֶת מִצְרַיְמָה.

רָאוּ הָאַחִים אֶת הָאֹרְחָה. קָם יְהוּדָה וְאָמַר אֶל אֶחָיו: לְכוּ וְנִמְכְּרָה אֶת יוֹסֵף לַיִּשְׁמְעֵאלִים, וְיָדֵנוּ אַל תְּהִי בוֹ[1] כִּי אָחִינוּ הוּא.

דִּבְרֵי יְהוּדָה הָיוּ טוֹבִים בְּעֵינֵי אֶחָיו, וְהֵם שָׁמְעוּ לוֹ. הָלְכוּ אֶל הַבּוֹר אֲשֶׁר בּוֹ הִשְׁלִיכוּ אֶת יוֹסֵף וְהֶעֱלוּ אֶת יוֹסֵף מִתּוֹךְ הַבּוֹר. בָּאוּ אֶל הַיִּשְׁמְעֵאלִים וּמָכְרוּ לָהֶם אֶת יוֹסֵף.

שָׁבוּ הָאַחִים לֶאֱכֹל, וְהַיִּשְׁמְעֵאלִים לָקְחוּ אֶת יוֹסֵף מִצְרַיְמָה.

1. לָמָּה יָשְׁבוּ הָאַחִים? 2. כַּאֲשֶׁר אָכְלוּ אֵיפֹה הָיָה יוֹסֵף? 3. מָה רָאוּ? 4. אָנָה הָלְכָה הָאֹרְחָה? 5. מִי אָמַר לִמְכֹּר אֶת יוֹסֵף? 6. לָמָּה? 7. מִי הֶעֱלָה אֶת יוֹסֵף מִתּוֹךְ הַבּוֹר? 8. מֶה עָשׂוּ אֲחֵי יוֹסֵף בּוֹ? 9. כַּאֲשֶׁר הָלְכוּ הַיִּשְׁמְעֵאלִים מֶה עָשׂוּ הָאַחִים? 10. אָנָה לָקְחוּ הַיִּשְׁמְעֵאלִים אֶת יוֹסֵף?

(To be followed by Reading 8.)

---

1 On the spirantization of ב see Reading 2 note 1.

Reading 8

if, *in alternatives* or	אִם
my son	בְּנִי
animal	חַיָּה
he mourned	(*hitpa'el*) הִתְאַבֵּל
days	יָמִים (יוֹם s)
many, much	רַבִּים (רַב s)
his daughters	בְּנוֹתָיו (בַּת s)
to console, to comfort	(*pi'el*) לְנַחֵם
he was consoled, comforted	(*hitpa'el*) הִתְנַחֵם
he-goat	שָׂעִיר
he slaughtered	שָׁחַט
he brought	הֵבִיא (בּוֹא *hif'il*)
he gave, put	נָתַן
her, it (fs di obj)	אֹתָהּ
blood	דָּם (דַּם־)
then	אָז
he recognized	הִכִּיר (נכר *hif'il*)
pray look at (it)!	הַכֶּר־נָא!
your son	בִּנְךָ

לָקְחוּ הָאַחִים שָׂעִיר אֶחָד וְשָׁחֲטוּ אֹתוֹ. הֵבִיאוּ אֶת כְּתֹנֶת יוֹסֵף וְנָתְנוּ אֹתָהּ בְּדַם הַשָּׂעִיר. אָז שָׁבוּ אֶל עֵמֶק חֶבְרוֹן.

הֵבִיאוּ הָאַחִים אֶת כְּתֹנֶת יוֹסֵף אֶל יַעֲקֹב אֲבִיהֶם. אָמְרוּ לוֹ: זֹאת מָצָאנוּ; הַכֶּר־נָא הַכְּתֹנֶת בִּנְךָ הִיא אִם לֹא?

כַּאֲשֶׁר רָאָה יַעֲקֹב אֶת הַכֻּתֹּנֶת הִכִּיר אֹתָהּ וְאָמַר: כְּתֹנֶת בְּנִי! חַיָּה רָעָה אָכְלָה אֶת יוֹסֵף!

יָשַׁב יַעֲקֹב עַל הָאָרֶץ וְהִתְאַבֵּל עַל בְּנוֹ יָמִים רַבִּים. קָמוּ כָּל בָּנָיו וּבְנוֹתָיו לְנַחֵם אֹתוֹ, וְיַעֲקֹב לֹא הִתְנַחֵם.

1. מֶה עָשׂוּ הָאַחִים בַּשָּׂעִיר? 2. מֶה עָשׂוּ בַּכֻּתֹּנֶת? 3. אָנָה שָׁבוּ? 4. אֶל מִי הֵבִיאוּ אֶת הַכֻּתֹּנֶת? 5. מָה אָמְרוּ לְיַעֲקֹב? 6. לָמָּה אָמַר יַעֲקֹב כִּי (that) חַיָּה רָעָה אָכְלָה אֶת יוֹסֵף? 7. מֶה עָשָׂה אָז יַעֲקֹב? 8. מִי בִקֵּשׁ לְנַחֵם אֹתוֹ? 9. לָמָּה לֹא הִתְנַחֵם?

(*To be followed by §12, p. 58.*)

Reading 9

his wife	אִשְׁתּוֹ	Egyptian	מִצְרִי
imprisoned, prisoner	אָסוּר	Potiphar	פּוֹטִיפַר
jail	בֵּית אֲסוּרִים	officer	שַׂר
place	מָקוֹם (מְקוֹם־)	Pharaoh	פַּרְעֹה
after	אַחַר	servant, slave	עֶבֶד
he commited an offense, sinned	חָטָא	he became	הָיָה לְ־
chief butler	שַׂר הַמַּשְׁקִים	——'s anger was kindled against	חָרָה אַף־ בְּ־
chief baker	שַׂר הָאוֹפִים		
king	מֶלֶךְ	on account of, because of	עַל דְּבַר־

הַיִּשְׁמְעֵאלִים הֵבִיאוּ אֶת יוֹסֵף מִצְרַיְמָה. שָׁם מָכְרוּ אֹתוֹ לְאִישׁ מִצְרִי, לְפוֹטִיפַר שַׂר פַּרְעֹה. יָשַׁב יוֹסֵף בְּבֵית פּוֹטִיפַר וְהָיָה לוֹ לְעֶבֶד.

יוֹם אֶחָד חָרָה אַף פּוֹטִיפַר בְּיוֹסֵף עַל דְּבַר אִשְׁתּוֹ, כִּי אָהֲבָה אִשְׁתּוֹ אֶת יוֹסֵף. נָתַן פּוֹטִיפַר אֶת יוֹסֵף בְּבֵית הָאֲסוּרִים, בַּמָּקוֹם אֲשֶׁר שָׁם אֲסוּרֵי הַמֶּלֶךְ אֲסוּרִים.

אַחַר הַדְּבָרִים הָאֵלֶּה חָטְאוּ שַׂר הַמַּשְׁקִים וְשַׂר הָאוֹפִים לְמֶלֶךְ מִצְרַיִם. חָרָה אַף פַּרְעֹה בַּשָּׂרִים, וְנָתַן אֹתָם בְּבֵית הָאֲסוּרִים, בַּמָּקוֹם אֲשֶׁר שָׁם יוֹסֵף אָסוּר.

שַׂר בֵּית הָאֲסוּרִים נָתַן אֶת יוֹסֵף לְשָׂרֵי פַּרְעֹה, וְהוּא הָיָה לָהֶם לְעֶבֶד כָּל הַיָּמִים אֲשֶׁר הָיוּ שָׁם.

1. אָנָה הֵבִיאוּ הַיִּשְׁמְעֵאלִים אֶת יוֹסֵף? 2. לְמִי מָכְרוּ אֹתוֹ? 3. מֶה הָיָה יוֹסֵף לְפוֹטִיפַר? 4. עַל מָה חָרָה אַף פּוֹטִיפַר בְּיוֹסֵף? 5. מֶה עָשָׂה לוֹ? 6. מִי חָטָא לְמֶלֶךְ מִצְרַיִם? 7. מֶה עָשָׂה לָהֶם הַמֶּלֶךְ? 8. מֶה עָשָׂה יוֹסֵף בְּבֵית הָאֲסוּרִים?

(*To be followed by Reading 10.*)

Reading 10

no(t), *negating noun sentences*	אֵין־[1]	night	לַ֫יְלָה m
he interpreted	פָּתַר	each	אִישׁ
God	אֱלֹהִים	he knew	יָדַע
he will return (trans)	יָשִׁיב (*hif'il* שׁוּב)	interpretation	פִּתְרוֹן
he returned (trans)	הֵשִׁיב	their dreams	חֲלוֹמוֹתֵיהֶם
also, too	גַּם	morning	בֹּ֫קֶר
he will put to death	יָמִית (*hif'il* מוּת)	that	כִּי (conj)
he put to death	הֵמִית	face	פָּנִים (פְּנֵי־)
just as...so	כַּאֲשֶׁר... כֵּן	your faces	פְּנֵיכֶם
		today	הַיּוֹם
how?	אֵיךְ?		

לַ֫יְלָה אֶחָד חָלְמוּ שָׂרֵי פַּרְעֹה אִישׁ חֲלוֹמוֹ, וְלֹא יָדְעוּ אֶת פִּתְרוֹן חֲלוֹמוֹתֵיהֶם. בַּבֹּ֫קֶר רָאָה יוֹסֵף כִּי פְּנֵי הַשָּׂרִים רָעִים. שָׁאַל אֹתָם יוֹסֵף: לָ֫מָּה פְּנֵיכֶם רָעִים הַיּוֹם? אָמְרוּ לוֹ: חֲלוֹם חָלַמְנוּ בַּלַּ֫יְלָה, וְאֵין אֲנַחְנוּ יוֹדְעִים אֶת פִּתְרוֹנִים. אָמַר יוֹסֵף: הֲלוֹא לֵאלֹהִים פִּתְרוֹנִים! סַפְּרוּ־נָא לִי.

סִפֵּר שַׂר הַמַּשְׁקִים אֶת חֲלוֹמוֹ; שָׁמַע יוֹסֵף וְאָמַר: זֶה פִּתְרוֹנוֹ: יָשִׁיב אֹתְךָ פַּרְעֹה אֶל בֵּיתְךָ וְאֶל מְקוֹמְךָ.

כַּאֲשֶׁר רָאָה שַׂר הָאוֹפִים כִּי לְטוֹב פָּתַר, סִפֵּר גַּם הוּא אֶת חֲלוֹמוֹ לְיוֹסֵף. שָׁמַע יוֹסֵף וּפָתַר: אֹתְךָ יָמִית פַּרְעֹה.

וְהִנֵּה כַּאֲשֶׁר פָּתַר יוֹסֵף כֵּן הָיָה: אֶת שַׂר הַמַּשְׁקִים הֵשִׁיב מֶ֫לֶךְ מִצְרַ֫יִם אֶל מְקוֹמוֹ וְאֶל בֵּיתוֹ, וְאֶת שַׂר הָאוֹפִים הֵמִית, כַּאֲשֶׁר פָּתַר יוֹסֵף.

וְיוֹסֵף יָשַׁב עוֹד בְּבֵית הָאֲסוּרִים.

---

1 Construct of אַ֫יִן "nought."

1. לָמָּה הָיוּ פְּנֵי הַשָּׂרִים רָעִים? 2. מַה שָּׁאַל אֹתָם יוֹסֵף? 3. מָה אָמְרוּ לוֹ? 4. אֵיךְ יָדַע יוֹסֵף אֶת פִּתְרוֹן חֲלוֹמוֹתֵיהֶם? 5. אֵיךְ פָּתַר אֶת חֲלוֹם שַׂר הַמַּשְׁקִים? 6. לָמָּה סִפֵּר שַׂר הָאוֹפִים אֶת חֲלוֹמוֹ לְיוֹסֵף? 7. אֵיךְ פָּתַר יוֹסֵף אֶת חֲלוֹמוֹ? 8. מֶה עָשָׂה פַּרְעֹה לַשָּׂרִים?

(*To be followed by §13, p. 61.*)

Reading 11

after them (f)	אַחֲרֵיהֶן	he stood	עָמַד
near	קָרוֹב	by	עַל
wise man	חָכָם (cs pl חַכְמֵי־	the river (Nile)	הַיְאוֹר
he spoke	דִּבֵּר	he came/went up	עָלָה
saying, *introduces quotation; often best left untranslated*	inf לֵאמֹר	coming up	pt fpl עוֹלוֹת
Hebrew	עִבְרִי	seven	f שֶׁבַע
with us	עִמָּנוּ	appearance, looks	מַרְאֶה
before, in the presence of	לִפְנֵי (ל + פְּנֵי)	good-looking	fpl יְפוֹת מַרְאֶה[1]
		bad-looking	fpl רָעוֹת מַרְאֶה[1]
		he pastured	רָעָה

אַחַר הַדְּבָרִים הָאֵלֶּה חָלַם פַּרְעֹה חֲלוֹם. בַּחֲלוֹמוֹ הוּא עוֹמֵד עַל הַיְאוֹר, וְהִנֵּה מִן הַיְאוֹר עוֹלוֹת שֶׁבַע פָּרוֹת יְפוֹת מַרְאֶה, וְהַפָּרוֹת רָעוּ בַּשָּׂדֶה. אַחֲרֵיהֶן עָלוּ שֶׁבַע פָּרוֹת רָעוֹת מַרְאֶה, וְהֵנָּה עָמְדוּ קָרוֹב אֶל הַפָּרוֹת יְפוֹת הַמַּרְאֶה. אָז אָכְלוּ הַפָּרוֹת רָעוֹת הַמַּרְאֶה אֶת הַפָּרוֹת יְפוֹת הַמַּרְאֶה.

בַּבֹּקֶר סִפֵּר פַּרְעֹה אֶת חֲלוֹמוֹ לְחַכְמֵי מִצְרַיִם, וְלֹא הָיָה אִישׁ בְּכָל חַכְמֵי מִצְרַיִם אֲשֶׁר יָדַע לִפְתֹּר אֹתוֹ לְפַרְעֹה.

אָז דִּבֶּר שַׂר הַמַּשְׁקִים אֶל פַּרְעֹה לֵאמֹר: נַעַר עִבְרִי הָיָה עִמָּנוּ בְּבֵית הָאֲסוּרִים, וְהוּא יָדַע לִפְתֹּר לָנוּ חֲלוֹמוֹת אֲשֶׁר חָלַמְנוּ, וְכַאֲשֶׁר פָּתַר לָנוּ כֵּן הָיָה.

הֵבִיאוּ אֶת יוֹסֵף מִבֵּית הָאֲסוּרִים, וְיוֹסֵף עָמַד לִפְנֵי פַּרְעֹה.

1. אֵיפֹה הָיָה פַּרְעֹה עוֹמֵד בַּחֲלוֹמוֹ? 2. מָה רָאָה עוֹלֶה מִן הַיְאוֹר? 3. מֶה עָשׂוּ הַפָּרוֹת? 4. אֶל מִי סִפֵּר פַּרְעֹה אֶת חֲלוֹמוֹ? לָמָּה? 5. מַה סִפֵּר שַׂר הַמַּשְׁקִים לְפַרְעֹה? 6. לָמָּה הֵבִיאוּ אֶת יוֹסֵף לִפְנֵי פַּרְעֹה?

(*To be followed by Reading 12.*)

---

[1] Lit., "beautiful/bad (in respect) of appearance." The distinction between the changeable *qâmeṣ* of יָפוֹת, יְפוֹת־ and the unchangeable one of רָעוֹת is explained in §25.

Reading 12

now	עַתָּה	about you	עָלֶיךָ
let him place, appoint	(נָתַן) juss יִתֵּן	he answered	עָנָה
let him gather	(אָסַף) juss יֶאֱסֹף	year	שָׁנָה (שָׁנִים, שְׁנֵי־)
food	אֹכֶל	they (f) (are)	הֵנָּה
they will die	יָמוּתוּ (מוּת)	plenty, abundance	שָׂבָע
people	עַם	will be (pl)	יִהְיוּ
his servants	עֲבָדָיו (עֶבֶד)	famine	רָעָב
spirit	רוּחַ	(it) will make an end of	יְכַלֶּה (כִּלָּה *pi'el*)
I have appointed	נָתַתִּי (נָתַן)		

אָמַר פַּרְעֹה אֶל יוֹסֵף: חֲלוֹם חָלַמְתִּי, וְאֵין אִישׁ בְּכָל חַכְמֵי מִצְרַיִם יוֹדֵעַ לִפְתֹּר אֹתוֹ לִי; וַאֲנִי שָׁמַעְתִּי עָלֶיךָ כִּי פּוֹתֵר חֲלוֹמוֹת אַתָּה. עָנָה יוֹסֵף: לֵאלֹהִים פִּתְרוֹנִים.

סִפֵּר פַּרְעֹה אֶת חֲלוֹמוֹ לְיוֹסֵף. שָׁמַע יוֹסֵף אֶת הַחֲלוֹם וְאָמַר: אֶת אֲשֶׁר אֱלֹהִים עוֹשֶׂה הִגִּיד לְפַרְעֹה: שֶׁבַע הַפָּרוֹת הַטּוֹבוֹת שֶׁבַע שָׁנִים הֵנָּה, וְשֶׁבַע הַפָּרוֹת הָרָעוֹת שֶׁבַע שָׁנִים הֵנָּה. הִנֵּה שֶׁבַע שָׁנִים בָּאוֹת – שָׂבָע גָּדוֹל בְּכָל אֶרֶץ מִצְרַיִם. אַחֲרֵיהֶן יִהְיוּ שֶׁבַע שְׁנֵי רָעָב, וְהָרָעָב יְכַלֶּה אֶת הָאָרֶץ. וְעַתָּה יִתֵּן פַּרְעֹה אִישׁ חָכָם עַל הָאָרֶץ וְיֶאֱסֹף אֶת אֹכֶל הַשָּׁנִים הַטּוֹבוֹת, וְלֹא יָמוּתוּ עַם הָאָרֶץ בָּרָעָב.

דִּבְרֵי יוֹסֵף הָיוּ טוֹבִים בְּעֵינֵי פַרְעֹה. אָמַר הַמֶּלֶךְ אֶל עֲבָדָיו: הֲנִמְצָא אִישׁ כָּזֶה אֲשֶׁר רוּחַ אֱלֹהִים בּוֹ?

וְאֶל יוֹסֵף אָמַר: רְאֵה נָתַתִּי אֹתְךָ עַל כָּל אֶרֶץ מִצְרָיִם!

1. לָמָּה סִפֵּר פַּרְעֹה אֶת חֲלוֹמוֹ לְיוֹסֵף? 2. מָה אָמַר יוֹסֵף עַל הַחֲלוֹם? 3. מָה אָמַר עַל שֶׁבַע הַפָּרוֹת הַטּוֹבוֹת? 4. עַל שֶׁבַע הַפָּרוֹת הָרָעוֹת? 5. עַל כִּי אָכְלוּ הַפָּרוֹת הָרָעוֹת אֶת הַטּוֹבוֹת? 6. אֵיךְ לֹא יָמוּתוּ עַם הָאָרֶץ? 7. מָה אָמַר פַּרְעֹה אֶל עֲבָדָיו עַל יוֹסֵף? 8. לָמָּה נָתַן פַּרְעֹה אֶת יוֹסֵף עַל הָאָרֶץ?

(To be followed by §14, p. 64.)

Reading 13

(to) there	(term שָׁם + ־ָה) שָׁמָּה	city	fpl עָרִים ,s עִיר
he obtained, procured [rations (שֶׁבֶר)]	שָׁבַר	field(s) of	שְׂדֵה־ (שָׂדֶה)
we shall live	נִחְיֶה (חָיָה)	lands	אֲרָצוֹת (אֶרֶץ)
we shall die	נָמוּת (מוּת)	bread, food	לֶחֶם
ten	m עֲשָׂרָה	rations, food supply (in an emergency)	שֶׁבֶר
he sent	שָׁלַח	you stare at one another (helplessly)	(*hitpa'el* רָאָה) תִּתְרָאוּ
lest	פֶּן	there is	(opposite of אֵין) יֵשׁ
(it) will befall	יִקְרֶה (קָרָה)	he went/came down	יָרַד
disaster, terrible accident	אָסוֹן	go down!	רְדוּ!
how many/much?	כַּמָּה		

שֶׁבַע שָׁנִים הָיָה שָׂבָע בָּאָרֶץ, וְיוֹסֵף אָסַף אֶת אֹכֶל הַשָּׁנִים הַטּוֹבוֹת וְנָתַן אֹתוֹ בֶּעָרִים בְּכָל אֶרֶץ מִצְרַיִם: אֹכֶל שְׂדֵה הָעִיר נָתַן בְּתוֹכָהּ. אַחַר הַשָּׁנִים הָאֵלֶּה בָּאוּ שְׁנֵי הָרָעָב, כַּאֲשֶׁר אָמַר יוֹסֵף. בְּכָל הָאֲרָצוֹת הָיָה רָעָב, וּבְאֶרֶץ מִצְרַיִם הָיָה לֶחֶם.

רָאָה יַעֲקֹב כִּי יֵשׁ שֶׁבֶר בְּמִצְרַיִם וְאָמַר לְבָנָיו: לָמָּה תִּתְרָאוּ? הִנֵּה שָׁמַעְתִּי כִּי יֵשׁ שֶׁבֶר בְּמִצְרַיִם; רְדוּ שָׁמָּה וְשִׁבְרוּ לָנוּ מִשָּׁם וְנִחְיֶה וְלֹא נָמוּת!

יָרְדוּ אֲחֵי יוֹסֵף, עֲשָׂרָה, לִשְׁבֹּר מִמִּצְרַיִם. וְאֶת בִּנְיָמִין, אֲחִי יוֹסֵף, לֹא שָׁלַח יַעֲקֹב כִּי אָמַר פֶּן יִקְרֶה אֹתוֹ אָסוֹן.

בָּאוּ בְּנֵי יַעֲקֹב מִצְרַיְמָה בְּתוֹךְ הַבָּאִים, כִּי הָיָה הָרָעָב בְּאֶרֶץ כְּנָעַן.

1. כַּמָּה שְׁנֵי שָׂבָע הָיוּ? 2. מֶה עָשָׂה יוֹסֵף בַּשָּׁנִים הָאֵלֶּה? 3. מַה נָּתַן בְּתוֹךְ כָּל עִיר? 4. מַה בָּא אַחַר שְׁנֵי הַשָּׂבָע? 5. הֶהָיָה רָעָב בְּמִצְרַיִם? 6. לָמָּה שָׁלַח יַעֲקֹב אֶת בָּנָיו מִצְרַיְמָה? 7. אֶת מִי לֹא שָׁלַח? לָמָּה? 8. מִי עוֹד בָּא מִצְרַיְמָה?

(*To be followed by Reading 14.*)

Reading 14

your words, what you say	דִּבְרֵיכֶם (דָּבָר)
truth	אֱמֶת
whether (or not) you are telling the truth [lit., is truth with you (or not)?]	הַאֱמֶת עִמָּכֶם
die	inf abs מוֹת
you shall surely die	מוֹת תָּמוּתוּ
let him stay	יֵשֵׁב
go back!	שׁוּבוּ!
bring!	הָבִיאוּ!
when?	מָתַי?
before him	לְפָנָיו
he remembered	זָכַר
spy	מְרַגֵּל, מְרַגְּלִים
to you	אֲלֵיכֶם (אֶל)
to me	אֵלַי (אֶל)
my lord	אֲדוֹנִי (אָדוֹן)
your servants	עֲבָדֶיךָ
twelve (lit., two-teen)	שְׁנֵים עָשָׂר
with	אֶת־
you will be tested	תִּבָּחֲנוּ (בָּחַן *nif'al*)
they will be tested	יִבָּחֲנוּ
let him come	יָבוֹא

וְיוֹסֵף הוּא הַמּוֹכֵר שֶׁבֶר לְכָל עַם הָאָרֶץ.

בָּאוּ אֲחֵי יוֹסֵף וְהִשְׁתַּחֲווּ לְפָנָיו אַרְצָה. כַּאֲשֶׁר רָאָה יוֹסֵף אֶת אֶחָיו הִכִּיר אֹתָם, וְהֵם לֹא הִכִּירוּ אֹתוֹ. זָכַר יוֹסֵף אֶת חֲלוֹמוֹתָיו אֲשֶׁר חָלַם עֲלֵיהֶם, וְאָמַר אֶל אֶחָיו: מְרַגְּלִים אַתֶּם! לִרְאוֹת אֶת הָאָרֶץ בָּאתֶם!

עָנוּ לוֹ הָאֲנָשִׁים: לֹא אֲדוֹנִי, עֲבָדֶיךָ בָּאוּ לִשְׁבֹּר אֹכֶל! שְׁנֵים עָשָׂר עֲבָדֶיךָ אַחִים אֲנַחְנוּ, בְּנֵי אִישׁ אֶחָד בְּאֶרֶץ כְּנַעַן. הַקָּטֹן אֶת אָבִינוּ הַיּוֹם וְהָאֶחָד אֵינֶנּוּ.

אָמַר לָהֶם יוֹסֵף: הוּא אֲשֶׁר דִּבַּרְתִּי אֲלֵיכֶם לֵאמֹר: מְרַגְּלִים אַתֶּם! בְּזֹאת תִּבָּחֲנוּ: יָבוֹא אֲחִיכֶם הַקָּטֹן אֵלַי, וְיִבָּחֲנוּ דִּבְרֵיכֶם הַאֱמֶת עִמָּכֶם; וְאִם לֹא, מוֹת תָּמוּתוּ! אֲחִיכֶם הָאֶחָד יֵשֵׁב בְּבֵית הָאֲסוּרִים, וְאַתֶּם שׁוּבוּ, הָבִיאוּ שֶׁבֶר לְבָתֵּיכֶם, וְאֶת אֲחִיכֶם הַקָּטֹן הָבִיאוּ אֵלַי וְלֹא תָּמוּתוּ.

1. מֶה עָשׂוּ אֲחֵי יוֹסֵף לְפָנָיו? 2. מִי הִכִּיר אֶת מִי? 3. מָתַי זָכַר יוֹסֵף אֶת חֲלוֹמוֹתָיו? 4. מָה אָמַר יוֹסֵף עַל אֶחָיו? 5. כַּמָּה אַחִים עָמְדוּ

לִפְנֵי יוֹסֵף, וְכַמָּה אָמְרוּ כִּי הָיוּ? 6. מָה אָמְרוּ עַל הָאַחִים אֲשֶׁר לֹא
הֵם שָׁם? 7. בַּמֶּה יִבָּחֲנוּ דִּבְרֵי הָאַחִים? 8. הֲיָשׁוּבוּ כָּל הָאַחִים אֶל
אֶרֶץ כְּנַעַן?

(*To be followed by §15, p. 69.*)

Reading 15

away from them מֵאִתָּם (מִן + אִתָּם)
he bound, fettered אָסַר
he filled מִלֵּא
sack שַׂק
to return (trans) (*hif'il* שׁוּב) לְהָשִׁיב
silver, money כֶּסֶף
their silver, money כַּסְפָּם
to give לָתֵת (נָתַן)
way, road דֶּרֶךְ
he lifted, carried, carried off נָשָׂא
donkey חֲמוֹר

guilty אָשֵׁם, אֲשֵׁמִים
we saw רָאִינוּ (רָאָה)
distress צָרָה
life, being, person נֶפֶשׁ
his mortal distress צָרַת נַפְשׁוֹ
he pleaded with (*hitpa'el* חנן) הִתְחַנֵּן אֶל
on account of this, therefore עַל כֵּן
child יֶלֶד
interpreter מֵלִיץ
between them בֵּינוֹתָם (בֵּין)
(i.e., between him and them)

אָמְרוּ הָאֲנָשִׁים אִישׁ אֶל אָחִיו: אֲשֵׁמִים אֲנַחְנוּ עַל יוֹסֵף אָחִינוּ אֲשֶׁר רָאִינוּ אֶת צָרַת נַפְשׁוֹ כַּאֲשֶׁר הִתְחַנֵּן אֵלֵינוּ וְלֹא שָׁמַעְנוּ אֵלָיו. עַל כֵּן בָּאָה אֵלֵינוּ הַצָּרָה הַזֹּאת! עָנָה אֹתָם רְאוּבֵן לֵאמֹר: הֲלוֹא אָמַרְתִּי אֲלֵיכֶם אַל תֶּחֶטְאוּ בַּיֶּלֶד, וְלֹא שְׁמַעְתֶּם!

וְהֵם לֹא יָדְעוּ כִּי שׁוֹמֵעַ יוֹסֵף כִּי הַמֵּלִיץ בֵּינוֹתָם.

אָז לָקַח יוֹסֵף מֵאִתָּם אֶת שִׁמְעוֹן וְאָסַר אֹתוֹ.

אָמַר יוֹסֵף לַעֲבָדָיו לְמַלֵּא אֶת שַׂקֵּי הָאֲנָשִׁים שֶׁבֶר וּלְהָשִׁיב אֶת כַּסְפָּם, כֶּסֶף אִישׁ אֶל שַׂקּוֹ, וְגַם אֹכֶל לַדֶּרֶךְ אָמַר לָתֵת לָהֶם. וְכֵן עָשׂוּ: מִלְאוּ אֶת שַׂקֵּיהֶם שֶׁבֶר וְהֵשִׁיבוּ אֶת כַּסְפָּם כֶּסֶף אִישׁ אֶל שַׂקּוֹ וְגַם אֹכֶל לַדֶּרֶךְ נָתְנוּ לָהֶם.

קָמוּ הָאַחִים, נָשְׂאוּ אֶת שִׁבְרָם עַל חֲמוֹרֵיהֶם, וְהָלְכוּ מִשָּׁם אַרְצָה כְּנַעַן.

1. אֵיךְ פָּתְרוּ הָאַחִים אֶת צָרָתָם? 2. מַה זָּכַר רְאוּבֵן? 3. מִי עָמַד בֵּינוֹת הָאַחִים וְיוֹסֵף? 4. מֶה עָשָׂה יוֹסֵף לְשִׁמְעוֹן? 5. מָה אָמַר יוֹסֵף לָתֵת לְאֶחָיו? 6. מֶה עָשׂוּ עֲבָדָיו? 7. אֵיךְ נָשְׂאוּ הָאַחִים אֶת שִׁבְרָם?

(To be followed by Reading 16.)

Reading 16

we were/are הָיִינוּ (הָיָה)
I shall know אֵדַע
take! קְחוּ! (לָקַח)
he opened פָּתַח
mouth פֶּה (פִּי־)
he feared, was afraid יָרֵא
you will take תִּקְחוּ (לָקַח)

things that befell, happenings קוֹרוֹת pt fpl (קָרָה)
lord of, *cs pl used in sense of s — the so-called pl of majesty* אֲדוֹנֵי־
hard things, *used adverbially* — harshly קָשׁוֹת fpl (קָשֶׁה s)
regard... as... נָתַן אֶת... כְּ...
he will go down יֵרֵד (יָרַד)

כַּאֲשֶׁר שָׁבוּ הָאַחִים אֶל יַעֲקֹב אֲבִיהֶם הִגִּידוּ לוֹ אֶת כָּל הַקּוֹרוֹת אֹתָם בְּמִצְרַיִם לֵאמֹר: דִּבֶּר הָאִישׁ אֲדוֹנֵי הָאָרֶץ אִתָּנוּ קָשׁוֹת, וְנָתַן אֹתָנוּ כִּמְרַגְּלִים. אָמַרְנוּ אֵלָיו: לֹא הָיִינוּ מְרַגְּלִים! שְׁנֵים עָשָׂר עֲבָדֶיךָ אַחִים אֲנַחְנוּ: הָאֶחָד אֵינֶנּוּ וְהַקָּטֹן הַיּוֹם אֶת אָבִינוּ בְּאֶרֶץ כְּנַעַן. אָמַר אֵלֵינוּ הָאִישׁ אֲדוֹנֵי הָאָרֶץ: בְּזֹאת אֵדַע כִּי אֱמֶת דִּבְרֵיכֶם: אֲחִיכֶם הָאֶחָד יֵשֵׁב אִתִּי, וְאֶת שֶׁבֶר רְעַב בָּתֵּיכֶם קְחוּ וּלְכוּ, וְהָבִיאוּ אֶת אֲחִיכֶם הַקָּטֹן אֵלַי וְאֵדַע כִּי לֹא מְרַגְּלִים אַתֶּם.

כַּאֲשֶׁר פָּתְחוּ הָאֲנָשִׁים אֶת שַׂקֵּיהֶם מָצְאוּ אִישׁ אֶת כַּסְפּוֹ בְּפִי שַׂקּוֹ. רָאוּ הֵם וַאֲבִיהֶם אֶת כַּסְפָּם וְיָרֵאוּ.

אָז אָמַר אֲלֵיהֶם יַעֲקֹב: יוֹסֵף אֵינֶנּוּ וְשִׁמְעוֹן אֵינֶנּוּ וְאֶת בִּנְיָמִין תִּקְחוּ! עָלַי הָיוּ כָּל אֵלֶּה! לֹא יֵרֵד בְּנִי עִמָּכֶם.

1. מַה סִפְּרוּ הָאַחִים לְיַעֲקֹב? 2. אֵיךְ דִּבֶּר אֲלֵיהֶם אֲדוֹנֵי הָאָרֶץ? 3. כְּמָה נָתַן אֹתָם? 4. בַּמֶּה יָדַע הָאִישׁ כִּי אֱמֶת עִמָּהֶם? 5. מַה מָּצְאוּ כַּאֲשֶׁר פָּתְחוּ אֶת שַׂקֵּיהֶם? 6. לָמָּה יָרְאוּ? 7. לָמָּה אָמַר יַעֲקֹב כִּי לֹא יֵרֵד בִּנְיָמִין עִמָּהֶם מִצְרַיְמָה?

(*To be followed by* §*16, p. 74.*)

Reading 17

I will be responsible for him	אֶעֶרְבֶנּוּ (עָרַב)	it was, it came to pass	וַיְהִי (הָיָה) impf cons
if (it must be) so	אִם כֵּן	they finished	כִּלּוּ (כִּלָּה *pi'el*
do!	עֲשׂוּ! (עָשָׂה)	he said	וַיֹּאמֶר (אָמַר) impf cons
your hand	יֶדְכֶם	you will see	תִּרְאוּ (רָאָה)
present	מִנְחָה	releasing, letting go	מְשַׁלֵּחַ (שִׁלַּח *pi'el*
returned	מוּשָׁב pass pt (שׁוּב *hǒf'al*	we shall go down	נֵרֵד (יָרַד)
compassion	רַחֲמִים	he inquired about	שָׁאַל לְ־
I am bereaved (of child)	שָׁכֹלְתִּי	living	חַי pt (חָיָה)
(variant at end of verse	שָׁכָלְתִּי)	let's get up	נָקוּמָה coh (קוּם)

וַיְהִי כַּאֲשֶׁר כִּלּוּ לֶאֱכֹל אֶת הַשֶּׁבֶר אֲשֶׁר הֵבִיאוּ מִמִּצְרָיִם וַיֹּאמֶר יַעֲקֹב אֶל בָּנָיו: שֻׁבוּ שִׁבְרוּ לָנוּ עוֹד אֹכֶל.

וַיֹּאמֶר אֵלָיו יְהוּדָה: הֲלוֹא אָמַר לָנוּ הָאִישׁ: לֹא תִרְאוּ פָנַי אִם אֵין אֲחִיכֶם אִתְּכֶם. אִם מְשַׁלֵּחַ אַתָּה אֶת אֲחִינוּ אִתָּנוּ נֵרֵד וְנִשְׁבֹּר לְךָ אֹכֶל; וְאִם אֵינְךָ מְשַׁלֵּחַ אֹתוֹ לֹא נֵרֵד.

וַיֹּאמֶר יַעֲקֹב: לָמָּה הִגַּדְתֶּם לָאִישׁ כִּי עוֹד לָכֶם אָח?

וַיֹּאמְרוּ: שָׁאוֹל שָׁאַל[1] הָאִישׁ לָנוּ וּלְבֵיתֵנוּ לֵאמֹר: הַעוֹד אֲבִיכֶם חַי? הֲיֵשׁ לָכֶם אָח? הֲיָדוֹעַ נֵדַע[1] כִּי יֹאמַר: הָבִיאוּ אֶת אֲחִיכֶם!

וַיֹּאמֶר יְהוּדָה אֶל אָבִיו: שְׁלַח אֶת הַנַּעַר אִתִּי וְנָקוּמָה וְנֵלְכָה, וְנִחְיֶה וְלֹא נָמוּת. אָנֹכִי אֶעֶרְבֶנּוּ, מִיָּדִי תְּבַקְשֶׁנּוּ!

וַיֹּאמֶר אֲלֵיהֶם יַעֲקֹב: אִם כֵּן זֹאת עֲשׂוּ: קְחוּ בְּיֶדְכֶם מִנְחָה לָאִישׁ, וְאֶת הַכֶּסֶף הַמּוּשָׁב בְּפִי שַׂקֵּיכֶם תָּשִׁיבוּ בְּיֶדְכֶם. וְאֶת אֲחִיכֶם קָחוּ. וֵאלֹהִים יִתֵּן לָכֶם רַחֲמִים לִפְנֵי הָאִישׁ. וַאֲנִי, כַּאֲשֶׁר שָׁכֹלְתִּי שָׁכָלְתִּי.

---

1 See §11.1.

1. מָתַי אָמַר יַעֲקֹב לְבָנָיו לָשׁוּב מִצְרַיְמָה? 2. לָמָּה אָמַר לָהֶם לָשׁוּב? 3. מַה בִּקֵּשׁ יְהוּדָה מֵאָבִיו? 4. מַה שָּׁאַל יַעֲקֹב אֶת בָּנָיו? 5. לָמָּה הִגִּידוּ לָאִישׁ בְּמִצְרַיִם כִּי עוֹד לָהֶם אָח? 6. מָתַי שָׁמַע יַעֲקֹב לְבָנָיו וְנָתַן עַל יָדָם אֶת בִּנְיָמִין? 7. מָה עוֹד אָמַר כִּי יִקְחוּ בְּיָדָם? 8. מַה בִּקֵּשׁ מֵאֱלֹהִים? 9. וְאִם לֹא יָשׁוּב גַּם בִּנְיָמִין?

(*To be followed by Reading 18.*)

Reading 18

opening, doorway פֶּתַח

please, my lord בִּי אֲדוֹנִי
asking permission to address a superior

he put (שִׂים) שָׂם

it is well with - שָׁלוֹם לְ־

hidden treasure, windfall מַטְמוֹן

he brought (*hif'il* בּוֹא) impf cons וַיָּבֵא

water מַיִם

they prepared (*hif'il* כּוּן) impf cons וַיָּכִינוּ

(when) he saw (רָאָה) impf cons וַיַּרְא

steward (lit., he who is over the household) אֲשֶׁר עַל הַבַּיִת

bring! (*hif'il* בּוֹא) הָבֵא!

they will eat (אָכַל) יֹאכְלוּ

noon (*ṣŏho-*) צָהֳרַיִם

brought (*hŏf'al* בּוֹא) pass pt מוּבָא

they were afraid (יָרֵא) impf cons וַיִּירְאוּ

the first time, at first בַּתְּחִלָּה

they came up to (נגשׁ) impf cons וַיִּגְּשׁוּ

וַיִּקְחוּ הָאֲנָשִׁים אֶת הַמִּנְחָה וְאֶת בִּנְיָמִין וַיָּקוּמוּ וַיֵּרְדוּ מִצְרַיְמָה; וַיָּבוֹאוּ וַיַּעַמְדוּ לִפְנֵי יוֹסֵף.

וַיַּרְא יוֹסֵף אֹתָם וַיֹּאמֶר לָאִישׁ אֲשֶׁר עַל בֵּיתוֹ: הָבֵא אֶת הָאֲנָשִׁים הַבַּיְתָה; כִּי אִתִּי יֹאכְלוּ הָאֲנָשִׁים בַּצָּהֳרָיִם.

וַיִּרְאוּ הָאַחִים כִּי מוּבָאִים הֵם בֵּיתָה יוֹסֵף וַיִּירְאוּ. וַיֹּאמְרוּ: עַל דְּבַר הַכֶּסֶף הַמּוּשָׁב בְּשַׂקֵּינוּ אֲנַחְנוּ מוּבָאִים. וַיִּגְּשׁוּ אֶל הָאִישׁ אֲשֶׁר עַל בֵּית יוֹסֵף וַיְדַבְּרוּ אֵלָיו בְּפֶתַח הַבַּיִת לֵאמֹר: בִּי אֲדוֹנִי, יָרוֹד יָרַדְנוּ בַּתְּחִלָּה לִשְׁבֹּר אֹכֶל. וַיְהִי כַּאֲשֶׁר פָּתַחְנוּ אֶת שַׂקֵּינוּ וַנִּמְצָא אֶת כַּסְפֵּנוּ כֶּסֶף אִישׁ בְּפִי שַׂקּוֹ! לֹא יָדַעְנוּ מִי שָׂם אֹתוֹ בְּשַׂקֵּנוּ וְהִנֵּה הוּא בְּיָדֵנוּ לַהֲשִׁיבוֹ אֵלֶיךָ.

וַיֹּאמֶר הָאִישׁ: שָׁלוֹם לָכֶם, אַל תִּירְאוּ! אֱלֹהֵיכֶם נָתַן לָכֶם מַטְמוֹן בְּשַׂקֵּיכֶם, כַּסְפְּכֶם בָּא אֵלָי.

וַיָּבֵא הָאִישׁ אֹתָם בֵּיתָה יוֹסֵף וַיִּתֵּן לָהֶם מַיִם, וְאֹכֶל נָתַן לַחֲמוֹרֵיהֶם. וַיָּכִינוּ אֶת הַמִּנְחָה כִּי שָׁמְעוּ כִּי שָׁם יֹאכְלוּ בַּצָּהֳרָיִם.

1. מַה לָּקְחוּ אִתָּם הָאַחִים מִצְרַיְמָה? 2. לָמָּה אָמַר יוֹסֵף לְהָבִיא אֹתָם הַבַּיְתָה? 3. לָמָּה יָרְאוּ הָאַחִים? 4. אֵיפֹה דִּבְּרוּ אֶל הָאִישׁ אֲשֶׁר עַל הַבָּיִת? 5. מַה סִפְּרוּ לוֹ? 6. מַה אָמַר הָאִישׁ עַל הַכֶּסֶף אֲשֶׁר הָיָה בְּפִי שַׂקֵּיהֶם? 7. מָה אָמַר עַל הַכֶּסֶף אֲשֶׁר הֵבִיאוּ בַּתְּחִלָּה? 8. מַה נָּתַן לָהֶם וְלַחֲמוֹרֵיהֶם?

(*To be followed by §17, p. 78.*)

Reading 19

he hurried; *often* *adverbial* he quickly, hastily — וַיְמַהֵר (מִהַר)
into the (his) room — הַחַדְרָה (הַחֶדֶר + ָ-ה term)
alone — לְבַד
  by himself — לְבַדּוֹ
  by themselves — לְבַדָּם
he came out — וַיֵּצֵא (יָצָא)
they drank — וַיִּשְׁתּוּ (שָׁתָה)

he returned — וַיָּשָׁב (שׁוּב)
they prepared — הֵכִינוּ (כּוּן *hif ʻil*)
he raised his eyes; *here*, he looked about — נָשָׂא אֶת עֵינָיו
he wept — בָּכָה
  to weep — לִבְכּוֹת
grew hot — נִכְמַר (כמר *nif ʻal*)
  his feelings were stirred — נִכְמְרוּ רַחֲמָיו

they became drunk — וַיִּשְׁכְּרוּ (שָׁכַר)

וַיְהִי בַצָּהֳרַיִם וַיָּשָׁב יוֹסֵף אֶל בֵּיתוֹ לֶאֱכֹל. וַיָּבִיאוּ לוֹ הָאֲנָשִׁים אֶת הַמִּנְחָה אֲשֶׁר הֵכִינוּ וַיִּתְּנוּ אֹתָהּ לְפָנָיו וַיִּקָּחֶהָ מִיָּדָם, וַיִּשְׁתַּחֲווּ לוֹ אַרְצָה. וַיִּשְׁאַל לָהֶם לְשָׁלוֹם וַיֹּאמֶר: הֲשָׁלוֹם לַאֲבִיכֶם הַזָּקֵן, הַעוֹדֶנּוּ חַי? וַיֹּאמְרוּ: שָׁלוֹם לְעַבְדְּךָ לְאָבִינוּ, עוֹדֶנּוּ חַי.

נָשָׂא יוֹסֵף אֶת עֵינָיו וַיַּרְא אֶת בִּנְיָמִין אָחִיו בֶּן אִמּוֹ וַיְבַקֵּשׁ לִבְכּוֹת כִּי נִכְמְרוּ רַחֲמָיו אֶל אָחִיו הַקָּטֹן. וַיְמַהֵר יוֹסֵף וַיָּבֹא הַחַדְרָה. שָׁם בָּכָה לְבַדּוֹ.

וַיֵּצֵא וַיֹּאמֶר לַעֲבָדָיו: שִׂימוּ לֶחֶם וְנֹאכַל! וַיָּשִׂימוּ לוֹ לְבַדּוֹ וּלְאֶחָיו לְבַדָּם וְלַמִּצְרִים הָאוֹכְלִים אִתּוֹ לְבַדָּם. וַיֵּשְׁבוּ אֶחָיו לְפָנָיו וַיֹּאכְלוּ עִמּוֹ, וַיִּשְׁתּוּ וַיִּשְׁכְּרוּ עִמּוֹ.

1. מָתַי שָׁב יוֹסֵף? 2. מֶה עָשׂוּ הָאַחִים בַּמִּנְחָה? 3. לִשְׁלוֹם מִי שָׁאַל יוֹסֵף? 4. מָה הִגִּידוּ לוֹ הָאַחִים עַל אָבִיו? 5. לָמָּה מִהַר יוֹסֵף לָבוֹא הַחַדְרָה? 6. מָה אָמַר לַעֲבָדָיו כַּאֲשֶׁר יָצָא מִן הַחֶדֶר? 7. אֵיךְ שָׂמוּ אֶת הָאֹכֶל? 8. מֶה עָשׂוּ אֲחֵי יוֹסֵף עִמּוֹ?

(To be followed by Reading 20.)

Reading 20

you will overtake	(*hif'il* נשג) תַּשִּׂיג	he ordered	(*pi'el* צִוָּה) וַיְצַו
he overtook	הִשִּׂיג	they are able	יוּכְלוּ (יָכֹל)
you did	עֲשִׂיתֶם	to carry	לָשֵׂאת (נָשָׂא)
he stole	גָּנַב	(wine) cup	גָּבִיעַ (גְּבִיעַ־)
he divined	נִחֵשׁ	he did	וַיַּעַשׂ (עָשָׂה)
far be it from us to do, God forbid that we do	חָלִילָה לָּנוּ מֵעֲשׂוֹת	became light	אוֹר
it will be found	(*nif'al*) יִמָּצֵא	they were sent off	(*pu'al*) שֻׁלְּחוּ
		he pursued	רָדַף אַחֲרֵי

וַיְצַו יוֹסֵף אֶת אֲשֶׁר עַל בֵּיתוֹ לֵאמֹר: מַלֵּא אֶת שַׂקֵּי הָאֲנָשִׁים אֹכֶל כַּאֲשֶׁר יוּכְלוּ לָשֵׂאת, וְשִׂים כֶּסֶף אִישׁ בְּפִי שַׂקּוֹ. וְאֶת גְּבִיעִי, גְּבִיעַ הַכֶּסֶף, תָּשִׂים בְּפִי שַׂק הַקָּטֹן עִם כֶּסֶף שִׁבְרוֹ. וַיַּעַשׂ הָאִישׁ כַּאֲשֶׁר צִוָּה יוֹסֵף.

הַבֹּקֶר אוֹר וְהָאֲנָשִׁים שֻׁלְּחוּ. הֵם יָצְאוּ אֶת הָעִיר וְיוֹסֵף צִוָּה אֶת אֲשֶׁר עַל בֵּיתוֹ לֵאמֹר: קוּם רְדֹף אַחֲרֵי הָאֲנָשִׁים! וְכַאֲשֶׁר תַּשִּׂיג אֹתָם וְאָמַרְתָּ אֲלֵיהֶם: לָמָּה עֲשִׂיתֶם אֶת הַדָּבָר הַזֶּה, לִגְנֹב אֶת גְּבִיעַ אֲדֹנִי! הֲלֹא זֶה אֲשֶׁר יִשְׁתֶּה אֲדֹנִי בּוֹ וְהוּא נַחֵשׁ יְנַחֵשׁ בּוֹ!

וַיֵּצֵא הָאִישׁ וַיִּרְדֹּף אַחֲרֵיהֶם. וַיַּשִּׂגֵם וַיְדַבֵּר אֲלֵיהֶם אֶת הַדְּבָרִים הָאֵלֶּה. וַיֹּאמְרוּ אֵלָיו: חָלִילָה לָּנוּ מֵעֲשׂוֹת כַּדָּבָר הַזֶּה! הִנֵּה הַכֶּסֶף אֲשֶׁר מָצָאנוּ בְּפִי שַׂקֵּינוּ הֱשִׁיבֹנוּ אֵלֶיךָ מֵאֶרֶץ כְּנַעַן, וְאֵיךְ נִגְנֹב מִבֵּית אֲדוֹנֶיךָ דָּבָר! הָאִישׁ אֲשֶׁר יִמָּצֵא אִתּוֹ הַגָּבִיעַ יָמוּת, וְגַם אֲנַחְנוּ נִהְיֶה לַאֲדוֹנִי לַעֲבָדִים!

The following sentences are factually incorrect; rewrite correctly.

1. יוֹסֵף צִוָּה לְמַלֵּא אֶת הַשַּׂקִּים מַיִם וְלָשִׂים אֶת גְּבִיעוֹ בְּשַׂק רְאוּבֵן. 2. הָאֲנָשִׁים שֻׁלְּחוּ בַּלַּיְלָה. 3. עֶבֶד יוֹסֵף דִּבֵּר אֶל הָאַחִים אֶת דִּבְרֵי יוֹסֵף לִפְנֵי אֲשֶׁר יָצְאוּ אֶת הָעִיר. 4. יוֹסֵף אֵינֶנּוּ עוֹשֶׂה דָּבָר בַּגָּבִיעַ. 5. כַּאֲשֶׁר גָּנְבוּ הָאַחִים אֶת הַכֶּסֶף הָשָּׁב בְּשַׂקֵּיהֶם כֵּן גָּנְבוּ אֶת הַגָּבִיעַ. 6. אִם יִמָּצֵא הַגָּבִיעַ עִם הָאַחִים יָמוּתוּ כֻּלָּם.

(*To be followed by §18, p. 84.*)

Reading 21

they took/brought down	וַיּוֹרִידוּ (ירד *hif'il* ; pf הוֹרִיד	they fell	וַיִּפְּלוּ (נָפַל)
saddlebag	אַמְתַּחַת	deed	מַעֲשֶׂה
he searched	חִפֵּשׂ	like me	כָּמוֹנִי
he began	הֵחֵל (חלל *hif'il*	we shall justify ourselves	נִצְטַדָּק (צדק *hitpa'el*
he finished	כִּלָּה (*pi'el*)	iniquity	עָוֹן (עֲוֹן־)
he tore	קָרַע	lo! we (are)	הִנֶּנּוּ
clothes, garment	שִׂמְלָה	it was found	נִמְצָא (*nif'al*)

וַיְמַהֲרוּ וַיּוֹרִידוּ אִישׁ אַמְתַּחְתּוֹ אַרְצָה, וַיִּפְתְּחוּ. וַיְחַפֵּשׂ הָאִישׁ: בַּגָּדוֹל הֵחֵל וּבַקָּטֹן כִּלָּה. וַיִּמָּצֵא הַגָּבִיעַ בְּאַמְתַּחַת בִּנְיָמִין.

וַיִּרְאוּ הָאֲנָשִׁים אֶת הַגָּבִיעַ וַיִּקְרְעוּ אֶת שִׂמְלוֹתָם. וַיָּשׁוּבוּ הָעִירָה. וַיָּבוֹא יְהוּדָה וְאֶחָיו בֵּיתָה יוֹסֵף – וְהוּא עוֹדֶנּוּ שָׁם – וַיִּפְּלוּ לְפָנָיו אַרְצָה.

וַיֹּאמֶר אֲלֵיהֶם יוֹסֵף: מָה הַמַּעֲשֶׂה הַזֶּה אֲשֶׁר עֲשִׂיתֶם, לִגְנֹב אֶת גְּבִיעִי! הֲלוֹא יְדַעְתֶּם כִּי נַחֵשׁ יְנַחֵשׁ אִישׁ אֲשֶׁר כָּמוֹנִי? וַיַּעַן יְהוּדָה וַיֹּאמַר: מַה נֹּאמַר לַאדֹנִי? מַה נְּדַבֵּר וּמַה נִּצְטַדָּק? הָאֱלֹהִים מָצָא אֶת עֲוֹן עֲבָדֶיךָ; הִנֶּנּוּ עֲבָדִים לַאדֹנִי, גַּם אֲנַחְנוּ גַּם אֲשֶׁר נִמְצָא הַגָּבִיעַ בְּיָדוֹ.

וַיֹּאמֶר יוֹסֵף: חָלִילָה לִּי מֵעֲשׂוֹת זֹאת! הָאִישׁ אֲשֶׁר נִמְצָא הַגָּבִיעַ בְּיָדוֹ הוּא לְבַדּוֹ יִהְיֶה לִּי עֶבֶד, וְאַתֶּם לְכוּ עֲלוּ בְשָׁלוֹם אֶל אֲבִיכֶם.

1. מֶה עָשׂוּ הָאַחִים בְּאַמְתְּחוֹתֵיהֶם? 2. אֵיךְ חִפֵּשׂ הָאִישׁ? 3. אֵיפֹה נִמְצָא הַגָּבִיעַ? 4. אַחַר זֹאת מֶה עָשׂוּ? 5. עַל פִּי (according to) דִּבְרֵי יוֹסֵף אֵיךְ יָדַע כִּי גָּנְבוּ הֵם אֶת הַגָּבִיעַ? 6. מָה אָמַר יְהוּדָה עַל צָרָתָם? 7. עַל פִּי דִּבְרֵי יְהוּדָה מַה יֵּעָשֶׂה לָהֶם? וְעַל פִּי יוֹסֵף?

(To be followed by Reading 22.)

Reading 22

וַיִּגַּשׁ	(נגשׁ)	he came up to, approached
אַל יִחַר אַפְּךָ	juss (חָרָה)	don't be angry
וַיִּוָּתֵר	(יתר *nif'al* ; נוֹתַר pf)	he remained, was left
הוֹרִידֻהוּ!	(ירד *hif'il*	bring him down!
עָלִינוּ	(עָלָה)	we went up
לָרֶדֶת	(יָרַד)	to go down
שְׁנַיִם	m	two
רְאִיתִיו	(רָאִיתִי + ו)	I've seen him
עַד		until, up to
הֵנָּה		to here, now
וְהוֹרַדְתֶּם	pf cons	you will bring down
שֵׂיבָתִי	(שֵׂיבָה)	my gray hair
יָגוֹן		grief
שְׁאוֹלָה	(term ־ָה + שְׁאוֹל)	to Sheol (the netherworld)
עָרַב... מֵעִם...		he took...on pledge from..., he was responsible for... to...
עַתָּה		now
יֵשֶׁב	juss (יָשַׁב)	let him stay
תַּחַת		instead of
יַעַל	juss (עָלָה)	let him go up

וַיִּגַּשׁ אֵלָיו יְהוּדָה וַיֹּאמַר: בִּי אֲדוֹנִי, יְדַבֶּר־נָא עַבְדְּךָ דָבָר בְּאָזְנֵי אֲדוֹנִי וְאַל יִחַר אַפְּךָ בְּעַבְדֶּךָ.

אֲדוֹנִי שָׁאַל אֶת עֲבָדָיו לֵאמֹר: הֲיֵשׁ לָכֶם אָב אוֹ אָח? וַנֹּאמֶר אֶל אֲדוֹנִי: יֶשׁ־לָנוּ אָב זָקֵן וְיֶלֶד זְקֻנִים קָטֹן וְאָחִיו מֵת וַיִּוָּתֵר הוּא לְבַדּוֹ לְאִמּוֹ, וְאָבִיו אָהֵב אֹתוֹ. וַתֹּאמֶר אֶל עֲבָדֶיךָ: הוֹרִידֻהוּ אֵלַי וְאָשִׂימָה עֵינִי עָלָיו.

כַּאֲשֶׁר עָלִינוּ אֶל אָבִינוּ וַנַּגֶּד־לוֹ אֶת דִּבְרֵי אֲדוֹנִי.

וַיֹּאמֶר אָבִינוּ: שֻׁבוּ שִׁבְרוּ לָנוּ עוֹד אֹכֶל. וַנֹּאמֶר: לֹא נוּכַל לָרֶדֶת אִם אֵין אָחִינוּ הַקָּטֹן אִתָּנוּ. וַיֹּאמֶר אֵלֵינוּ אָבִינוּ: אַתֶּם יְדַעְתֶּם כִּי שְׁנַיִם יָלְדָה לִי אִשְׁתִּי. וַיֵּצֵא הָאֶחָד מֵאִתִּי וְלֹא רְאִיתִיו עַד הֵנָּה; וּלְקַחְתֶּם גַּם אֶת זֶה מֵעִמִּי וְקָרָהוּ אָסוֹן בַּדֶּרֶךְ, וְהוֹרַדְתֶּם אֶת שֵׂיבָתִי בְּיָגוֹן שְׁאוֹלָה.

עַבְדְּךָ עָרַב אֶת הַנַּעַר מֵעִם אָבִי. וְעַתָּה, יֵשֶׁב־נָא עַבְדְּךָ תַּחַת הַנַּעַר עֶבֶד לַאדֹנִי וְהַנַּעַר יַעַל עִם אֶחָיו. כִּי אֵיךְ אֶעֱלֶה אֶל אָבִי וְהַנַּעַר אֵינֶנּוּ אִתִּי? פֶּן אֶרְאֶה בָּרָע אֲשֶׁר יִמְצָא אֶת אָבִי.

1. עַל פִּי דִבְרֵי יְהוּדָה מַה שָּׁאַל יוֹסֵף וּמֶה עָנוּ לוֹ אֶחָיו? 2. מַה בִּקֵּשׁ אָז יוֹסֵף? 3. לָמָּה לֹא יָכְלוּ הָאַחִים לָרֶדֶת אִם אֵין בִּנְיָמִין אִתָּם? 4. לָמָּה יָרֵא יַעֲקֹב לְשַׁלַּח אֶת בִּנְיָמִין? 5. מָתַי שִׁלַּח אֹתוֹ? 6. מַה בִּקֵּשׁ יְהוּדָה מִיּוֹסֵף? 7. לָמָּה לֹא יַעֲלֶה יְהוּדָה אִם אֵין בִּנְיָמִין אִתּוֹ?

(*To be followed by §19, p. 88.*)

Reading 23

לְהִתְאַפֵּק	to restrain himself
קָרָא	he called, cried
הוֹצִיאוּ! (*hif'il* יצא)	take out! clear out!
מֵעָלַי (מִן + עָלַי)	from (attendance) upon me
הִתְוַדַּע (*hitpa'el* ידע)	he made himself known
בְּהִתְוַדַּע יוֹסֵף	lit., in the-making-himself-known of J. = when J. made himself known
נִבְהַל (*nif'al*)	he was terrified
אַל יִחַר בְּעֵינֵיכֶם	don't let it vex you (lit., let it not burn in your eyes)
מִחְיָה	sustenance
זֶה שְׁנָתַיִם	it is two years now
קֶרֶב	midst
חָמֵשׁ f	five
לְהַחֲיוֹת (*hif'il* חיה)	to keep alive
כֹּה	thus
רְדָה! (יָרַד)	come down! (§10.9)
גֹּשֶׁן	Goshen
כִּלְכֵּל	he sustained
כָּבוֹד (כְּבוֹד־)	honor
צַוָּאר (צַוְּארֵי־)	neck
נִשֵּׁק	he kissed

וְלֹא יָכֹל יוֹסֵף לְהִתְאַפֵּק עוֹד וַיִּקְרָא: הוֹצִיאוּ כָל אִישׁ מֵעָלָי! וְלֹא עָמַד אִישׁ אִתּוֹ בְּהִתְוַדַּע יוֹסֵף אֶל אֶחָיו.

וַיֹּאמֶר יוֹסֵף אֶל אֶחָיו: אֲנִי יוֹסֵף, הַעוֹד אָבִי חָי?

וְלֹא יָכְלוּ אֶחָיו לַעֲנוֹת אֹתוֹ כִּי נִבְהֲלוּ מִפָּנָיו. וַיֹּאמֶר יוֹסֵף לְאֶחָיו: גְּשׁוּ אֵלַי! וַיִּגָּשׁוּ. וַיֹּאמֶר: אֲנִי יוֹסֵף אֲחִיכֶם אֲשֶׁר מְכַרְתֶּם אֹתִי מִצְרַיְמָה. וְעַתָּה אַל יִחַר בְּעֵינֵיכֶם כִּי מְכַרְתֶּם אֹתִי הֵנָּה כִּי לְמִחְיָה שְׁלָחַנִי אֱלֹהִים לִפְנֵיכֶם. כִּי זֶה שְׁנָתַיִם הָרָעָב בְּקֶרֶב הָאָרֶץ, וְעוֹד חָמֵשׁ שָׁנִים יִהְיֶה רָעָב, וַיִּשְׁלָחֵנִי אֱלֹהִים לִפְנֵיכֶם לְהַחֲיוֹת אֶתְכֶם. וְעַתָּה מַהֲרוּ וַעֲלוּ אֶל אָבִי וַאֲמַרְתֶּם אֵלָיו: כֹּה אָמַר בִּנְךָ יוֹסֵף: שָׂמַנִי אֱלֹהִים לְאָדוֹן לְכָל מִצְרַיִם, רְדָה אֵלַי אַל תַּעֲמֹד, וְיָשַׁבְתָּ בְּאֶרֶץ גֹּשֶׁן וְהָיִיתָ קָרוֹב אֵלַי, וְכִלְכַּלְתִּי אֹתְךָ שָׁם. וְהִגַּדְתֶּם לְאָבִי אֶת כָּל כְּבוֹדִי בְּמִצְרַיִם וְאֵת כָּל אֲשֶׁר רְאִיתֶם, וּמִהַרְתֶּם וְהוֹרַדְתֶּם אֶת אָבִי הֵנָּה!

וַיִּפֹּל עַל צַוְּארֵי בִנְיָמִין וַיֵּבְךְּ, וּבִנְיָמִין בָּכָה עַל צַוָּארָיו. וַיְנַשֵּׁק לְכָל אֶחָיו וַיֵּבְךְּ עֲלֵיהֶם, וְאַחֲרֵי־כֵן דִּבְּרוּ אֶחָיו אִתּוֹ.

1. מַה קָּרָא יוֹסֵף לִפְנֵי הִתְוַדְּעוֹ אֶל אֶחָיו? 2. עַל מִי שָׁאַל יוֹסֵף בְּהִתְוַדְּעוֹ? 3. לָמָּה לֹא יָכְלוּ אֶחָיו לַעֲנוֹתוֹ? 4. מָה אָמַר יוֹסֵף עַל הֱיוֹתוֹ בְּמִצְרַיִם? 5. זֶה כַּמָּה שָׁנִים הָיָה הָרָעָב, וְעוֹד כַּמָּה שָׁנִים יִהְיֶה? 6. מַה בִּקֵּשׁ יוֹסֵף מֵאֶחָיו לַעֲשׂוֹת? 7. מָה אָמַר יוֹסֵף כִּי יַעֲשֶׂה לְאָבִיו? 8. מֶה עָשָׂה יוֹסֵף אַחַר דַּבְּרוֹ אֶל אֶחָיו? 9. מָתַי יָכְלוּ אֶחָיו לְדַבֵּר אִתּוֹ?

(*To be followed by Reading 24.*)

Reading 24

sound, voice, report	קוֹל	ruling, ruler	מוֹשֵׁל pt
was heard	נִשְׁמַע (שׁמע *nif'al*)	it grew numb, failed	וַיָּפָג (פוג)
it was good, pleasing	וַיִּיטַב (יטב)	heart	לֵב (לִבִּי w suf)
wagon	עֲגָלָה	he believed	הֶאֱמִין (אמן *hif'il*)
little ones	טַף (טַפִּי w suf)	to carry	לָשֵׂאת (נָשָׂא)
the best of	טוּב	it revived	וַתְּחִי (חָיָה)
at the command of	עַל פִּי	enough	רַב
provisions	צֵידָה	before	בְּטֶרֶם

וְהַקּוֹל נִשְׁמַע בְּבֵית פַּרְעֹה לֵאמֹר: בָּאוּ אֲחֵי יוֹסֵף! וַיִּיטַב הַדָּבָר בְּעֵינֵי פַרְעֹה וּבְעֵינֵי עֲבָדָיו. וַיֹּאמֶר פַּרְעֹה אֶל יוֹסֵף: אֱמֹר אֶל אַחֶיךָ: זֹאת עֲשׂוּ: קְחוּ לָכֶם מֵאֶרֶץ מִצְרַיִם עֲגָלוֹת לְטַפְּכֶם וְלִנְשֵׁיכֶם, וַעֲלִיתֶם אַרְצָה כְּנַעַן, וּנְשָׂאתֶם אֶת אֲבִיכֶם וְאֶת בָּתֵּיכֶם וּבָאתֶם. הִנֵּה טוּב אֶרֶץ מִצְרַיִם לָכֶם הוּא!

וַיִּתֵּן לָהֶם יוֹסֵף עֲגָלוֹת עַל פִּי פַרְעֹה, וַיִּתֵּן לָהֶם צֵידָה לַדָּרֶךְ. וַיְשַׁלַּח אֶת אֶחָיו וַיֵּלֵכוּ.

וַיַּעֲלוּ מִמִּצְרַיִם וַיָּבוֹאוּ אַרְצָה כְּנַעַן אֶל יַעֲקֹב אֲבִיהֶם. וַיַּגִּידוּ לוֹ לֵאמֹר: עוֹד יוֹסֵף חַי! וְהוּא מוֹשֵׁל בְּכָל אֶרֶץ מִצְרָיִם! וַיָּפָג לִבּוֹ כִּי לֹא הֶאֱמִין לָהֶם. וַיְדַבְּרוּ אֵלָיו אֶת כָּל דִּבְרֵי יוֹסֵף וַיְסַפְּרוּ לוֹ אֶת כָּל כְּבוֹדוֹ, וַיַּרְא אֶת הָעֲגָלוֹת אֲשֶׁר שָׁלַח יוֹסֵף לָשֵׂאת אֹתוֹ וַיַּאֲמֵן לָהֶם, וַתְּחִי רוּחַ יַעֲקֹב אֲבִיהֶם. וַיֹּאמֶר: רַב, עוֹד יוֹסֵף בְּנִי חָי. אֵלְכָה וְאֶרְאֶנּוּ בְּטֶרֶם אָמוּת.

1. מָה הַקּוֹל אֲשֶׁר נִשְׁמַע בְּבֵית פַּרְעֹה? 2. מַה צִּוָּה פַּרְעֹה לָתֵת לָאַחִים? לָמָּה? 3. מַה שָּׂם פַּרְעֹה לִפְנֵי בֵּית יַעֲקֹב? 4. מָה הִגִּידוּ הָאַחִים לְיַעֲקֹב? 5. לָמָּה פָּג לִבּוֹ? 6. מָתַי הֶאֱמִין לָהֶם? 7. מַה בִּקֵּשׁ לַעֲשׂוֹת בְּטֶרֶם יָמוּת?

(*To be followed by §20, p. 93.*)

AIDS TO READING THE BIBLE

ORIENTATION IN THE HEBREW BIBLE

The name

The collection of biblical writings is most often called merely סְפָרִים (s סֵפֶר) "books" in Hebrew literature of antiquity. Greek-speaking Jews mediated this term to the world as *biblia*, "books," whence — through Latin and Old French — our "Bible."

The earliest notice of the tripartition of biblical writings comes from the end of the 2nd century B.C.E. In the preface to the Greek translation of the originally Hebrew "Wisdom of Ben-Sira" the translator praises the author's learning in "the Law, the Prophets, and the rest of the books." This division corresponds to the Hebrew designations תּוֹרָה, נְבִיאִים, וּ(שְׁאָר) כְּתוּבִים "Torah, Prophets, and (the rest of the) Writings." Abbreviated as תנ״ך (*Tanaḵ*, *T^{e}naḵ*), it is the most common of Hebrew names for the Bible.

The three parts

The Torah ("instruction," but Grecized as "the law," i.e., the constitution of the Jewish commonwealth) comprises the earliest traditions of Israel. It was considered of Mosaic origin certainly no later than the 5th century B.C.E. Beginning with an account of the Creation, attention is gradually focused on the early history of Israel, which is described from patriarchal times to the death of Moses, on the eve of the people's entry into Canaan.

The various strands of tradition embodying the prose, poetry, and law collections of the Torah reached a form essentially the same as their present one probably during the 5th century B.C.E., at which time the Torah was canonized. Critical examination of these traditions confirms their antiquity and general historical worth.

The Prophets are subdivided into "Former Prophets" נְבִיאִים רִאשׁוֹנִים and "Latter Prophets" נְבִיאִים אַחֲרוֹנִים. The Former Prophets comprise the historical records of Israel from its conquest of Canaan (end of the 13th century) to the Babylonian exile (first deportation, 597; fall of Jerusalem, 586). The varied materials of these books were selected and arranged with a view to providing an understanding of the Divine will at work in Israel's history. Because the viewpoint is to a large extent that of the early prophets, the writing of these anonymous books was early ascribed to them.

The records of prophetic utterances began to be kept about 750 B.C.E., when Amos began his prophetic career. The poetic and prose sermons of the "literary prophets" (Amos to Malachi, middle of the 5th century B.C.E.) comprise the Latter Prophets.

The significance of this literature was heightened by the catastrophic fall of Judah and the ensuing Babylonian exile (586-538 B.C.E.). For the restored community of postexilic times, the Prophets furnished the historic example and the warning of what would befall Israel when it was disloyal to God. Probably by the end of the 3rd century B.C.E., the Prophets had become canonical.

The (rest of the) Writings comprise a heterogeneous collection of wisdom, poetic, and later historical literature. Here are, for example, Psalms, Proverbs, Job, Song of Songs, as well as Ezra-Nehemiah (the account of the return from Babylonia) and Chronicles (a later edition of the history of pre-exilic Israel). While there is a good deal of early (pre-exilic) material here (e.g., many of the Psalms and Proverbs), much of this literature does not antedate the Restoration (538 B.C.E). Part of the book of Daniel — the latest biblical book — dates to Maccabean times (about 165 B.C.E). During the 1st and 2nd centuries C.E. the canonicity of a few of these works was still in question. A 3rd-century Talmudic list is the first to record the canon of 24 books as we now have it.

The structure of the Torah

Since we shall be reading from the Torah, a closer look at its structure is now in order.

The Torah was divided into fifths (for easy handling when written on the parchment scrolls of antiquity), hence the whole is often called חֲמִשָּׁה חֻמְשֵׁי תוֹרָה "the five fifths (s חֹמֶשׁ) of the Torah" = Greek *penta* ("five") *teuchos* ("roll" of writing material), whence our "Pentateuch."

Following ancient Near-Eastern custom, each fifth is called in Hebrew by its first (significant) word(s): בְּרֵאשִׁית "In the beginning," (וְאֵלֶּה) שְׁמוֹת "(Now these are) the names of," וַיִּקְרָא "Then [God] called," בְּמִדְבַּר "In the wilderness of," and (וְאֵלֶּה הַ)דְּבָרִים "(Now these are the) words."

But this is not the most anciently attested method. The Alexandrian Jews, who, some time in the 3rd century B.C.E. translated the Torah into Greek (the *Septuagint*), titled each part by a rough characterization of its content: *Genesis* "The beginning [of the world]," *Exodos* "The departure [from Egypt]," *Leuitikon* "Levitical [and priestly] matters," *Arithmoi* "Numbers [of the census of Israel]," and *Deuteronomion* "Second (i.e., repetition by Moses before his death of the) Law." The Latinized forms of these titles have reached us through the Vulgate (made by Jerome at the end of the 4th century), the standard Christian Bible of the Middle Ages.

The Jewish custom of a weekly public reading of the Torah is attested as early as the 1st century, and then it is considered to be a custom of great antiquity. The 1st-century historian Josephus writes:

> For ignorance he [Moses] left no pretext. He appointed the Law to be the most excellent and necessary form of instruction, ordaining, not that it should be heard once for all, or twice, or on several occasions, but that every week men should desert their other occupations and assemble to listen to the Law and to obtain a thorough and accurate knowledge of it, a practice which all other legislators seem to have neglected.[1]

Accordingly the Torah was divided into sections which were read through, either in the course of three years — the old Palestinian custom — or in one year — the Babylonian custom — which now prevails. Each of the 54 sections of the one-year cycle — called in Hebrew פָּרָשָׁה (pl פָּרָשִׁיּוֹת) or סִדְרָה (pl סְדָרוֹת) — is entitled by its first significant word(s). In the runninghead of most printings, the name of the *påråšå* follows that of the book. The weekly Sabbath reading of the *påråšå* is

---

[1] *Against Apion* II, 175; translated by H. St. J. Thackeray in the Loeb Classical Library, Cambridge, Mass.: Harvard University Press, n.d.

apportioned among seven readers, each of whom, in early times, read his portion; these portions are marked in some printings by ordinal numbers written small in the text or margin.

The paragraphing is found already in the 1st-century Torah fragments from the Wilderness of Judah. It is formally observed only in Torah scrolls. In printed Bibles the traditional paragraphs are indicated by a letter indicating the size of the space between paragraphs: פ [for פְּתוּחָה "open (section)"] indicating a large space, ס [for סְתוּמָה "closed (section)"] indicating a smaller one.[2]

The verse division (not the numbering) is quite ancient, for the meaning often depends on it. A fixed verse division existed by Mishnaic times (3rd century C.E.), although discrepancies persist among various authorities as to the precise number and disposition of the verses.

The chapter division and the numbering of verses were initiated by Christians. Chapters first appeared in the Vulgate in the 13th century, verse numbers in the 16th. From there both were adopted by printers of Hebrew Bibles in the 16th and 17th centuries.

The genealogy of our texts

Before the discovery in 1947 of the scrolls from the Wilderness of Judah, the earliest fragments of Hebrew Bible manuscripts came from about the 8th-9th centuries. Earlier copies perished, owing to the Jewish law requiring that worn-out copies be withdrawn from use, to be disposed of either by burial or by storage in a synagogue lumber-room. In the latter case, such scrolls as were not consumed by rodents were

---

[2] In many printings a triple פפפ or ססס marks the break between the weekly *påråšiyyoṯ*. It is followed by a number [in Arabic and/or Hebrew numerals (Hebrew letters serve as numerals)] indicating which of the 54 the new *påråšå* is.

usually lost when the synagogue itself was abandoned or demolished. Most of the surviving 8th-9th century manuscript fragments come from just this sort of a lumber-room, discovered in a still-used Cairo synagogue by Solomon Schechter at the end of the 19th century.

The lineage of our text, however, ascends to the same scholars of Tiberias who developed the present system of vocalization (§2.4). These scholars, called Massoretes ("text-traditionists" from מַסּוֹרָה "text-tradition"), labored for centuries to produce a standard text of the Bible. Their efforts were crowned in the work of the last members of the Ben Asher family of Tiberias who, in the 9th-10th centuries, created the archetypes of all subsequent texts. Owing chiefly to the lifelong researches of Paul Kahle, several Ben Asher texts scattered over Europe and the Near East have been identified, comprising the entire Hebrew Bible. The best recent editions of the Bible have been based on these texts.

Kahle himself participated in the standard scholarly edition of the Bible, the Kittel-Kahle *Biblia Hebraica* (3rd edition, Stuttgart, 1937). The basis for this text is a Ben Asher manuscript (or rather a copy of such a manuscript) dating to 1008/09, now in Leningrad. In 1957 the British and Foreign Bible Society published an edition edited by Norman Snaith based on other manuscripts that Snaith believes to represent the true Ben Asher text and which is substantially similar to Kahle's.

Most present-day Hebrew Bibles, however, are based on the much later, second Rabbinic Bible (מִקְרָאוֹת גְּדוֹלוֹת), edited by Jacob Ben Hayyim and printed at Venice by Daniel Bomberg in 1524-25. Ben Hayyim worked with the best manuscripts then available; but these were late, and he himself was troubled by their dissensions. Of the successive editions of Ben Hayyim's text, that of Van der Hooght

(Amsterdam & Utrecht, 1705) became the basis of those of today. The edition of Meir Letteris (Vienna, 1852) has been reprinted many times over in the type of the British and Foreign Bible Society (first printing: Berlin, 1866). The Hebrew Publishing Company Bible is such a reprint.

NOTES ON THE HEBREW TEXT OF GENESIS 37, 42-45

Genesis 37

Verse 1. וַיֵּשֶׁב יַעֲקֹב "Jacob, however, settled." As indicated by the impf cons, the verse continues the narrative left off in 36: 8.

2. שָׁנָה. Numbered nouns with the numbers 2-10 are usually in the plural (חָמֵשׁ שָׁנִים 45: 6, עֲשָׂרָה חֲמוֹרִים 45: 23). With the numbers 11-19 they may also be in the plural אַחַד עָשָׂר כּוֹכָבִים 37: 9), though if they are items frequently numbered (e.g., אִישׁ, יוֹם, or, as here, שָׁנָה) they appear in the singular.

וְהוּא נַעַר... אָבִיו. The relation of this clause to the preceding is problematic. Two suggested interpretations are: (1) to take each of its phrases as paralleling corresponding phrases in the first clause: יוֹסֵף בֶּן שְׁבַע עֶשְׂרֵה שָׁנָה ‖ וְהוּא נַעַר; הָיָה רֹעֶה אֶת אֶחָיו בַּצֹּאן ‖ אֶת בְּנֵי בִלְהָה וְאֶת בְּנֵי זִלְפָּה נְשֵׁי אָבִיו "Joseph, at seventeen years of age, used to tend the flocks with his brothers — being a mere lad — with the sons of B. and the sons of Z., his father's wives"; (2) to give נַעַר

a special sense (which it has elsewhere), "servant," and render: "being a helper with (to) the sons of B., etc."

דִּבָּתָם רָעָה. רָעָה is a predicate of דִּבָּתָם, defining its quality: "the report of them, (it being) bad." Cf. our objective predicate: "I bought the book *bound*." Render: "bad reports about them."

3. וְיִשְׂרָאֵל אָהַב "now Israel loved." The flow of the narrative is interrupted to tell of a background (prior) circumstance; hence the verb reverts to the perfect (see § 16.2).

וְעָשָׂה לוֹ [on the stress, see § 29.2 (b)] "and he had made." The verb is not conceived of as consequent upon אָהַב (not: "because he loved him he made him"; that would have been expressed by the impf cons וַיַּעַשׂ), but as in an independent clause coordinate with the preceding one.

4. וַיִּרְאוּ אֶחָיו... וַיִּשְׂנְאוּ אֹתוֹ "when his brothers saw... they hated him." Of two coordinate impf cons verbs, the first is frequently subordinate to the second as a temporal clause. So, e.g., vs 10 וַיְסַפֵּר... וַיִּגְעַר בּוֹ "when he told it... (his father) scolded him"; vs 21 וַיִּשְׁמַע רְאוּבֵן וַיַּצִּלֵהוּ "when Reuben heard it he tried to rescue him." Cf. note on vs 25.

דַּבְּרוֹ. An unusual case of the suf representing the indirect, rather than the direct, object (the same usage in הֲשִׁבֵנִי "bring back (word) to me" 37:14).

7. וְהִנֵּה. הִנֵּה makes the narrative graphic and vivid and enables the reader to enter into the surprise or satisfaction of the speaker or actor concerned. It is regularly employed in narrating dreams. The opening clause is usually (as here) participial — setting the scene against which the action takes place.

אֲלֻמִּים "sheaves" in general; אֲלֻמָּה "a particular, single sheaf"; אֲלֻמּוֹת "sheaves" in particular.

תְּסֻבֶּינָה. From סבב; on the impf see §10.2.

וַתִּשְׁתַּחֲוֶיןָ. ןָ defectively written (§2.3) for ־נָה.

8. הֲמָלֹךְ ... אִם מָשׁוֹל. See §11.1.

12. אֶת. Dots over letters are an ancient scribal device for calling attention to the dotted matter. Dots were employed to indicate what ought to be struck out or to point to some peculiarity of meaning — which of the two is involved in this case is difficult to say. (A rabbinic comment fancifully suggests that the dots point to the fact that "they really went to tend to *themselves*," i.e., to their own interests, not their father's).

17. שָׁמַעְתִּי אוֹמְרִים "I heard them say"; supply the object as in vs 25, לְהוֹרִיד "to bring them down."

דֹּתָיְנָה – דֹּתָן. ־ָן and ־ַיִן interchange as place-name endings.

20. וְעַתָּה "now then." ו often expresses an informal inference or consequence, especially at the beginning of a speech. So too 44:8 וְאֵיךְ נִגְנֹב "how then could we steal."

21. לֹא נַכֶּנּוּ נָפֶשׁ "we mustn't kill him!" (lit., "we mustn't strike him mortally"). נָפֶשׁ is an objective complement, defining the part of the object (־ֶנּוּ "him") specially affected by the action, namely "life."

22. ... לְמַעַן. A parenthetical aside.

25. לֶאֱכָל־לֶחֶם. See §29.2(a).

וַיִּשְׂאוּ עֵינֵיהֶם וַיִּרְאוּ "lifting up their eyes, they saw." The subordinate temporal clause (see note to vs 4 וַיִּרְאוּ אֶחָיו) may sometimes be rendered more neatly by the English participial construction. So too vs 30 וַיָּשָׁב אֶל אֶחָיו וַיֹּאמַר "returning to his brothers, he said," vs 33 וַיַּכִּירָהּ וַיֹּאמֶר "recognizing it, he said."

וָלֹט. As a rule the copula is vocalized וָ before a monosyllable or a word stressed on the first syllable when that word has a disjunctive accent. So too 44:31 וָמֵת [pf cons whose *wåw* is vocalized like the copula (§16.6)], and compare Genesis 8:22 וְקֹר וָחֹם וְקַיִץ וָחֹרֶף וְיוֹם וָלַיְלָה "cold and heat, summer and winter, day and night."

28. וַיִּמְשְׁכוּ וַיַּעֲלוּ "they pulled up" (lit., "they pulled and brought up"). The second verb, indicating direction of motion, is used adverbially.

עֶשְׂרִים כָּסֶף "twenty shekels of silver"; similarly in 45:22 שְׁלֹשׁ מֵאוֹת כֶּסֶף "300 shekels of silver."

30. אָנָה אֲנִי בָא. The sense is: "what am I to do now?"

32. הַכְּתֹנֶת. That the interrogative ה should be followed by a long consonant is very unusual (for the normal vocalization of the interrogative ה see vocabulary of Reading 3).

33. טָרֹף טֹרַף יוֹסֵף. See §11.1.

36. וְהַמְּדָנִים מָכְרוּ. See §16.2(b).

Genesis 42

1. יֶשׁ־. "There *was*..." in Egypt, in contrast to Canaan.

2. שִׁבְרוּ... וְנִחְיֶה וְלֹא נָמוּת "procure food... that we may live and not die." Result or purpose clauses are expressed by *wåw* before a voluntative verb (cohortative, imperative, jussive); e.g., 42:34 וְהָבִיאוּ... וְאֵדְעָה "bring... that I may know," 42:18 זֹאת עֲשׂוּ וִחְיוּ "do this and so live" (if you do this you will live") 42:16 שִׁלְחוּ... וְיִקַּח... וְיִבָּחֲנוּ "send... to take... that (your words) may be tested."

In many cases, as here, the voluntative verb has no distinctive form; the context (e.g., a preceding imperative) is generally a sufficient indication of a result or purpose clause.

A negative result or purpose clause — such as וְלֹא נָמוּת "that we may not die" — does not of course employ a voluntative verb.

3. עֲשָׂרָה. "Ten (in number)."

6. וְיוֹסֵף הוּא הַשַּׁלִּיט "now it was Joseph who was the ruler...." Generally the predicate of a noun sentence or clause does not have the article (see § 5.6); when it does, the emphasis which is thereby added is best rendered by "it was/is... who/which...," etc. [Cf. 45:12 פִּי הַמְדַבֵּר "it is my mouth (and not another's) that is speaking."] Further emphasis is given by הוּא; lit., "Now Joseph (note the disjunctive of וְיוֹסֵף), it was he who was the ruler."

7. קָשׁוֹת "harsh things," here adverbial "harshly." For indefinite or abstract expressions the feminine is commonly used: 42:29 הַקֹּרֹת "the things that happened," 44:4 רָעָה "evil" (noun), טוֹבָה "good" (noun).

10. וַעֲבָדֶיךָ. Opposition is expressed by the *wåw*: "the fact is, rather, that..."

11. לֹא הָיוּ "have never been," § 9.3 end.

13. עֲבָדֶיךָ... אֲנַחְנוּ. The change from 3 pers (הָיוּ in vs 11) to 1 pers when using the self-appellation is normal in Hebrew. Cf. the similar changes in 44:7–9. When a superior is respectfully addressed as אֲדֹנִי a similar inconsistency between 3 and 2 pers is found: 44:18ff. יְדַבֶּר נָא עַבְדְּךָ דָבָר בְּאָזְנֵי אֲדֹנִי וְאַל יִחַר אַפְּךָ בְּעַבְדֶּךָ... אֲדֹנִי שָׁאַל אֶת עֲבָדָיו... וַתֹּאמֶר אֶל עֲבָדֶיךָ "Please, my lord, let your servant have a word with my lord, and don't be angry with

your servant.... My lord asked his servants... then you said to your servants...."

14. הוּא אֲשֶׁר דִּבַּרְתִּי אֲלֵיכֶם לֵאמֹר "it is just as I spoke to you, when I said...."

15. חֵי פַרְעֹה אִם תֵּצְאוּ מִזֶּה... הֵנָּה "(I swear) by Pharaoh's life! you shall not leave this place unless your youngest brother comes here." The oath is introduced by אִם and takes the form of an "if" clause; the "then" clause, which contains a self-imprecation, the teeth of the oath, is left unspoken. Literally, then: "If you leave this place except with the coming of your youngest brother here (may I be cursed)!"

16. הֵאָסְרוּ "submit to imprisonment!"

חֵי פַרְעֹה כִּי מְרַגְּלִים אַתֶּם "(I swear) by Pharaoh's life that you are spies!" (Only verb clauses are introduced by אִם, as in vs 15.)

21. אֲשֶׁר רָאִינוּ. It is not clear to what אֲשֶׁר is attached; if to אֲנַחְנוּ, then render "(we) who saw" ("for we saw"); but if to אָחִינוּ, the clause is to be construed אָחִינוּ אֲשֶׁר (אֶת) צָרַת נַפְשׁוֹ בְּהִתְחַנְנוֹ אֵלֵינוּ רָאִינוּ "whose mortal distress when he pleaded with us we saw."

צָרַת נַפְשׁוֹ "his mortal distress." The suffix refers to the whole construction: "his distress-with-regard-to-life." Similarly below, vs 35 צְרוֹר כַּסְפּוֹ "his money-bag," צְרֹרוֹת כַּסְפֵּיהֶם "their money-bags," 44:2 כֶּסֶף שִׁבְרוֹ "his ration-money."

22. וְגַם "so now...." גַּם sometimes expresses consequence in the sense of "measure for measure."

23. הַמֵּלִיץ. The article may be used with items which, though as yet not mentioned, are associated so closely with a given situation that the writer assumes their presence there all along to be well known.

הַמֵּלִיץ "the interpreter (who customarily mediated between Joseph and foreigners)." English idiom requires "an interpreter."

25. וַיְצַו... וַיְמַלְאוּ[1]... וּלְהָשִׁיב "he gave orders... to fill... and to give back...." Two ways of expressing the complement of צִוָּה are here combined: וַיְצַו וַיְמַלְאוּ and וַיְצַו לְהָשִׁיב.

וַיַּעַשׂ לָהֶם כֵּן "it was so done for them." The subject is indefinite (the medieval Hebrew grammarians supplied it as הָעוֹשֶׂה "the doer"); "one did so for them," best rendered by English passive.

28. וַיֶּחֶרְדוּ אִישׁ אֶל אָחִיו "they turned trembling to one another." חָרַד cannot normally govern the preposition אֶל since it does not in itself convey an idea of motion *toward* anything. אֶל depends, rather, on some inexplicit verb expressing a movement made by the brothers אִישׁ אֶל אָחִיו — such as turning the head toward or looking at — which was accompanied by trembling. Such a construction as חָרַד אֶל which implies more than the words say explicitly is called a *pregnant construction.* Another pregnant construction is 43:33 וַיִּתְמְהוּ הָאֲנָשִׁים אִישׁ אֶל רֵעֵהוּ "the men looked at one another in astonishment."

31. לֹא הָיִינוּ "we have never been," §9.3 end.

32. שְׁנֵים עָשָׂר אֲנַחְנוּ "we are twelve," "there are twelve of us."

33. שֶׁבֶר רַעֲבוֹן=רַעֲבוֹן as in vs 19.

34. כִּי לֹא מְרַגְּלִים אַתֶּם "that you are not spies (but honest men)." Noun clauses are normally negated by אֵין: 37:29 אֵין יוֹסֵף בַּבּוֹר "Joseph was not in the pit," and the word order אֵין – subject – predicate is preserved even after כִּי: I Kings 21:15 כִּי אֵין נָבוֹת חַי "for Naboth is not alive," Esther 3:5 כִּי אֵין מָרְדְּכַי כֹּרֵעַ "that Mordecai did not kneel." But when, as here, it is desired to negate the

---

1 On the absence of *dåḡeš* in the ל (though the verb is *pi'el*) see § 22.4, note 1.

predicate forcefully, not only is the word order reversed to predicate–subject, לֹא is employed as the negative particle, its force falling on the immediately following predicate rather than on the whole clause. A rising inflection in the voice on "spies" will render the effect of these changes in English.

36. אֹתִי שִׁכַּלְתֶּם "it is I (not yourselves!) whom you have bereaved"; see §27.7. Hence Reuben's response in vs 37.

כֻלָּנָה "all these things" i.e., these troubles. The form is that taken by כֻּלָּן in a major pause; for the feminine, see note on vs 7 above.

38. וּקְרָאָהוּ אָסוֹן ... וְהוֹרַדְתֶּם "if disaster befalls him... you will bring down...." Conditions are often expressed by simple juxtaposition of the "if" and the "then" clauses, each preceded by ו (in this case *wāw*-consecutive with the perfect) to bring out the correlation of clauses. Cf. 44:22 וְעָזַב אֶת אָבִיו וָמֵת "if he should leave his father, he will die"; 44:29 וּלְקַחְתֶּם גַּם אֶת זֶה... וְקָרָהוּ אָסוֹן וְהוֹרַדְתֶּם "if you take this one too... and disaster befalls him, you will bring down...."

Genesis 43

3. הָעֵד הֵעִד בָּנוּ "he solemnly/strictly/clearly warned us."

4–5. אִם יֶשְׁךָ מְשַׁלֵּחַ, וְאִם אֵינְךָ מְשַׁלֵּחַ "if you really mean to let our brother go... but if you do not mean to let him go." יֵשׁ and אֵין here express disposition or nondisposition to do something.

7. שָׁאוֹל שָׁאַל, הֲיָדוֹעַ נֵדַע. See §11.1.

8. ... שִׁלְחָה. See §10.9.

9. אִם לֹא הֲבִיאֹתִיו, וְהִצַּגְתִּיו, וְחָטָאתִי. The verbs concern future time but are perfects; hence future perfects: "if (at that time) I shall

not have brought him to you and set him before you, I shall have incurred life-long guilt toward you." Render: "if I do not bring him to you and set him before you, I shall stand guilty before you all my life."

14. יִתֵּן לָכֶם רַחֲמִים לִפְנֵי הָאִישׁ "may He show you compassion (when you are) in the presence of the man," i.e., by inclining the man to be favorable toward you.

אֲחִיכֶם אַחֵר. We expect אֲחִיכֶם הָאַחֵר; has the article been omitted for the sake of euphony (to avoid adding another laryngal)? Cf. 42:19 אֲחִיכֶם אֶחָד as compared with vs 33 אֲחִיכֶם הָאֶחָד [but perhaps there the intent is first "any one of your brothers," but when the brothers narrate the tale, "the one (that Joseph did in fact imprison) of your brothers"].

כַּאֲשֶׁר שָׁכֹלְתִּי שָׁכָלְתִּי "if I am to be bereaved, I must be bereaved." On שָׁכָלְתִּי see §29.1(e).

15. וּמִשְׁנֶה כֶּסֶף. Note that in vs 12 the word order is reversed. Numbers too may precede or follow the noun: שְׁלֹשָׁה יָמִים or יָמִים שְׁלֹשָׁה.

מִצְרַיְמָה = מִצְרַיִם; cf. vs 18 בֵּיתָה יוֹסֵף = בֵּית יוֹסֵף; similarly in vs 19 בְּפֶתַח הַבָּיִת = פֶּתַח הַבָּיִת.

16. טְבֹחַ טֶבַח "slaughter an animal," lit., "slaughter a slaughtering." טֶבַח is a *cognate accusative*, i.e., a direct object noun derived from the verb — a very common usage in Hebrew.

20. יָרֹד יָרַדְנוּ. The force of the inf abs is unclear.

27. הֲשָׁלוֹם אֲבִיכֶם הַזָּקֵן "is your aged father well?" lit., "is your aged father well-being?" The predicate of a nominal sentence need not be wholly applicable in substance to the subject; it is enough

if, as here, something of it is shared in common with the subject. The reply in vs 28 שָׁלוֹם לְעַבְדְּךָ לְאָבִינוּ is of course a different construction: "your servant our father enjoys (is possessed of) well-being."

28. וַיִּקְּדוּ. Root קדד

29. יָחְנְךָ. Root חנן

30. The main clause is וַיְמַהֵר יוֹסֵף... וַיָּבֹא הַחַדְרָה; כִּי begins the clause giving the reason.

31. וַיִּתְאַפַּק. See §29.1(e).

32. יוּכְלוּן. The ן is an archaic ending attached occasionally to the vowel afformatives of the impf; cf 44:23 תֹסִפוּן (note final stress).

33. וַיִּתְמְהוּ... אִישׁ אֶל רֵעֵהוּ. On this pregnant construction see note on 42:28.

34. וַיִּשָּׂא מַשְׂאוֹת "he had portions carried," i.e., at his command. Or render as a passive: "portions were carried"; see note to 42:25 וַיַּעַשׂ לָהֶם כֵּן.

חָמֵשׁ יָדוֹת "by five shares," i.e., it was five times as large.

Genesis 44

3,4. הַבֹּקֶר אוֹר וְהָאֲנָשִׁים שֻׁלְּחוּ "when morning dawned, the men were sent off." הֵם יָצְאוּ אֶת הָעִיר... וְיוֹסֵף אָמַר "when they had left the city, Joseph said...." וְהִשַּׂגְתָּם וְאָמַרְתָּ אֲלֵיהֶם "and when you overtake them, say to them...." These are three examples of temporal expressions, in which the temporal and the main clause are merely juxtaposed and linked by ו, the simplest and most elegant manner of expressing such a relation in Hebrew. Cf. note to 37:4 וַיִּרְאוּ אֶחָיו.

לֹא הִרְחִיקוּ "without/not having gone very far": a circumstantial verb clause, qualifying יָצְאוּ; it is identifiable by being set off from the main clause without וְ. Another such circumstantial verb clause appears in vs 12: וַיְחַפֵּשׂ בַּגָּדוֹל הֵחֵל וּבַקָּטֹן כִּלָּה "he searched them, beginning with the eldest and ending with the youngest."

5. וְהוּא נַחֵשׁ יְנַחֵשׁ בּוֹ "by which in fact he usually divines"; or "about which he'd certainly divine" (cf. vs 15).

הֲרֵעֹתֶם. Root רעע. הֲרֵעֹתֶם אֲשֶׁר עֲשִׂיתֶם lit., "you did evil (in that) which you did"; render: "you did evil in so doing."

8. וְאֵיךְ נִגְנֹב "how then could we steal"; see note to 37:20 and §10.3.

9. וְגַם אֲנַחְנוּ "moreover the rest of us." Similarly וְאַתֶּם in vss 10 and 17 is "the rest of you"; so too in 42:19.

10. גַּם עַתָּה כְדִבְרֵיכֶם כֶּן הוּא "though what you say is right"; lit., "though now it is right as you say."

14. וַיָּבֹא יְהוּדָה וְאֶחָיו... וַיִּפְּלוּ With a subject composed of two (or more) coordinate nouns, a verb that precedes may agree with only the first noun, but a verb that follows is generally in the plural.

18. בְּאָזְנֵי אֲדֹנִי "in the hearing of my lord." The sense of the whole clause is: "Please permit me to speak, and give what I have to say a favorable hearing." It does not mean, "Let me have a private word with you."

On the changes of person in these verses see note to 42:13.

כָמוֹךָ כְּפַרְעֹה "you and Pharaoh are alike." The sense of כ...כ is not merely "a is like b," but includes the idea that "b is like a."

20. אֲהֵבוֹ "loves him"; see §9.3 end and note the stative vowel ֵ that reappears when אָהַב takes a suffix.

22. וְעָזַב...וָמֵת. See note to 42:38.

26. וְאָחִינוּ הַקָּטֹן אֵינֶנּוּ אִתָּנוּ "unless our youngest brother is with us"; lit., "our youngest brother not being with us." This is a circum-

stantial noun clause, usually linked by ו to the main clause; cf. vs 30 וְהַנַּעַר אֵינֶנּוּ אִתָּנוּ "the lad not being with us" = "without the lad" and similarly in vs 34.

27. **אַתֶּם יְדַעְתֶּם.** The independent pronoun is used with finite verbs to add emphasis (cf. vs 17 הוּא יִהְיֶה "he *alone* will be"). Here Jacob wishes to recall to his sons what they know full well but seem to have disregarded; אַתֶּם יְדַעְתֶּם almost: "let me remind you."

כִּי שְׁנַיִם "only two sons"; cf. §27.7.

29. **...וּלְקַחְתֶּם.** See note to 42:38.

30. וְנַפְשׁוֹ קְשׁוּרָה בְנַפְשׁוֹ "and his whole being is so bound up with him."

32. כִּי עַבְדְּךָ עָרַב "now it was your servant who took the lad on pledge"; §27.5(c). Here Judah supplies the motive for his princely offer in the next verse.

34. פֶּן "(I could not) lest...."

Genesis 45

1. **לְכֹל.** ל "for" here conveys the idea "as was proper in the presence of."

2. וַיִּתֵּן אֶת קֹלוֹ בִּבְכִי "he wept loud and freely"; the phrase expresses giving vent to pent-up emotion.

4. **אֲשֶׁר מְכַרְתֶּם אֹתִי.** Note how the retrospective אֹתִי agrees with אֲנִי יוֹסֵף rather than with אֲחִיכֶם — the rule in relative clauses.

6. אֵין חָרִישׁ וְקָצִיר "there will be no yield from tilling." חָרִישׁ and קָצִיר are combined here into one concept; not that there will be no plowing *or* harvesting (even in famine the farmer may plow his field in hope of a return), but that there will be no plowing that produces a harvest.

7. לָשׂוּם לָכֶם שְׁאֵרִית "to establish for you a remnant"; i.e., to insure that you and yours survive.

לְהַחֲיוֹת אֶתְכֶם=וּלְהַחֲיוֹת לָכֶם. The presence of לָכֶם is probably due to the influence of לָשׂוּם לָכֶם.

לִפְלֵיטָה גְּדֹלָה. Unclear; it has been understood either as "to (become) a great band of survivors" — alluding perhaps to the numerous future progeny of these survivors of famine — or "for a great escape" — alluding to the marvelous manner of their deliverance.

12. פִּי הַמְדַבֵּר. See note on 42:6.

19. וְאַתָּה צֻוֵּיתָה "you are charged (to bid them)."

23. כַּזֹּאת "as follows."

26. וְכִי. Not part of the quotation. It may be understood either as unexpectedly introducing indirect speech, or better, as dependent upon וַיַּגִּדוּ... לֵאמֹר and taking up the direct speech anew.

QUESTIONS FOR REVIEW

GENESIS 37

עֲנֵה:

1. לָמָּה שָׂנְאוּ אֲחֵי יוֹסֵף אֹתוֹ, וְלָמָּה קִנְאוּ בוֹ? 2. מַה פִּתְרוֹנֵי חֲלוֹמוֹת יוֹסֵף? 3. לָמָּה שָׁלַח יַעֲקֹב אֶת יוֹסֵף שְׁכֶמָה? 4. אֵיךְ מָצָא יוֹסֵף אֶת אֶחָיו בְּדוֹתָן? 5. אֵיךְ הִצִּיל רְאוּבֵן אֶת יוֹסֵף מִיַּד אֶחָיו? 6. אֵיךְ כִּסּוּ הָאַחִים מִיַּעֲקֹב אֶת אֲשֶׁר עָשׂוּ לְיוֹסֵף? 7. לָמָּה מֵאֵן יַעֲקֹב לְהִתְנַחֵם?

מִי אָמַר אֶל מִי וּמָתַי?

1. אֶת אַחַי אָנֹכִי מְבַקֵּשׁ. 2. הִנֵּה בַּעַל הַחֲלוֹמוֹת הַלָּזֶה בָּא. 3. אַל תִּשְׁפְּכוּ דָם. 4. אָחִינוּ בְּשָׂרֵנוּ הוּא.

GENESIS 42

עֲנֵה:

1. לָמָּה לֹא שָׁלַח יַעֲקֹב אֶת בִּנְיָמִין אֶת אֶחָיו מִצְרַיְמָה? 2. מָה הִגִּידוּ הָאַחִים לְיוֹסֵף? 3. מַה בֵּין דִּבְרֵי יוֹסֵף לְאֶחָיו לִפְנֵי אֲשֶׁר הָיוּ בַּמִּשְׁמָר לִדְבָרָיו אַחֲרֵי אֲשֶׁר הָיוּ שָׁם שְׁלֹשֶׁת יָמִים? 4. אֵיךְ פָּתְרוּ הָאַחִים אֶת דְּבַר צָרָתָם? אֵיךְ פָּתַר אֹתוֹ רְאוּבֵן? 5. מַה מִּכָּל הַקּוֹרוֹת אֹתָם בְּמִצְרַיִם לֹא הִגִּידוּ בְּנֵי יַעֲקֹב לַאֲבִיהֶם? 6. לָמָּה אָמַר רְאוּבֵן: אֶת שְׁנֵי בָנַי תָּמִית?

מִי אָמַר אֶל מִי וּמָתַי?

1. מֵאַיִן בָּאתֶם? 2. וְגַם דָּמוֹ הִנֵּה נִדְרָשׁ. 3. אֲחִיכֶם הָאֶחָד הַנִּיחוּ אִתִּי.

GENESIS 43

עֲנֵה:

1. לָמָּה בִּקֵּשׁ יְהוּדָה מִיַּעֲקֹב כִּי יְשַׁלַּח אֶת בִּנְיָמִין? 2. לָמָּה הִגִּידוּ לָאִישׁ כִּי עוֹד לָהֶם אָח? 3. מָה אָמַר יְהוּדָה לְיַעֲקֹב כַּאֲשֶׁר עָרַב אֶת בִּנְיָמִין מִמֶּנּוּ? 4. מַה זִּמְרַת אֶרֶץ כְּנַעַן? 5. כַּמָּה כֶּסֶף הֵשִׁיבוּ הָאַחִים בְּיָדָם? לָמָּה? 6. לָמָּה יָרְאוּ כַּאֲשֶׁר הוּבְאוּ בֵּיתָה יוֹסֵף? 7. אֵיךְ פָּתַר לָהֶם הָאִישׁ אֶת דְּבַר הַכֶּסֶף אֲשֶׁר נִמְצָא בְּשַׂקֵּיהֶם? 8. מֶה עָשָׂה לָהֶם כַּאֲשֶׁר הֵבִיא אֹתָם הַבַּיְתָה? 9. עַל מַה בָּכָה יוֹסֵף? 10. עַל מַה תָּמְהוּ הָאַחִים?

Utilize in a sentence :

רָחַץ. עַד. נִכְמְרוּ רַחֲמָיו. הִתְאַפֵּק. תּוֹעֵבָה. רָבָה.

GENESIS 44

עֲנֵה:

1. מַה צִּוָּה יוֹסֵף לָשִׂים בְּאַמְתְּחוֹת הָאַחִים? 2. מַה יַּעֲשֶׂה יוֹסֵף בַּגָּבִיעַ – עַל פִּי הָאִישׁ אֲשֶׁר עַל בֵּית יוֹסֵף? 3. עַל פִּי דִּבְרֵי הָאַחִים מַה לַּעֲשׂוֹת בָּאִישׁ אֲשֶׁר יִמָּצֵא הַגָּבִיעַ בְּיָדוֹ? וְעַל פִּי דִּבְרֵי יוֹסֵף? 4. לָמָּה לֹא יוּכַל יְהוּדָה לַעֲלוֹת אֶל אָבִיו אִם הַנַּעַר אֵינֶנּוּ אִתּוֹ?

מִי אָמַר אֶל/עַל מִי וּמָתַי?

1. לָמָּה שִׁלַּמְתֶּם רָעָה תַּחַת טוֹבָה? 2. וְאַתֶּם תִּהְיוּ נְקִיִּם. 3. כָמוֹךָ כְּפַרְעֹה. 4. נַפְשׁוֹ קְשׁוּרָה בְנַפְשׁוֹ. 5. טָרֹף טֹרַף.

Utilize in a sentence :

מִלֵּא. רָדַף. שִׁלֵּם. זָהָב. גָּנַב. נָקִי. עָזַב. שְׁנַיִם. יָלַד. עָלָה.

GENESIS 45

עֲנֵה:

1. לָמָּה לֹא יָכֹל יוֹסֵף לְהִתְאַפֵּק עוֹד? 2. אֵיךְ פָּתַר יוֹסֵף אֶת דְּבַר רִדְתּוֹ מִצְרַיְמָה? 3. מָה הָיָה יוֹסֵף בְּמִצְרַיִם? 4. מַה בִּקֵּשׁ לַעֲשׂוֹת לְאָבִיו וּלְבֵיתוֹ? 5. מָתַי יָכְלוּ יוֹסֵף וְאֶחָיו לְדַבֵּר אִישׁ אֶל רֵעֵהוּ? 6. מַה צִוָּה פַּרְעֹה לַעֲשׂוֹת לְבֵית יַעֲקֹב וְלֵאמֹר לָהֶם? 7. מַה נָּתַן יוֹסֵף לְאֶחָיו וּמַה שָּׁלַח אֶל אָבִיו? 8. מָתַי הֶאֱמִין יַעֲקֹב כִּי עוֹד יוֹסֵף חַי?

Utilize in a sentence:

הִתְוַדַּע. נִצָּב. קוֹל. נִבְהַל. שְׁנָתַיִם. טַף. חֲלִיפָה. חָס.

* * * * * * *

VOCABULARY REVIEW

Give synonyms:

עָמַד. נָתַן. קֶרֶב. שְׁאֵרִית. תּוֹךְ. בַּעַל. שַׁלִּיט. עָמַס. חֵלֶב הָאָרֶץ. אֹכֶל. בֶּגֶד. נִשְׁאַר. יָגוֹן. צָרָה. דָּרַשׁ. טָבַח. צָעִיר. מָלַךְ עַל. הָרַג.

Give antonyms:

שָׂבָע. רָחוֹק. לָתֵת. עָנָה. יֵשׁ. בְּכוֹר. טוֹבָה. חַי. הֵרִיק. יָצָא. הֵחֵל. מְעַט. לַעֲלוֹת. מֵאַיִן? אָסַר. לְהָמִית. אָהַב. הֶעֱלָה. עֶבֶד.

Translate:

The numbers: 1, 2, 3, 5, 10, 11, 12, 17, 20, 300; *give a noun with each.*

Parts of the body: (*where possible supply an associated verb*) gray hair, face, eye/s, ear/s, mouth, neck, hips, feet, flesh, blood, heart, hand/s.

Parts of day and concepts of time: day, night, morning, noon, year, two years, one time, twice, afterward.

Verbs of motion: come, go, come/go up, — down, — in, — out, — back; bring up, — down, — out, — back; pass; arise; pursue; overtake.

Family and age: father, mother, son, daughter, brother, little ones, child, lad, firstborn, youngest, old man, family, household.

Utterance: say, tell, speak, narrate, call, weep, scold, ask, answer, order, sound (voice).

Emotion: love, hate, be afraid, be terrified, tremble, be astonished, have feelings stirred, restrain oneself, console, be consoled, have pity (regard) for, be angry at, be wrought up at.

GLOSSARY

GENESIS 37, 42-45

Words are listed in alphabetical order; שׂ precedes שׁ. Verbs are defined in the English infinitive form.

A parenthesis with chapter and verse followed by n refers to the section "Notes on the Hebrew Text."

אָב (§14.5) *father*, in 45:8 *counsellor*

אֲבָל *the truth is, that...*, affirming what one would gladly deny

אָבֵל *be in mourning*; *hitpa'el* הִתְאַבֵּל *mourn for* (עַל)

אָדוֹן, suf לַאדֹנִי, אֲדֹנִי *lord, master*; cs pl אֲדֹנֵי־ is used with s meaning

אָהֵב, אָהַב *love*

אוֹ *or*

אוּלַי *perhaps*

אוֹר *become light*

אֹזֶן, du אָזְנַיִם, אָזְנֵי־ f *ear*

אָח (§14.5) *brother*; אִישׁ אֶל אָחִיו *one to the other*

אֶחָד (אַחַד־) m *one*; אַחַד עָשָׂר "*one-teen*" (*eleven*)

אַחֵר *(an)other*

אַחַר, אַחֲרֵי־ *after*; אַחֲרֵי כֵן *afterward*

אֵיךְ *how?*

אֵין (cs of אַיִן *nought*; §15.8) *no, not* negating noun sentence (42:34 n)

אֵיפֹה *where?*

אִישׁ, אֲנָשִׁים, אַנְשֵׁי־ *a man, one, each*; אִישׁ אֶל אָחִיו *one to the other*

אַךְ *surely!*

אָכַל, impf יֹאכַל [§21.4(b)] pf 3fs w suf 3ms אֲכָלָתְהוּ *eat*

אֹכֶל *food*

אַל *(do) not* w juss

אֶל (§15.4) *to, into*

אֵל *god*; אֵל שַׁדַּי *El Shadday* (usually rendered *God Almighty*); שַׁדַּי is a divine epithet of as yet undetermined meaning; אֵל שַׁדַּי is an antique name of God used chiefly in stories of patriarchal times

אֵלֶּה *these*

אֱלֹהִים pl of majesty, *God*

אֲלֻמָּה, אֲלֻמִּים, אֲלֻמּוֹת (37:7n) *sheaf*

אלם, *pi'el* אִלֵּם *bind* (sheaves)

אֵם, suf אִמּוֹ *mother*

אִם *if, or;* introduces an oath (42:15n)

אמן, *nif'al* impf יֵאָמֵן *be verified, proven true*; *hif'il* pf הֶאֱמִין *consider true, believe*

אָמַר, impf יֹאמַר [§21.4(b)] *say, command*; the inf cs לֵאמֹר, usually rendered *saying*, often has no meaning beyond that of our colon or comma with quotation marks marking a direct address

אֱמֶת *truth*

אַמְתַּחַת *saddlebag*

אָנָה *whither?*

אֲנִי, אָנֹכִי *I;* pl אֲנַחְנוּ *we*

אָסוֹן *disaster, terrible accident*

אָסַף [§21.4(a)] *gather*

אָסַר *bind, imprison; nif'al* impf יֵאָסֵר *be imprisoned*

אַף *nose, anger;* חָרָה אַפּוֹ בְּ־ *his anger was kindled against;* אַפַּיִם du *face* (=פָּנִים)

אֵפוֹא particle *then;* אִם כֵּן אֵפוֹא *if so, then....*

אפק, *hitpa'el* הִתְאַפֵּק, וַיִּתְאַפַּק [§29.1(e)] *restrain oneself*

אֹרְחָה *caravan*

אֶרֶץ w art הָאָרֶץ, w term אַרְצָה f *land, ground*

אִשָּׁה, אֵשֶׁת־, נָשִׁים, נְשֵׁי־ *woman, wife* also used for *concubine*

אָשֵׁם *be guilty*

אֲשֶׁר word of relation *that, which, who*

אֵת (§14.6) (*together*) *with* מֵאֵת (*away*) *from*

אֵת (§14.6) the sign of the definite direct object; precedes direct object defined either by (1) the art (2) being in the cs (3) having a pron suf (4) being a proper name

אָתוֹן, אֲתֹנוֹת *she-donkey*

בּ (§14.6) (1) *in, at, upon.* (2) prefixed to the object of some verbs; e.g., רָעָה, מָשַׁל, גָּעַר. (3) *by* בְּזֹאת תִּבָּחֵנוּ *by this will you be tested*

בֶּגֶד, בְּגָדִים *clothing*

בהל, *nif'al* נִבְהַל *be terrified*

בּוֹא, pf בָּא (§17.2) *come; hif'il* הֵבִיא (§17.3) *bring*; *hŏf'al* הוּבָא *be brought*

בּוֹר, בּוֹרוֹת *pit, cistern*

בחן, *nif'al* impf יִבָּחֵן *be tested*

בָּטְנִים *pistachios*

בִּי אֲדֹנִי formula craving permission to open a conversation with a superior, *please, my lord*

בֵּין־, בֵּינוֹת־ *between*

בַּיִת, בֵּית־, suf בֵּיתוֹ, pl בָּתִּים, בָּתֵּי־ *house, household*

בָּכָה, impf יִבְכֶּה, וַיֵּבְךְּ *weep, bewail*

בְּכוֹר *firstborn, oldest son*

בְּכִי *weeping*

בְּכֹרָה *seniority* (lit., *firstborn status*)

בִּלְהָה *Bilhah*, one of Jacob's concubines, the maid of Rachel

בִּלְתִּי *except, unless*, only with a noun clause

בֵּן, בֶּן־, בָּנִים, בְּנֵי־ (§14.5) *son;* בֶּן שְׁבַע עֶשְׂרֵה שָׁנָה *son of* 17 *years* (17 *years old*)

בִּנְיָמִין *Benjamin*

בְּעִיר collective *beasts*

בַּעַל *owner, master;* בַּעַל חֲלוֹמוֹת *dreamer*

בֶּצַע *gain, profit*

בֹּקֶר *morning*

בָּקָר *cattle*

בקשׁ, *pi'el* בִּקֵּשׁ *seek, want, demand*

בָּר *grain*

בָּשָׂר *flesh*

בַּת, בָּנוֹת (§15.3) *daughter*

גָּבִיעַ, גְּבִיעַ־, suf גְּבִיעִי *cup*

גָּדוֹל *big, old* (mature)

גלל, *hitpolel* הִתְגֹּלֵל *find a pretext against* (עַל)

גִּלְעָד *Gilead*

גַּם *also, even*, 44:10 *even though;* גַּם...גַּם *both... and*

גָּמָל, גְּמַלִּים *camel*

גָּנַב *steal*

גָּעַר, impf יִגְעַר *rebuke, scold* (בְּ־)

גֹּשֶׁן *Goshen*, district in NE Egypt

דִּבָּה *report*

דבר, *pi'el* דִּבֶּר *speak*

דָּבָר *thing, matter, word, something said*

דְּבַשׁ *honey*

דָּם *blood*

דֶּרֶךְ f *way*

דָּרַשׁ *require; nif'al* 42:22 דָּמוֹ... נִדְרָשׁ *his blood* (i.e., an accounting for the shedding of his innocent blood) *is being required*

דֹּתָן w term דֹּתָיְנָה *Dothan*

הֲ (for vocalization see vocabulary to Reading 3) interrogative particle; prefixed to the first word of a statement it makes it a question, הֲמָלֹךְ תִּמְלֹךְ עָלֵינוּ? *Would you indeed be king over us?* in indirect questions *whether*, 42:16 יִבָּחֲנוּ דִּבְרֵיכֶם הַאֱמֶת אִתְּכֶם *let your words be tested (to see) whether you are telling the truth;* 43:6 לְהַגִּיד לָאִישׁ הַעוֹד לָכֶם אָח *telling the man whether you had another brother*

הַ, הָ, הֶ (§5) art *the*, w pt *who, which, that*

הוּא m הוּא (הִיא) f (§7.1) 3s pron *he she, it;* as a demonstrative *that*

הָיָה impf יִהְיֶה, וַיְהִי (§19.4) *be, become*

הַלָּזֶה = הַזֶּה

הָלַךְ, impf יֵלֵךְ, וַיֵּלֶךְ (§20.4) *go;* the

imv לֵךְ (לְכָה) לְכוּ is often used to exhort, *come!*

הֵם, הֵמָּה m הֵנָּה f 3 pl pron *they*

הִנֵּה = הֵן

הֵנָּה *hither;* temporally *now* as in עַד הֵנָּה *until now*

הִנֵּה *lo!* הִנְנִי *lo! I (here I am)* הִנֶּנּוּ *lo! we (are)*

הָרַג *kill*

וְ, וּ, וָ, וַ (on vocalization see § 4 exercise vocabulary, p. 36, note 1, 37 : 25n) the copula *and;* it may express, according to context, *but, yet, so that, or, while,* and the like

זֶה m זֹאת f (1) *this,* מִזֶּה *from this place* (2) with expressions of time *already, by now,* 43:10 זֶה פַעֲמָיִם *already twice;* 45:6 זֶה שְׁנָתַיִם *it is two years now*

זָהָב *gold*

זָכַר *remember*

זִלְפָּה *Zilpah,* Leah's maid, a concubine of Jacob

זִמְרָה collective *choice products*

זְקֻנִים *old age;* בֶּן־זְקֻנִים *son of old age*

חֶבְרוֹן *Hebron*

חֶדֶר, w term חַדְרָה *private chamber, room*

חוּס, juss 3fs תָּחֹס *pity, have compassion for* (עַל), 45:20 וְעֵינְכֶם אַל תָּחֹס עַל כְּלֵיכֶם *let your eye not pity (never mind about) your household stuff*

חָטָא, impf יֶחֱטָא *sin against* (בְּ־); *stand guilty before* (לְ־)

חֵי־ (cs of *חַי appearing otherwise in the pl חַיִּים *life*) in oaths: *(by) the life of...* e.g., 42:15 חֵי פַרְעֹה *(I swear) by Pharaoh's life!*

חָיָה, impf יִחְיֶה, impf cons 3fs וַתְּחִי, pt חַי (§19.4) *live, revive; hif'il* inf cs לְהַחֲיוֹת *keep alive, preserve*

חַיָּה *beast;* חַיָּה רָעָה *wild beast*

חֵלֶב *fat,* figuratively used in חֵלֶב הָאָרֶץ *the fat (best) of the land*

חָלַם *dream*

חֲלוֹם, חֲלוֹמוֹת *a dream*

חָלִילָה in חָלִילָה לְ־ מִ־(מֵ־), e.g., 44:7 חָלִילָה לַעֲבָדֶיךָ מֵעֲשׂוֹת *far be it from your servants to (God forbid that we) do*

חלל, *hif'il* הֵחֵל *begin*

חֲלִפָה *change of clothing, suit*

חֲמוֹר *donkey*

חָמֵשׁ f חֲמִשָּׁה m *five*

חָנַן, impf יָחֹן juss, w 2ms suf יָחְנְךָ *be gracious toward; hitpa'el* הִתְחַנֵּן *implore favor for oneself, plead with* (אֶל)

חפשׂ, *pi'el* חִפֵּשׂ *search*

חָרַד, impf יֶחֱרַד *tremble; look trembling at* (אֶל)

חָרָה, juss יִחַר *burn, be kindled.* (אַף anger) *against* (בְּ־), 44:18 אַל יִחַר אַפְּךָ בְּעַבְדֶּךָ *don't be angry with your servant;* 45:5 אַל יִחַר בְּעֵינֵיכֶם *don't let it vex you*

חָרִישׁ *plowing*

טָבַח *slaughter*

טֶבַח *a slaughtering* of animals

טַבָּח in (שַׂר) הַטַּבָּחִים *(captain of) the bodyguard*

טָבַל *dip*

טוֹב *good;* f טוֹבָה is used as a noun *good* in 44:4

טוּב *the best (of)*

טָעַן *load*

טַף, suf טַפִּי *little ones*

טֶרֶם or בְּטֶרֶם *ere, before* w impf

טָרַף *tear in pieces* (said of wild beasts); pass *qal* pf טֹרַף *was torn in pieces* (§8.3 note 2)

יָגוֹן *grief*

יָד f (1) du יָדַיִם, יְדֵי־ *hand;* עַל יָדִי *into my charge, custody;* בְּיַד־ w לָקַח, הֵשִׁיב, etc. *with.* (2) pl יָדוֹת *share*

יָדַע, impf יֵדַע (§20) *know; hitpa'el* הִתְוַדַּע *make oneself known*

יְהוּדָה *Judah*

יוֹם, יָמִים *day;* הַיּוֹם *now, at present;* כָּל הַיָּמִים *all one's life*

יוֹסֵף *Joseph*

יטב only impf, יִיטַב (§20.8) *be good, pleasing* וַיִּיטַב בְּעֵינֵי פַרְעֹה *it was good in the eyes of Pharaoh (Pharaoh was pleased)*

יָכֹל, impf יוּכַל (§20.6,7) *be able*

יָלַד *bear a child*

יֶלֶד *child*

יסף, *hif'il* הוֹסִיף *do again* or *more* w inf cs (with or without ל), 37:8 וַיֹּסִפוּ עוֹד שְׂנֹא אֹתוֹ *they did yet more (of) hating him (they hated him all the more;)* 44:23 לֹא תֹסִפוּן לִרְאוֹת פָּנָי *you shall not do more (of) seeing my face (you shall not see my face again)*

יַעֲקֹב *Jacob*

יָצָא, impf יֵצֵא (§20.3) *go* or *come out, leave; hif'il* הוֹצִיא *take* or *bring out*

יָרֵא, impf יִירָא (§20.5) *be afraid*

יָרַד, impf יֵרֵד (§20.3) *go* or *come down hif'il* הוֹרִיד *bring* or *take down*

יָרֵחַ *moon*

ירשׁ, *nif'al* impf 2ms תִּוָּרֵשׁ *come to want*

יִשְׂרָאֵל *Israel,* second name of Jacob

יֵשׁ, יֶשׁ־ *(there) is/are,* usually implies some emphasis; with suf it expresses the subj; e.g., 43:4 אִם יֶשְׁךָ מְשַׁלֵּחַ אֶת אָחִינוּ אִתָּנוּ *if you really mean to let our brother go with us*

יָשַׁב, impf יֵשֵׁב (§20.3) *sit, remain, dwell*

יִשְׁמְעֵאלִי *Ishmaelite*

יתר, *nif'al* impf יִוָּתֵר *be left*

כְּ, suf כָּמוֹךָ, כָּמֹנִי *like, as;* w inf cs *when;* 44:30 כְּבֹאִי *when I come;* 44:31 כִּרְאוֹתוֹ *when he sees*

כַּאֲשֶׁר (כְּ + אֲשֶׁר) *when, as*

כָּבֵד *be heavy, grievous*

כָּבוֹד *honor*

כֹּה *thus*

כּוֹכָב *star*

כון, pt כֵּן *be true, right honest, hif'il;* הֵכִין *make right, ready, put in order*

כִּי (1) conj *that* introducing object clause of verbs of seeing, hearing, knowing, saying, etc. וַיִּרְאוּ... כִּי אֹתוֹ אָהַב *they saw that he loved him.* (2) *for, because.* (3) *when* (= כַּאֲשֶׁר), 43:21 כִּי בָאנוּ *when we came;* 44:24 כִּי עָלִינוּ *when we went up.* (4) *but (rather)* 45:8. Combination: כִּי אִם *except;* כִּי עַתָּה expresses strong affirmation; *indeed now* (see לוּלֵא)

כֹּל, כָּל־ suf 1cpl כֻּלָּנוּ, 3 mpl כֻּלָּם, 3fpl כֻּלָּנָה, כֻּלָּן, *all*

כלה, *pi'el* כִּלָּה *finish, make an end of*

כְּלִי, כֵּלִים, כְּלֵי־ *vessel,* in pl *household stuff*

כִּלְכֵּל, *pilpel* of כּוּל *sustain, maintain*

כְּמוֹ־ see כְּ־

כמר, *nif'al* נִכְמַר *grow hot, be stirred* said of רַחֲמִים *tender feelings*

(I) כֵּן *thus, so;* אַחֲרֵי כֵן *afterwards*

(II) כֵּן *qal* pt כון *(up)right, honest*

כְּנַעַן Canaan

כסה, *pi'el* כִּסָּה *cover (up)*

כֶּסֶף, suf כַּסְפִּי, כַּסְפֵּיהֶם *silver, money*

כְּתֹנֶת, כְּתֹנֶת־ suf כֻּתָּנְתּוֹ *tunic;* כְּתֹנֶת פַּסִּים *ornamented tunic* (but see פַּס)

ל (see §14.6 and §4 exercise vocabulary) (1) *to, toward.* (2) transition *into* a new condition, 44:9 נִהְיֶה לַעֲבָדִים *we shall become slaves;* 45:8 וַיְשִׂימֵנִי לְאָב לְפַרְעֹה *he appointed me counsellor to Ph.* (3) *belonging to,* 45:10 כָּל אֲשֶׁר לָךְ *all that belongs to you.* (4) *in relation to,* 44:17 הוּא יִהְיֶה לִּי עָבֶד *he will be a slave in relation to me (he will be my slave).* (5) *about,* 43:7 שָׁאוֹל שָׁאַל הָאִישׁ לָנוּ וּלְמוֹלַדְתֵּנוּ *the man inquired closely about us and our family.* (6) *in a manner or condition,* 37:4 דַּבְּרוֹ לְשָׁלֹם *to speak to him in a friendly manner*

לֹא *no, not,* הֲלוֹא *is/are not...? was/were not..? did not...?* invites an affirmative answer

לֵב, suf לִבּוֹ *heart, sense,* 42:28 וַיֵּצֵא לִבָּם *their sense left them (they panicked)*

לְבַד (ל + בד) properly, *in a state of separation* לְבַדּוֹ *by himself, he alone;* לְבַדָּם *by themselves*

לוּלֵא (לוּ + לֹא) neg cond particle *had...not;* coordinate with כִּי עַתָּה

לֶחֶם *bread, food*

לֹט *ladanum,* an aromatic resin

לָמָּה *why? wherefore?*

לְמַעַן *for the sake of, in order to* + inf.

לָקַח (§22.4) *take*

לִפְנֵי (ל + פְּנֵי) *before, in the presence of*

מֵאָה, מֵאוֹת *hundred*

מֵאַיִן (מִן + אַיִן) *from where?*

מאן, *pi'el* מֵאֵן *refuse*

מְגוּרִים *state of being a sojourner;* אֶרֶץ מְגוּרִים *land where one is a sojourner*

מִדְבָּר *wilderness, plain* (used for pasturage)

מִדְיָנִי *Midianite, of Midian* (an Arab tribe); variant: מְדָנִי

מַה, מָה, מֶה *what?* (§5.3) 44:16 מַה נִּצְטַדָּק *how can we justify ourselves*

מהמה (*pilpel* of מהה) *hitpalpel* הִתְמַהְמַהּ *tarry, delay*

מהר, *pi'el* מִהַר *do hastily;* usually best rendered as an adverb *hastily, quickly* with its complementary verb: 43:30 וַיְמַהֵר יוֹסֵף... וַיָּבֹא הַחַדְרָה *J. hastily went into his private chamber*

מוֹלֶדֶת *family, kin*

מות, pf מֵת (§17.2) *die; hif'il* הֵמִית *put to death*

מָזוֹן *food*

מִחְיָה *sustenance*

מַטְמוֹן *a hidden treasure*

מַיִם *water*

מָכַר *sell*

מלא, *pi'el* מִלֵּא (§21.3) *fill*

מָלוֹן *lodging place*

מֵלִיץ *interpreter*

מָלַךְ *be king*

מִן, מִ·, מֵ (§15.8; ן usually assimilated except before the art) *from, of, out of;* expresses the comparative in 37:3 אָהַב אֶת יוֹסֵף מִכָּל בָּנָיו *he loved J. out of all* (*more than all*) *his sons;* has the sense *some* or *one* out of many in 42:16 שִׁלְחוּ מִכֶּם אֶחָד *send one of you;* 43:11 קְחוּ מִזִּמְרַת הָאָרֶץ *take some of the choice products of the land.* In combinations: מֵעַל *from off, away from,* מֵעִם = מֵאֵת (*away*) *from*

מִנְחָה *present* (to a superior)

מִסְפּוֹא *fodder*

מְעַט *a little bit, some*

מַעֲשֶׂה *deed*

מָצָא (§21) *find, come across, come upon; nif'al* impf יִמָּצֵא *be found*

מִצְרִי *Egyptian*

מִצְרַיִם *Egypt*

מְרַגֵּל (*pi'el* pt of רִגֵּל) *a spy*

מַשְׂאֵת, מַשְׂאַת־, מַשְׂאֹת *present* from host to guest

מִשְׁגֶּה *mistake, oversight*

מָשַׁךְ *draw, drag*

מָשַׁל *rule over* (בְּ־)

מִשְׁמָר *jail, guardhouse*

מִשְׁנֶה *double amount, extra*

מִשְׁקָל *weight,* כַּסְפֵּנוּ בְּמִשְׁקָלוֹ *our money in its full weight*

מָתְנַיִם *loins, hips*

נָא particle of entreaty or exhortation; *pray! now*

נגד, *hif'il* הִגִּיד *tell*

נגשׁ, pf נִגַּשׁ, impf יִגַּשׁ [§22.2(b)] *draw near to, come up to* (אֶל)

נוח, *hif'il* הִנִּיחַ imv mpl הַנִּיחוּ *set down, leave*

נחם, *pi'el* נִחַם *comfort, console; hitpa'el* הִתְנַחֵם *be comforted, consoled*

אֲנַ֫חְנוּ = נַ֫חְנוּ
נחשׁ, *pi'el* נִחֵשׁ *(to) divine*
נְכֹאת a spice, possibly *tragacanth gum*
נכה, *hif'il* הִכָּה impf יַכֶּה (§22.6) *smite*
נכל, *hiṯpa'el* הִתְנַכֵּל *plot against* (אֶת)
נכר, *hif'il* הִכִּיר (§22.2) *recognize, look at closely* to see whether or not one recognizes; *hiṯpa'el* הִתְנַכֵּר *act as a stranger*
נָסַע *set out, journey*
נַ֫עַר *a youth, lad*
נָפַל, impf יִפֹּל (§22.2) *fall; hiṯpa'el* הִתְנַפֵּל *attack* (עַל)
נֶ֫פֶשׁ, suf נַפְשׁוֹ *soul, life, being*
נצב, *nif'al* נִצַּב *stand (up); נִצַּב עַל stand in attendance upon* a king or other high official
נצג, *hif'il* הִצִּיג *set down*, more forceful than שִׂים
נצל, *hif'il* הִצִּיל *rescue, save*
נָקִי, נְקִיִּם *clear, innocent*
נָשָׂא, impf יִשָּׂא (§22.5) *lift, carry off, away*
נשג, *hif'il* הִשִּׂיג *overtake*
נָשִׁים see אִשָּׁה
נשק, *pi'el* נִשֵּׁק *kiss*
נָתַן, impf יִתֵּן (§22.3) *put, give;* 42:30 נָתַן אֶת... כְּ־ *regard...as*
סָבַב, impf וַיִּסֹּב ,יִסֹּב, 3fpl תְּסֻבֶּ֫ינָה *turn about, surround*
סָחַר, impf יִסְחַר *travel about;* pt סוֹחֵר (סֹחֲרִים) *trader.*
ספר, *pi'el* סִפֵּר *relate*
סָרִיס, סְרִיס־ *court official*
עֶ֫בֶד *servant, slave, minister, courtier*
עָבַר *pass by*
עִבְרִי *Hebrew*
עֲגָלָה, עֲגָלוֹת *wagon*
עַד *until*
עוד, *hif'il* הֵעֵד *warn* (בְּ־)
עוֹד (§15.8) *still, yet, besides, again*
עָוֹן, עֲוֹן־ *iniquity*
עֵז, עִזִּים f *goat*
עָזַב *leave*
עַ֫יִן, suf עֵינִי, du עֵינַ֫יִם f *eye*
עִיר, עָרִים f *town*
עַל (§15.4) *upon, over, about, on account of*. Combinations: עַל דְּבַר *on account of, because of;* עַל כֵּן *therefore;* עַל פִּי *according to, by the command of*
עָלָה, impf יַעֲלֶה, juss יַ֫עַל *go* or *come up; hif'il* הֶעֱלָה impf cons 3mpl וַיַּעֲלוּ *bring* or *take up*
עַם *people*
עִם (§14.6) *with*
עָמַד *stand, tarry*
עָמַס *load* (object) *upon* (עַל)
עֵ֫מֶק *valley*
עָנָה, impf יַעֲנֶה ,וַ֫יַּעַן *answer, speak up*
עצב, *nif'al* יֵעָצֵב *be grieved*
עָרַב *stand surety for, be responsible for, take on pledge from* (מֵעִם)
עֶרְוָה *pudenda* עֶרְוַת הָאָ֫רֶץ *the secret parts of the land*

עָשָׂה, impf וַיַּעַשׂ, יַעֲשֶׂה *do, make*

עָשָׂר m עֶשְׂרֵה f *-teen*

שְׁבַע־עֶשְׂרֵה f *seventeen*

אַחַד־עָשָׂר m "*one-teen*" (*eleven*)

שְׁנֵים־עָשָׂר m "*two-teen*" (*twelve*)

עֶשֶׂר f עֲשָׂרָה m *ten* עֶשְׂרִים *twenty*

עַתָּה *now*

פֶּה, פִּי־, 1cs suf פִּי *mouth;* עַל פִּי see עַל

פוג, impf cons וַיָּפָג *grow numb, fail*

פּוֹטִיפַר *Potiphar*, Egyptian official

פְּלֵיטָה *an escape*, or *survivors* escaped from a calamity

פֶּן *lest*

פָּנִים, פְּנֵי־, suf 1cs פָּנַי 3ms פָּנָיו *face, presence;* לִפְנֵי־ *before*

פַּס in כְּתֹנֶת פַּסִּים, meaning uncertain; traditional guesses; *varicolored strip(e)s, palm* of hand, *sole* of foot, hence *tunic reaching to extremities*

פַּעַם f *time;* du פַּעֲמַיִם *twice*

פַּרְעֹה *Pharaoh*, Egyptian royal title ("the great house")

פשט, *hif'il* הִפְשִׁיט *divest* of

פָּתַח impf יִפְתַּח *open*

פֶּתַח, *opening, doorway*

צֹאן *sheep, flock(s)*

צֵדָה *provisions*

צדק, *hitpa'el* הִצְטַדֵּק (§18.5) נִצְטַדָּק [§29.1(e)] *justify oneself*

צָהֳרַיִם *noon*

צַוָּאר, suf צַוָּארָיו, pl cs צַוְּארֵי־ used as s *neck*

צוה, *pi'el* צִוָּה, impf יְצַוֶּה, וַיְצַו *charge, order; pu'al* pf 2ms צֻוֵּיתָה *be charged* with a command to others.

צָעִיר *small, young*

צְעִרָה *youth*, "*juniority*"

צָרָה *distress, trouble*

צְרוֹר, צְרֹרוֹת *bundle, pouch* (of money)

צְרִי *balsam* (*balm*)

קדד, impf יִקֹּד *bow the head*

קוֹל *voice, report*

קוּם *arise, get up;* with another verb, *make a move to* and the like, 37:35 וַיָּקֻמוּ... לְנַחֲמוֹ *they tried to console him*

קָטֹן, קָטָן [§29.1(e)] *small, young*

קנא, *pi'el* קִנֵּא *be wrought up at, jealous of* (בְּ־)

קָצִיר *harvesting*

(I) קָרָא, impf יִקְרָא *call*

(II) קָרָא = קרה pf w suf קְרָאָהוּ, impf w suf יִקְרָאֶנּוּ *befall, happen to*

קֶרֶב *midst*

קָרֵב *be* or *draw near*

קָרוֹב *near*

קָרָה, impf יִקְרֶה *befall, happen to;* pt fpl קֹרֹת (קוֹרוֹת) *happening, things that befall*

קָרַע *tear* (trans)

קָשֶׁה *hard, harsh;* fpl קָשׁוֹת is used adverbially *harshly*

קָשַׁר, pass pt fs קְשׁוּרָה *bind, tie*

רָאָה, impf יִרְאֶה, וַיַּרְא *see, behold* (אֶת, בְּ־); *hitpa'el* impf 2mpl תִּתְרָאוּ *stare at one another* at a loss as to what to do

רְאוּבֵן *Reuben*

רַב, רַבִּים *much, many;* as exclamation *enough!*

רָבָה, impf cons 3fs וַתֵּרֶב *be much, great,* 43:34 וַתֵּרֶב... מִ־... *was greater than*

רָגַז *be agitated, quarrel*

רֶגֶל, du רַגְלַיִם f *foot*

רָדַף *pursue*

רוּחַ *spirit*

רַחֲמִים suf רַחֲמָיו *compassion, tender feelings*

רָחַץ *wash*

רחק, *hif'il* הִרְחִיק *be* or *go very far*

רָחֹק, *(a)far*

ריק, *hif'il* הֵרִיק *empty out*

רָע *evil;* as a noun (also f רָעָה), *evil, calamity*

רֵעַ, suf רֵעֵהוּ *fellow, companion;* אִישׁ אֶל רֵעֵהוּ *one to the other*

רָעָב *famine*

רְעָבוֹן, רַעֲבוֹן־ *hunger, famine*

רָעָה *pasture, tend* (sheep) (אֶת, בְּ־)

רעע, *hif'il* 2mpl הֲרֵעֹתֶם *do evil, do harm,* 44:5 הֲרֵעֹתֶם אֲשֶׁר עֲשִׂיתֶם *you did evil in so doing*

רֵק, (rt ריק) *empty*

שָׂדֶה *field, countryside*

שִׂים, שׂוּם *set, put, appoint as* (לְ־)

שֵׂיבָה *gray hairs*

שִׂמְלָה, שְׂמָלוֹת, שִׂמְלוֹת־ *clothing, garment*

שָׂנֵא *hate*

שָׂעִיר, שְׂעִיר־ *buck* (of goats עִזִּים)

שַׂק, suf שַׂקּוֹ, pl שַׂקִּים *sack, sackcloth* for mourning

שַׂר *chief, official;* שַׂר הַטַּבָּחִים *captain of the bodyguard*

שָׁאַל, impf יִשְׁאַל *ask, inquire after* (לְ־)

שְׁאֹל *Sheol,* the netherworld abode of the dead

שאר, *nif'al* נִשְׁאַר *remain, be left*

שְׁאֵרִית *remnant*

שֶׁבַע, שְׁבַע־ f *seven* שְׁבַע־עֶשְׂרֵה f *seventeen*

שֶׁבֶר, suf שִׁבְרוֹ *rations, emergency food supply;* properly שֶׁבֶר רְעָבוֹן (42:19) "breakhunger"

שָׁבַר (denominative of שֶׁבֶר) *obtain, procure* food (אֹכֶל, שֶׁבֶר) in an emergency; *hif'il* pt מַשְׁבִּיר *supply* food in an emergency

שַׁדַּי see אֵל

שׁוּב (§17.2) *come* or *go back, return* (intrans); *hif'il* הֵשִׁיב (§17.3) *bring back, return; hŏf'al* הוּשַׁב pt מוּשָׁב (§17.4 note) *given back, returned*

שחוה, *hitpa'lel* הִשְׁתַּחֲוָה (see Reading 3, note) *prostrate oneself*

שָׁחַט *slaughter*

שָׁכֹל *be bereaved of child(ren); pi'el* שִׁכֵּל *cause to be bereaved, make childless*

שְׁכֶם *Shechem*

שָׁכַר *become drunk, carouse*

שָׁלוֹם, שְׁלוֹם־ *welfare, amity, wholeness,* 37:4 לֹא יָכְלוּ דַּבְּרוֹ לְשָׁלֹם *they could not speak to him amicably;* 37:14 רְאֵה אֶת שְׁלוֹם אַחֶיךָ *see how your brothers are faring;* 44:17 עֲלוּ לְשָׁלוֹם *go up intact, safe and sound*

שָׁלַח *send; pi'el* שִׁלַּח *send off, release, let go*

שַׁלִּיט *ruler*

שלך, *hif'il* הִשְׁלִיךְ *throw*

שְׁלִישִׁי *third*

שלם, *pi'el* שִׁלֵּם *(re)pay*

שָׁלשׁ, שְׁלשׁ־, f שְׁלשָׁה־ שְׁלשֶׁת־ m *three*

שָׁם *there,* שָׁמָּה *thither*

שָׁמַע, impf יִשְׁמַע *hear, understand; nif'al* נִשְׁמַע *be heard*

שִׁמְעוֹן *Simeon*

שָׁמַר *keep, watch, guard*

שֶׁמֶשׁ *sun*

שָׁנָה, du שְׁנָתַיִם, pl שָׁנִים or שָׁנוֹת *year*

שְׁנַיִם, cs שְׁנֵי־, שְׁנֵים־ m *two;* שְׁנֵים עָשָׂר "*two-teen*" (*twelve*)

שָׁפַךְ *spill, shed* (blood)

שָׁקֵד, שְׁקֵדִים *almond*

שָׁתָה *drink*

תָּוֶךְ, תּוֹךְ־ *midst;* בְּתוֹךְ *in the midst of, amongst*

תּוֹלָדוֹת, תֹּלְדוֹת־ *begettings, family history*

תּוֹעֵבָה *abomination, taboo*

תְּחִלָּה *first time* בַּתְּחִלָּה *the first time, previously*

תַּחַת *instead of, for*

תָּמַהּ *be astonished; look in astonishment at* (אֶל)

תָּעָה *wander about* (lost)

TABLES OF VERB AND NOUN INFLECTION

The Sound Verb

	QAL (§ 9–11)			NIF'AL (§ 18)	PI'EL (§ 12)	PU'AL (§ 12.3)	HIṮPA'EL (§ 18)	HIF'IL (§ 13)	HŎF'AL (§ 13.3)
1cs pf	שָׁמַרְתִּי	כָּבַדְתִּי	קָטֹנְתִּי	נִשְׁמַרְתִּי	סִפַּרְתִּי	סֻפַּרְתִּי	הִתְאַפַּקְתִּי	הִשְׁלַכְתִּי	הָשְׁלַכְתִּי
2m	שָׁמַרְתָּ	כָּבַדְתָּ	קָטֹנְתָּ	נִשְׁמַרְתָּ	סִפַּרְתָּ	סֻפַּרְתָּ	הִתְאַפַּקְתָּ	הִשְׁלַכְתָּ	הָשְׁלַכְתָּ
2f	שָׁמַרְתְּ	כָּבַדְתְּ	קָטֹנְתְּ	נִשְׁמַרְתְּ	סִפַּרְתְּ	סֻפַּרְתְּ	הִתְאַפַּקְתְּ	הִשְׁלַכְתְּ	הָשְׁלַכְתְּ
3m	שָׁמַר	כָּבֵד	קָטֹן	נִשְׁמַר	סִפֵּר	סֻפַּר	הִתְאַפֵּק	הִשְׁלִיךְ	הָשְׁלַךְ
3f	שָׁמְרָה	כָּבְדָה	קָטְנָה	נִשְׁמְרָה	סִפְּרָה	סֻפְּרָה	הִתְאַפְּקָה	הִשְׁלִיכָה	הָשְׁלְכָה
1cpl	שָׁמַרְנוּ	כָּבַדְנוּ	קָטֹנּוּ	נִשְׁמַרְנוּ	סִפַּרְנוּ	סֻפַּרְנוּ	הִתְאַפַּקְנוּ	הִשְׁלַכְנוּ	הָשְׁלַכְנוּ
2m	שְׁמַרְתֶּם	כְּבַדְתֶּם	קְטָנְתֶּם	נִשְׁמַרְתֶּם	סִפַּרְתֶּם	סֻפַּרְתֶּם	הִתְאַפַּקְתֶּם	הִשְׁלַכְתֶּם	הָשְׁלַכְתֶּם
2f	שְׁמַרְתֶּן	כְּבַדְתֶּן	קְטָנְתֶּן	נִשְׁמַרְתֶּן	סִפַּרְתֶּן	סֻפַּרְתֶּן	הִתְאַפַּקְתֶּן	הִשְׁלַכְתֶּן	הָשְׁלַכְתֶּן
3c	שָׁמְרוּ	כָּבְדוּ	קָטְנוּ	נִשְׁמְרוּ	סִפְּרוּ	סֻפְּרוּ	הִתְאַפְּקוּ	הִשְׁלִיכוּ	הָשְׁלְכוּ
1cs impf	אֶשְׁמֹר	אֶכְבַּד	אֶקְטַן	אֶשָּׁמֵר	אֲסַפֵּר	אֲסֻפַּר	אֶתְאַפֵּק	אַשְׁלִיךְ	אָשְׁלַךְ
2m	תִּשְׁמֹר	תִּכְבַּד	תִּקְטַן	תִּשָּׁמֵר	תְּסַפֵּר	תְּסֻפַּר	תִּתְאַפֵּק	תַּשְׁלִיךְ	תָּשְׁלַךְ
2f	תִּשְׁמְרִי	תִּכְבְּדִי	תִּקְטְנִי	תִּשָּׁמְרִי	תְּסַפְּרִי	תְּסֻפְּרִי	תִּתְאַפְּקִי	תַּשְׁלִיכִי	תָּשְׁלְכִי
3m	יִשְׁמֹר	יִכְבַּד	יִקְטַן	יִשָּׁמֵר	יְסַפֵּר	יְסֻפַּר	יִתְאַפֵּק	יַשְׁלִיךְ	יָשְׁלַךְ
3f	תִּשְׁמֹר	תִּכְבַּד	תִּקְטַן	תִּשָּׁמֵר	תְּסַפֵּר	תְּסֻפַּר	תִּתְאַפֵּק	תַּשְׁלִיךְ	תָּשְׁלַךְ
1cpl	נִשְׁמֹר	נִכְבַּד	נִקְטַן	נִשָּׁמֵר	נְסַפֵּר	נְסֻפַּר	נִתְאַפֵּק	נַשְׁלִיךְ	נָשְׁלַךְ
2m	תִּשְׁמְרוּ	תִּכְבְּדוּ	תִּקְטְנוּ	תִּשָּׁמְרוּ	תְּסַפְּרוּ	תְּסֻפְּרוּ	תִּתְאַפְּקוּ	תַּשְׁלִיכוּ	תָּשְׁלְכוּ
2f	תִּשְׁמֹרְנָה	תִּכְבַּדְנָה	תִּקְטַנָּה	תִּשָּׁמַרְנָה	תְּסַפֵּרְנָה	תְּסֻפַּרְנָה	תִּתְאַפֵּקְנָה	תַּשְׁלֵכְנָה	תָּשְׁלַכְנָה
3m	יִשְׁמְרוּ	יִכְבְּדוּ	יִקְטְנוּ	יִשָּׁמְרוּ	יְסַפְּרוּ	יְסֻפְּרוּ	יִתְאַפְּקוּ	יַשְׁלִיכוּ	יָשְׁלְכוּ
3f	תִּשְׁמֹרְנָה	תִּכְבַּדְנָה	תִּקְטַנָּה	תִּשָּׁמַרְנָה	תְּסַפֵּרְנָה	תְּסֻפַּרְנָה	תִּתְאַפֵּקְנָה	תַּשְׁלֵכְנָה	תָּשְׁלַכְנָה
coh	אֶ/נִשְׁמְרָה	אֶ/נִכְבְּדָה	אֶ/נִקְטְנָה	אִ/נִשָּׁמְרָה	אֲ/נְסַפְּרָה		אֶ/נִתְאַפְּקָה	אַ/נַשְׁלִיכָה	
juss								יַשְׁלֵךְ	
waw-cons								וַיַּשְׁלֵךְ	
ms imv	שְׁמֹר	כְּבַד		הִשָּׁמֵר	סַפֵּר		הִתְאַפֵּק	הַשְׁלֵךְ	
f	שִׁמְרִי	כִּבְדִי		הִשָּׁמְרִי	סַפְּרִי		הִתְאַפְּקִי	הַשְׁלִיכִי	
mpl	שִׁמְרוּ	כִּבְדוּ		הִשָּׁמְרוּ	סַפְּרוּ		הִתְאַפְּקוּ	הַשְׁלִיכוּ	
f	שְׁמֹרְנָה	כְּבַדְנָה		הִשָּׁמַרְנָה	סַפֵּרְנָה		הִתְאַפֵּקְנָה	הַשְׁלֵכְנָה	
inf abs	שָׁמוֹר	כָּבוֹד	קָטוֹן	נִשְׁמֹר, הִשָּׁמֵר	סַפֵּר, סַפֹּר		הִתְאַפֵּק	הַשְׁלֵךְ	
inf cs	(לִ)שְׁמֹר	(לִ)כְבֹּד	(לִ)קְטֹן	(לְ)הִשָּׁמֵר	(לְ)סַפֵּר		(לְ)הִתְאַפֵּק	(לְ)הַשְׁלִיךְ	
ms pt	שׁוֹמֵר	כָּבֵד	יָכֹל	נִשְׁמָר	מְסַפֵּר	מְסֻפָּר	מִתְאַפֵּק	מַשְׁלִיךְ	מָשְׁלָךְ
f	שׁוֹמֶרֶת (שׁוֹמְרָה)	כְּבֵדָה	יְכֹלָה	נִשְׁמֶרֶת	מְסַפֶּרֶת	מְסֻפֶּרֶת	מִתְאַפֶּקֶת	מַשְׁלֶכֶת (מַשְׁלִיכָה)	מָשְׁלֶכֶת
mpl	שׁוֹמְרִים	כְּבֵדִים	יְכֹלִים	נִשְׁמָרִים	מְסַפְּרִים	מְסֻפָּרִים	מִתְאַפְּקִים	מַשְׁלִיכִים	מָשְׁלָכִים
f	שׁוֹמְרוֹת	כְּבֵדוֹת	יְכֹלוֹת	נִשְׁמָרוֹת	מְסַפְּרוֹת	מְסֻפָּרוֹת	מִתְאַפְּקוֹת	מַשְׁלִיכוֹת	מָשְׁלָכוֹת
ms pt pass	שָׁמוּר								
f	שְׁמוּרָה								

Hollow Verbs (§ 17)

HŎF'AL	HIF'IL	HIṬPOLEL	POLAL	POLEL	NIF'AL	QAL			
הוּשַׁבְתִּי	הֲשִׁיבוֹתִי[2]	הִתְקוֹמַמְתִּי	קוֹמַמְתִּי	קוֹמַמְתִּי[1]	נְכוּנוֹתִי	שַׂמְתִּי	מַתִּי	שַׁבְתִּי	1cs pf
הוּשַׁבְתָּ	הֲשִׁיבוֹתָ	הִתְקוֹמַמְתָּ		קוֹמַמְתָּ	נְכוּנוֹתָ	שַׂמְתָּ	מַתָּ	שַׁבְתָּ	2m
הוּשַׁבְתְּ	הֲשִׁיבוֹת	הִתְקוֹמַמְתְּ		קוֹמַמְתְּ	נְכוּנוֹת	שַׂמְתְּ	מַתְּ	שַׁבְתְּ	2f
הוּשַׁב	הֵשִׁיב	הִתְקוֹמֵם	קוֹמַם	קוֹמֵם	נָכוֹן	שָׂם	מֵת	שָׁב	3m
הוּשְׁבָה	הֵשִׁיבָה	הִתְקוֹמְמָה		קוֹמְמָה	נָכוֹנָה	שָׂמָה	מֵתָה	שָׁבָה	3f
הוּשַׁבְנוּ	הֲשִׁיבוֹנוּ	הִתְקוֹמַמְנוּ		קוֹמַמְנוּ	נְכוּנוֹנוּ	שַׂמְנוּ	מַתְנוּ	שַׁבְנוּ	1cpl
הוּשַׁבְתֶּם	הֲשִׁיבוֹתֶם	הִתְקוֹמַמְתֶּם		קוֹמַמְתֶּם	נְכוּנוֹתֶם	שַׂמְתֶּם	מַתֶּם	שַׁבְתֶּם	2m
הוּשַׁבְתֶּן	הֲשִׁיבוֹתֶן	הִתְקוֹמַמְתֶּן		קוֹמַמְתֶּן	נְכוּנוֹתֶן	שַׂמְתֶּן	מַתֶּן	שַׁבְתֶּן	2f
הוּשְׁבוּ	הֵשִׁיבוּ	הִתְקוֹמְמוּ		קוֹמְמוּ	נָכוֹנוּ	שָׂמוּ	מֵתוּ	שָׁבוּ	3c
אוּשַׁב	אָשִׁיב	אֶתְקוֹמֵם	אֲקוֹמַם	אֲקוֹמֵם	אִכּוֹן	אָשִׂים	אָמוּת	אָשׁוּב	1cs impf
תּוּשַׁב	תָּשִׁיב	תִּתְקוֹמֵם		תְּקוֹמֵם	תִּכּוֹן	תָּשִׂים		תָּשׁוּב	2m
תּוּשְׁבִי	תָּשִׁיבִי	תִּתְקוֹמְמִי		תְּקוֹמְמִי	תִּכּוֹנִי	תָּשִׂימִי		תָּשׁוּבִי	2f
יוּשַׁב	יָשִׁיב	יִתְקוֹמֵם		יְקוֹמֵם	יִכּוֹן	יָשִׂים		יָשׁוּב	3m
תּוּשַׁב	תָּשִׁיב	תִּתְקוֹמֵם		תְּקוֹמֵם	תִּכּוֹן	תָּשִׂים		תָּשׁוּב	3f
נוּשַׁב	נָשִׁיב	נִתְקוֹמֵם		נְקוֹמֵם	נִכּוֹן	נָשִׂים		נָשׁוּב	1cpl
תּוּשְׁבוּ	תָּשִׁיבוּ	תִּתְקוֹמְמוּ		תְּקוֹמְמוּ	תִּכּוֹנוּ	תָּשִׂימוּ		תָּשׁוּבוּ	2m
תּוּשַׁבְנָה	תָּשֵׁבְנָה תְּשִׁיבֶיָּה	תִּתְקוֹמֵמְנָה		תְּקוֹמֵמְנָה	תִּכּוֹנָּה	תָּשֵׂמְנָה תְּשִׂימֶנָה		תָּשֹׁבְנָה תְּשׁוּבֶינָה	2 & 3f
יוּשְׁבוּ	יָשִׁיבוּ	יִתְקוֹמְמוּ		יְקוֹמְמוּ	יִכּוֹנוּ	יָשִׂימוּ		יָשׁוּבוּ	3m
	אָ/נָשִׁיבָה	אֶ/נִתְקוֹמְמָה		אֲ/נְקוֹמְמָה		אָ/נָשִׂימָה		אָ/נָשׁוּבָה	coh
	יָשֵׁב					יָשֵׂם		יָשֹׁב	juss
	וַיָּשֶׁב					וַיָּשֶׂם		וַיָּשָׁב	*waw*-cons
	הָשֵׁב	הִתְקוֹמֵם		קוֹמֵם	הִכּוֹן	שִׂים		שׁוּב	ms imv
	הָשִׁיבִי	הִתְקוֹמְמִי		קוֹמְמִי	הִכּוֹנִי	שִׂימִי		שׁוּבִי	f
	הָשִׁיבוּ	הִתְקוֹמְמוּ		קוֹמְמוּ	הִכּוֹנוּ	שִׂימוּ		שׁוּבוּ	mpl
	הָשֵׁבְנָה	הִתְקוֹמֵמְנָה		קוֹמֵמְנָה	הִכּוֹנָּה	שֵׂמְנָה		שֹׁבְנָה	f
	הָשֵׁב	הִתְקוֹמֵם		קוֹמֵם	נָכוֹן, הִכּוֹן	שׂוֹם		שׁוֹב	inf abs
	(לְ)הָשִׁיב	(לְ)הִתְקוֹמֵם		(לְ)קוֹמֵם	(לְ)הִכּוֹן	(לָ)שִׂים		(לָ)שׁוּב	inf cs
מוּשָׁב	מֵשִׁיב	מִתְקוֹמֵם	מְקוֹמָם	מְקוֹמֵם	נָכוֹן	שָׂם	מֵת	שָׁב	ms pt
מוּשָׁבָה	מְשִׁיבָה	מִתְקוֹמֶמֶת	מְקוֹמֶמֶת	מְקוֹמֶמֶת	נְכוֹנָה	שָׂמָה	מֵתָה	שָׁבָה	f
מוּשָׁבִים	מְשִׁיבִים	מִתְקוֹמְמִים	מְקוֹמָמִים	מְקוֹמְמִים	נְכוֹנִים	שָׂמִים	מֵתִים	שָׁבִים	mpl
מוּשָׁבוֹת	מְשִׁיבוֹת	מִתְקוֹמְמוֹת	מְקוֹמָמוֹת	מְקוֹמְמוֹת	נְכוֹנוֹת	שָׂמוֹת	מֵתוֹת	שָׁבוֹת	f

[2] הֲשִׁבֹתִי

[1] קִיַּמְתִּי

Final ה Verbs (§ 19)

HŎFʻAL	HIFʻIL	HIṮPAʻEL	PUʻAL	PIʻEL	NIFʻAL	QAL	
הָרְבֵּיתִי	הִרְבֵּיתִי (—בֵּ—)	הִתְרַצֵּיתִי[2]	צֻוֵּיתִי	צִוִּיתִי (—וֵ—)	נִבְנֵיתִי[1]	בָּכִיתִי	1cs pf
הָרְבֵּיתָ	הִרְבִּיתָ (—בֵּ—)	הִתְרַצִּיתָ	צֻוֵּיתָ	צִוִּיתָ	נִבְנֵיתָ	בָּכִיתָ	2m
הָרְבֵּית	הִרְבִּית (—בֵּ—)	הִתְרַצִּית	צֻוֵּית	צִוִּית	נִבְנֵית	בָּכִית	2f
הָרְבָּה	הִרְבָּה	הִתְרַצָּה	צֻוָּה	צִוָּה	נִבְנָה	בָּכָה	3m
הָרְבְּתָה	הִרְבְּתָה	הִתְרַצְּתָה	צֻוְּתָה	צִוְּתָה	נִבְנְתָה	בָּכְתָה	3f
הָרְבֵּינוּ	הִרְבִּינוּ	הִתְרַצִּינוּ	צֻוֵּינוּ	צִוִּינוּ	נִבְנֵינוּ	בָּכִינוּ	1cpl
הָרְבֵּיתֶם	הִרְבִּיתֶם (—בֵּ—)	הִתְרַצִּיתֶם	צֻוֵּיתֶם	צִוִּיתֶם	נִבְנֵיתֶם	בְּכִיתֶם	2m
הָרְבֵּיתֶן	הִרְבִּיתֶן (—בֵּ—)	הִתְרַצִּיתֶן	צֻוֵּיתֶן	צִוִּיתֶן	נִבְנֵיתֶן	בְּכִיתֶן	2f
הָרְבּוּ	הִרְבּוּ	הִתְרַצּוּ	צֻוּוּ	צִוּוּ	נִבְנוּ	בָּכוּ	3c
אָרְבֶּה	אַרְבֶּה	אֶתְרַצֶּה	אֲצֻוֶּה	אֲצַוֶּה	אֶבָּנֶה	אֶבְכֶּה	1cs impf
תָּרְבֶּה	תַּרְבֶּה	תִּתְרַצֶּה	תְּצֻוֶּה	תְּצַוֶּה	תִּבָּנֶה	תִּבְכֶּה	2m
תָּרְבִּי	תַּרְבִּי	תִּתְרַצִּי	תְּצֻוִּי	תְּצַוִּי	תִּבָּנִי	תִּבְכִּי	2f
יָרְבֶּה	יַרְבֶּה	יִתְרַצֶּה	יְצֻוֶּה	יְצַוֶּה	יִבָּנֶה	יִבְכֶּה	3m
תָּרְבֶּה	תַּרְבֶּה	תִּתְרַצֶּה	תְּצֻוֶּה	תְּצַוֶּה	תִּבָּנֶה	תִּבְכֶּה	3f
נָרְבֶּה	נַרְבֶּה	נִתְרַצֶּה	נְצֻוֶּה	נְצַוֶּה	נִבָּנֶה	נִבְכֶּה	1cpl
תָּרְבּוּ	תַּרְבּוּ	תִּתְרַצּוּ	תְּצֻוּוּ	תְּצַוּוּ	תִּבָּנוּ	תִּבְכּוּ	2m
תָּרְבֶּינָה	תַּרְבֶּינָה	תִּתְרַצֶּינָה	תְּצֻוֶּינָה	תְּצַוֶּינָה	תִּבָּנֶינָה	תִּבְכֶּינָה	2f
יָרְבּוּ	יַרְבּוּ	יִתְרַצּוּ	יְצֻוּוּ	יְצַוּוּ	יִבָּנוּ	יִבְכּוּ	3m
תָּרְבֶּינָה	תַּרְבֶּינָה	תִּתְרַצֶּינָה	תְּצֻוֶּינָה	תְּצַוֶּינָה	תִּבָּנֶינָה	תִּבְכֶּינָה	3f
	יֶרֶב	יִתְרַץ		יְצַו	יִבָּן	יֵבְךְּ	apoc
	הַרְבֵּה	הִתְרַצֵּה		צַוֵּה	הִבָּנֵה	בְּכֵה	ms imv
	הַרְבִּי	הִתְרַצִּי		צַוִּי	הִבָּנִי	בְּכִי	f
	הַרְבּוּ	הִתְרַצּוּ		צַוּוּ	הִבָּנוּ	בְּכוּ	mpl
	הַרְבֶּינָה	הִתְרַצֶּינָה		צַוֶּינָה	הִבָּנֶינָה	בְּכֶינָה	f
	הַרְבֵּה (הַרְבָּה)	הִתְרַצֵּה		צַוֹּה, צַוֵּה	נִבְנֹה	בָּכֹה	inf abs
	(לְ)הַרְבּוֹת	(לְ)הִתְרַצּוֹת		(לְ)צַוּוֹת	(לְ)הִבָּנוֹת	(לְ)בְכּוֹת	inf cs
מֻרְבֶּה	מַרְבֶּה	מִתְרַצֶּה	מְצֻוֶּה	מְצַוֶּה	נִבְנֶה	בּוֹכֶה	ms pt
מֻרְבָּה	מַרְבָּה	מִתְרַצָּה	מְצֻוָּה	מְצַוָּה	נִבְנָה	בּוֹכָה	f
מֻרְבִּים	מַרְבִּים	מִתְרַצִּים	מְצֻוִּים	מְצַוִּים	נִבְנִים	בּוֹכִים	mpl
מֻרְבּוֹת	מַרְבּוֹת	מִתְרַצּוֹת	מְצֻוּוֹת	מְצַוּוֹת	נִבְנוֹת	בּוֹכוֹת	f
						עָשׂוּי	ms pt pass
						עֲשׂוּיָה	f

[1] I was built

Initial י Verbs (§ 20)

ORIGINALLY INITIAL י					ORIGINALLY INITIAL ו			
HIF'IL	QAL	HŎF'AL	HIF'IL	NIF'AL	QAL			
הֵיטַ֫בְתִּי	(יטב)	הוּלַ֫דְתִּי	הוֹלַ֫דְתִּי	נוֹלַ֫דְתִּי	יָכֹ֫לְתִּי	יָרֵ֫אתִי	יָלַ֫דְתִּי	1cs pf
הֵיטַ֫בְתָּ			הוֹלַ֫דְתָּ	נוֹלַ֫דְתָּ				2m
הֵיטַבְתְּ			הוֹלַדְתְּ	נוֹלַדְתְּ				2f
הֵיטִיב		הוּלַד	הוֹלִיד	נוֹלַד				3m
הֵיטִ֫יבָה			הוֹלִ֫ידָה	נוֹלְדָה				3f
הֵיטַ֫בְנוּ			הוֹלַ֫דְנוּ	נוֹלַ֫דְנוּ				1cpl
הֵיטַבְתֶּם			הוֹלַדְתֶּם	נוֹלַדְתֶּם				2m
הֵיטַבְתֶּן			הוֹלַדְתֶּן	נוֹלַדְתֶּן				2f
הֵיטִ֫יבוּ			הוֹלִ֫ידוּ	נוֹלְדוּ				3c
אֵיטִיב	אִיטַב	אוּלַד	אוֹלִיד	אִוָּלֵד	אוּכַל	אִירָא	אֵלֵד	1cs impf
תֵּיטִיב	תִּיטַב		תּוֹלִיד	תִּוָּלֵד	תּוּכַל	תִּירָא	תֵּלֵד	2m
תֵּיטִ֫יבִי	תִּיטְבִי		תּוֹלִ֫ידִי	תִּוָּלְדִי	תּוּכְלִי	תִּירְאִי	תֵּלְדִי	2f
יֵיטִיב	יִיטַב		יוֹלִיד	יִוָּלֵד	יוּכַל	יִירָא	יֵלֵד	3m
תֵּיטִיב	תִּיטַב		תּוֹלִיד	תִּוָּלֵד	תּוּכַל	תִּירָא	תֵּלֵד	3f
נֵיטִיב	נִיטַב		נוֹלִיד	נִוָּלֵד	נוּכַל	נִירָא	נֵלֵד	1cpl
תֵּיטִ֫יבוּ	תִּיטְבוּ		תּוֹלִ֫ידוּ	תִּוָּלְדוּ	תּוּכְלוּ	תִּירְאוּ	תֵּלְדוּ	2m
תֵּיטֵ֫בְנָה	תִּיטַ֫בְנָה		תּוֹלֵ֫דְנָה	תִּוָּלַ֫דְנָה	תּוּכַ֫לְנָה	תִּירֶ֫אנָה	תֵּלַ֫דְנָה	2f
יֵיטִ֫יבוּ	יִיטְבוּ		יוֹלִ֫ידוּ	יִוָּלְדוּ	יוּכְלוּ	יִירְאוּ	יֵלְדוּ	3m
תֵּיטֵ֫בְנָה	תִּיטַ֫בְנָה		תּוֹלֵ֫דְנָה	תִּוָּלַ֫דְנָה	תּוּכַ֫לְנָה	תִּירֶ֫אנָה	תֵּלַ֫דְנָה	3f
וַיֵּ֫יטֶב	וַיִּ֫יטַב		וַיּ֫וֹלֶד	וַיִּוָּלֵד	וַיּוּכַל	וַיִּירָא	וַיֵּ֫לֶד	*waw*-cons
הֵיטֵב			הוֹלֵד	הִוָּלֵד		יְרָא	לֵד	ms imv
הֵיטִ֫יבִי			הוֹלִ֫ידִי	הִוָּלְדִי		יִרְאִי	לְדִי	f
הֵיטִ֫יבוּ			הוֹלִ֫ידוּ	הִוָּלְדוּ		יִרְאוּ	לְדוּ	mpl
הֵיטֵ֫בְנָה			הוֹלֵ֫דְנָה	הִוָּלַ֫דְנָה		יְרֶ֫אנָה	לֵ֫דְנָה	f
הֵיטֵב			הוֹלֵד	הִוָּלֵד		יָרוֹא	יָלוֹד	inf abs
(לְ)הֵיטִיב			(לְ)הוֹלִיד	(לְ)הִוָּלֵד		(לִ)ירֹא	(לָ)לֶ֫דֶת	inf cs
מֵיטִיב		מוּלָד	מוֹלִיד	נוֹלָד		יָרֵא	יוֹלֵד	ms pt
מֵיטִיבָה			מוֹלִידָה	נוֹלֶ֫דֶת				f
מֵיטִיבִים			מוֹלִידִים	נוֹלָדִים				mpl
מֵיטִיבוֹת			מוֹלִידוֹת	נוֹלָדוֹת				f

Initial נ *Verbs* (§ 22) | *Initial* א *Verbs* (§ 21)

HŎF'AL	HIF'IL	NIF'AL	QAL		QAL		
הֻכַּרְתִּי	הִכַּרְתִּי	נִגַּשְׁתִּי		נָפַלְתִּי	אָכַלְתִּי	אָסַפְתִּי	1cs pf
הֻכַּרְתָּ	הִכַּרְתָּ	נִגַּשְׁתָּ					2m
הֻכַּרְתְּ	הִכַּרְתְּ	נִגַּשְׁתְּ					2f
הֻכַּר	הִכִּיר	נִגַּשׁ					3m
הֻכְּרָה	הִכִּירָה	נִגְּשָׁה					3f
הֻכַּרְנוּ	הִכַּרְנוּ	נִגַּשְׁנוּ					1cpl
הֻכַּרְתֶּם	הִכַּרְתֶּם	נִגַּשְׁתֶּם					2m
הֻכַּרְתֶּן	הִכַּרְתֶּן	נִגַּשְׁתֶּן					2f
הֻכְּרוּ	הִכִּירוּ	נִגְּשׁוּ					3c
אֻכַּר	אַכִּיר	אֶנָּצֵל	אֶגַּשׁ	אֶפֹּל	אֹכַל	אֶאֱסֹף	1cs impf
תֻּכַּר	תַּכִּיר		תִּגַּשׁ	תִּפֹּל	תֹּאכַל	תֶּאֱסֹף	2m
תֻּכְּרִי	תַּכִּירִי		תִּגְּשִׁי	תִּפְּלִי	תֹּאכְלִי	תַּאַסְפִי	2f
יֻכַּר	יַכִּיר		יִגַּשׁ	יִפֹּל	יֹאכַל	יֶאֱסֹף	3m
תֻּכַּר	תַּכִּיר		תִּגַּשׁ	תִּפֹּל	תֹּאכַל	תֶּאֱסֹף	3f
נֻכַּר	נַכִּיר		נִגַּשׁ	נִפֹּל	נֹאכַל	נֶאֱסֹף	1cpl
תֻּכְּרוּ	תַּכִּירוּ		תִּגְּשׁוּ	תִּפְּלוּ	תֹּאכְלוּ	תַּאַסְפוּ	2m
תֻּכַּרְנָה	תַּכֵּרְנָה		תִּגַּשְׁנָה	תִּפֹּלְנָה	תֹּאכַלְנָה	תֶּאֱסֹפְנָה	2f
יֻכְּרוּ	יַכִּירוּ		יִגְּשׁוּ	יִפְּלוּ	יֹאכְלוּ	יַאַסְפוּ	3m
תֻּכַּרְנָה	תַּכֵּרְנָה		תִּגַּשְׁנָה	תִּפֹּלְנָה	תֹּאכַלְנָה	תֶּאֱסֹפְנָה	3f
	וַיַּכֵּר				וַיֹּאכַל וַיֹּאמֶר , וַיֹּאמַר		*waw*-cons
	הַכֵּר	הִנָּצֵל	גַּשׁ	נְפֹל	אֱכֹל	אֱסֹף	ms imv
	הַכִּירִי		גְּשִׁי	נִפְלִי	אִכְלִי	אִסְפִי	f
	הַכִּירוּ		גְּשׁוּ	נִפְלוּ	אִכְלוּ	אִסְפוּ	mpl
	הַכֵּרְנָה		גַּשְׁנָה	נְפֹלְנָה	אֱכֹלְנָה	אֱסֹפְנָה	f
	הַכֵּר		נָגוֹשׁ	נָפוֹל	אָכוֹל	אָסוֹף	inf abs
	(לְ)הַכִּיר	(לְ)הִנָּצֵל	(לָ)גֶשֶׁת	לִפֹּל	(לֶ)אֱכֹל, לֵאמֹר	(לֶ)אֱסֹף	inf cs
מֻכָּר	מַכִּיר	נִגָּשׁ		נוֹפֵל	אוֹכֵל	אוֹסֵף	ms pt
מֻכֶּרֶת	מַכֶּרֶת	נִגֶּשֶׁת					f
מֻכָּרִים	מַכִּירִים	נִגָּשִׁים					mpl
מֻכָּרוֹת	מַכִּירוֹת	נִגָּשׁוֹת					f

Final א *Verbs* (§ 21)

HŎF'AL	HIF'IL	HITPA'EL	PU'AL	PI'EL	NIF'AL	QAL	QAL	
הָמְצֵאתִי	הִמְצֵאתִי	הִתְמַלֵּאתִי	מֻלֵּאתִי	מִלֵּאתִי	נִמְצֵאתִי	שָׂנֵאתִי	מָצָאתִי	1cs pf
הָמְצֵאתָ	הִמְצֵאתָ	הִתְמַלֵּאתָ	מֻלֵּאתָ	מִלֵּאתָ	נִמְצֵאתָ	שָׂנֵאתָ	מָצָאתָ	2m
הָמְצֵאת	הִמְצֵאת	הִתְמַלֵּאת	מֻלֵּאת	מִלֵּאת	נִמְצֵאת	שָׂנֵאת	מָצָאת	2f
הָמְצָא	הִמְצִיא	הִתְמַלֵּא	מֻלָּא	מִלֵּא	נִמְצָא	שָׂנֵא	מָצָא	3m
הָמְצְאָה	הִמְצִיאָה	הִתְמַלְּאָה	מֻלְּאָה	מִלְּאָה	נִמְצְאָה	שָׂנְאָה	מָצְאָה	3f
הָמְצֵאנוּ	הִמְצֵאנוּ	הִתְמַלֵּאנוּ	מֻלֵּאנוּ	מִלֵּאנוּ	נִמְצֵאנוּ	שָׂנֵאנוּ	מָצָאנוּ	1cpl
הָמְצֵאתֶם	הִמְצֵאתֶם	הִתְמַלֵּאתֶם	מֻלֵּאתֶם	מִלֵּאתֶם	נִמְצֵאתֶם	שְׂנֵאתֶם	מְצָאתֶם	2m
הָמְצֵאתֶן	הִמְצֵאתֶן	הִתְמַלֵּאתֶן	מֻלֵּאתֶן	מִלֵּאתֶן	נִמְצֵאתֶן	שְׂנֵאתֶן	מְצָאתֶן	3f
הָמְצְאוּ	הִמְצִיאוּ	הִתְמַלְּאוּ	מֻלְּאוּ	מִלְּאוּ	נִמְצְאוּ	שָׂנְאוּ	מָצְאוּ	3c
אָמְצָא	אַמְצִיא	אֶתְמַלֵּא	אֲמֻלָּא	אֲמַלֵּא	אֶמָּצֵא	אֶשְׂנָא	אֶמְצָא	1cs impf
תָּמְצָא	תַּמְצִיא	תִּתְמַלֵּא	תְּמֻלָּא	תְּמַלֵּא	תִּמָּצֵא	תִּשְׂנָא	תִּמְצָא	2m
תָּמְצְאִי	תַּמְצִיאִי	תִּתְמַלְּאִי	תְּמֻלְּאִי	תְּמַלְּאִי	תִּמָּצְאִי	תִּשְׂנְאִי	תִּמְצְאִי	2f
יָמְצָא	יַמְצִיא	יִתְמַלֵּא	יְמֻלָּא	יְמַלֵּא	יִמָּצֵא	יִשְׂנָא	יִמְצָא	3m
תָּמְצָא	תַּמְצִיא	תִּתְמַלֵּא	תְּמֻלָּא	תְּמַלֵּא	תִּמָּצֵא	תִּשְׂנָא	תִּמְצָא	3f
נָמְצָא	נַמְצִיא	נִתְמַלֵּא	נְמֻלָּא	נְמַלֵּא	נִמָּצֵא	נִשְׂנָא	נִמְצָא	1cpl
תָּמְצְאוּ	תַּמְצִיאוּ	תִּתְמַלְּאוּ	תְּמֻלְּאוּ	תְּמַלְּאוּ	תִּמָּצְאוּ	תִּשְׂנְאוּ	תִּמְצְאוּ	2m
תָּמְצֶאנָה	תַּמְצֶאנָה	תִּתְמַלֶּאנָה	תְּמֻלֶּאנָה	תְּמַלֶּאנָה	תִּמָּצֶאנָה	תִּשְׂנֶאנָה	תִּמְצֶאנָה	2f
יָמְצְאוּ	יַמְצִיאוּ	יִתְמַלְּאוּ	יְמֻלְּאוּ	יְמַלְּאוּ	יִמָּצְאוּ	יִשְׂנְאוּ	יִמְצְאוּ	3m
תָּמְצֶאנָה	תַּמְצֶאנָה	תִּתְמַלֶּאנָה	תְּמֻלֶּאנָה	תְּמַלֶּאנָה	תִּמָּצֶאנָה	תִּשְׂנֶאנָה	תִּמְצֶאנָה	3f
	יַמְצֵא							juss
	הַמְצֵא	הִתְמַלֵּא		מַלֵּא	הִמָּצֵא	שְׂנָא	מְצָא	ms imv
	הַמְצִיאִי	הִתְמַלְּאִי		מַלְּאִי	הִמָּצְאִי	שִׂנְאִי	מִצְאִי	f
	הַמְצִיאוּ	הִתְמַלְּאוּ		מַלְּאוּ	הִמָּצְאוּ	שִׂנְאוּ	מִצְאוּ	mpl
	הַמְצֶאנָה	הִתְמַלֶּאנָה		מַלֶּאנָה	הִמָּצֶאנָה	שְׂנֶאנָה	מְצֶאנָה	f
	הַמְצֵא	הִתְמַלֵּא		מַלֵּא	נִמְצֹא, הִמָּצֵא	שָׂנוֹא	מָצוֹא	inf abs
	(לְ)הַמְצִיא	(לְ)הִתְמַלֵּא		(לְ)מַלֵּא	(לְ)הִמָּצֵא	(לִ)שְׂנֹא	(לִ)מְצֹא	inf cs
מֻמְצָא	מַמְצִיא	מִתְמַלֵּא	מְמֻלָּא	מְמַלֵּא	נִמְצָא	יָרֵא	מוֹצֵא	ms pt
מֻמְצֵאת	מַמְצֵאת	מִתְמַלֵּאת	מְמֻלֵּאת	מְמַלֵּאת	נִמְצֵאת	יְרֵאָה	מוֹצֵאת	f
מֻמְצָאִים	מַמְצִיאִים	מִתְמַלְּאִים	מְמֻלָּאִים	מְמַלְּאִים	נִמְצָאִים	יְרֵאִים	מוֹצְאִים	mpl
מֻמְצָאוֹת	מַמְצִיאוֹת	מִתְמַלְּאוֹת	מְמֻלָּאוֹת	מְמַלְּאוֹת	נִמְצָאוֹת	יְרֵאוֹת	מוֹצְאוֹת	f
							מָצוּא	ms pt pass
							מְצוּאָה	f

Middle Laryngal Verbs (§24) — Initial Laryngal Verbs (§23)

	Initial Laryngal Verbs (§23)					Middle Laryngal Verbs (§24)					
	QAL	QAL	NIF'AL	HIF'IL	HIF'IL	QAL	NIF'AL	PI'EL	PI'EL	PU'AL	HITPA'EL
1cs pf	עָמַדְתִּי	חָרַדְתִּי	נֶעֱצַבְתִּי	הֶאֱמַנְתִּי	הָעֳמַדְתִּי	שָׁאַלְתִּי	נִשְׁאַלְתִּי	מֵאַנְתִּי	מִהַרְתִּי	בֹּרַכְתִּי	הִתְבָּרַכְתִּי
2m	עָמַדְתָּ		נֶעֱצַבְתָּ	הֶאֱמַנְתָּ	הָעֳמַדְתָּ	שָׁאַלְתָּ	נִשְׁאַלְתָּ	מֵאַנְתָּ	מִהַרְתָּ	בֹּרַכְתָּ	הִתְבָּרַכְתָּ
2f	עָמַדְתְּ		נֶעֱצַבְתְּ	הֶאֱמַנְתְּ	הָעֳמַדְתְּ	שָׁאַלְתְּ	נִשְׁאַלְתְּ	מֵאַנְתְּ	מִהַרְתְּ	בֹּרַכְתְּ	הִתְבָּרַכְתְּ
3m	עָמַד		נֶעֱצַב	הֶאֱמִין	הָעֳמַד	שָׁאַל	נִשְׁאַל	מֵאֵן	מִהֵר	בֹּרַךְ	הִתְבָּרֵךְ
3f	עָמְדָה		נֶעֶצְבָה	הֶאֱמִינָה	הָעָמְדָה	שָׁאֲלָה	נִשְׁאֲלָה	מֵאֲנָה	מִהֲרָה	בֹּרְכָה	הִתְבָּרְכָה
1cpl	עָמַדְנוּ		נֶעֱצַבְנוּ	הֶאֱמַנּוּ	הָעֳמַדְנוּ	שָׁאַלְנוּ	נִשְׁאַלְנוּ	מֵאַנּוּ	מִהַרְנוּ	בֹּרַכְנוּ	הִתְבָּרַכְנוּ
2m	עֲמַדְתֶּם		נֶעֱצַבְתֶּם	הֶאֱמַנְתֶּם	הָעֳמַדְתֶּם	שְׁאַלְתֶּם	נִשְׁאַלְתֶּם	מֵאַנְתֶּם	מִהַרְתֶּם	בֹּרַכְתֶּם	הִתְבָּרַכְתֶּם
2f	עֲמַדְתֶּן		נֶעֱצַבְתֶּן	הֶאֱמַנְתֶּן	הָעֳמַדְתֶּן	שְׁאַלְתֶּן	נִשְׁאַלְתֶּן	מֵאַנְתֶּן	מִהַרְתֶּן	בֹּרַכְתֶּן	הִתְבָּרַכְתֶּן
3c	עָמְדוּ		נֶעֶצְבוּ	הֶאֱמִינוּ	הָעָמְדוּ	שָׁאֲלוּ	נִשְׁאֲלוּ	מֵאֲנוּ	מִהֲרוּ	בֹּרְכוּ	הִתְבָּרְכוּ
1cs impf	אֶעֱמֹד	אֶחֱרַד	אֵעָצֵב	אַאֲמִין	אָעֳמַד	אֶשְׁאַל	אֶשָּׁאֵל	אֲמָאֵן	אֲמַהֵר	אֲבֹרַךְ	אֶתְבָּרֵךְ
2m	תַּעֲמֹד	תֶּחֱרַד	תֵּעָצֵב	תַּאֲמִין	תָּעֳמַד	תִּשְׁאַל	תִּשָּׁאֵל	תְּמָאֵן	תְּמַהֵר	תְּבֹרַךְ	תִּתְבָּרֵךְ
2f	תַּעַמְדִי	תֶּחֶרְדִי	תֵּעָצְבִי	תַּאֲמִינִי	תָּעָמְדִי	תִּשְׁאֲלִי	תִּשָּׁאֲלִי	תְּמָאֲנִי	תְּמַהֲרִי	תְּבֹרְכִי	תִּתְבָּרְכִי
3m	יַעֲמֹד	יֶחֱרַד	יֵעָצֵב	יַאֲמִין	יָעֳמַד	יִשְׁאַל	יִשָּׁאֵל	יְמָאֵן	יְמַהֵר	יְבֹרַךְ	יִתְבָּרֵךְ
3f	תַּעֲמֹד	תֶּחֱרַד	תֵּעָצֵב	תַּאֲמִין	תָּעֳמַד	תִּשְׁאַל	תִּשָּׁאֵל	תְּמָאֵן	תְּמַהֵר	תְּבֹרַךְ	תִּתְבָּרֵךְ
1cpl	נַעֲמֹד	נֶחֱרַד	נֵעָצֵב	נַאֲמִין	נָעֳמַד	נִשְׁאַל	נִשָּׁאֵל	נְמָאֵן	נְמַהֵר	נְבֹרַךְ	נִתְבָּרֵךְ
2m	תַּעַמְדוּ	תֶּחֶרְדוּ	תֵּעָצְבוּ	תַּאֲמִינוּ	תָּעָמְדוּ	תִּשְׁאֲלוּ	תִּשָּׁאֲלוּ	תְּמָאֲנוּ	תְּמַהֲרוּ	תְּבֹרְכוּ	תִּתְבָּרְכוּ
2f	תַּעֲמֹדְנָה	תֶּחֱרַדְנָה	תֵּעָצַבְנָה	תַּאֲמֵנָּה	תָּעֳמַדְנָה	תִּשְׁאַלְנָה	תִּשָּׁאַלְנָה	תְּמָאֵנָּה	תְּמַהֵרְנָה	תְּבֹרַכְנָה	תִּתְבָּרֵכְנָה
3m	יַעַמְדוּ	יֶחֶרְדוּ	יֵעָצְבוּ	יַאֲמִינוּ	יָעָמְדוּ	יִשְׁאֲלוּ	יִשָּׁאֲלוּ	יְמָאֲנוּ	יְמַהֲרוּ	יְבֹרְכוּ	יִתְבָּרְכוּ
3f	תַּעֲמֹדְנָה	תֶּחֱרַדְנָה	תֵּעָצַבְנָה	תַּאֲמֵנָּה	תָּעֳמַדְנָה	תִּשְׁאַלְנָה	תִּשָּׁאַלְנָה	תְּמָאֵנָּה	תְּמַהֵרְנָה	תְּבֹרַכְנָה	תִּתְבָּרֵכְנָה
juss				יַאֲמֵן							
ms imv	עֲמֹד	חֲרַד	הֵעָצֵב	הַאֲמֵן		שְׁאַל	הִשָּׁאֵל	מָאֵן	מַהֵר		הִתְבָּרֵךְ
f	עִמְדִי	חִרְדִי	הֵעָצְבִי	הַאֲמִינִי		שַׁאֲלִי	הִשָּׁאֲלִי	מָאֲנִי	מַהֲרִי		הִתְבָּרְכִי
mpl	עִמְדוּ	חִרְדוּ	הֵעָצְבוּ	הַאֲמִינוּ		שַׁאֲלוּ	הִשָּׁאֲלוּ	מָאֲנוּ	מַהֲרוּ		הִתְבָּרְכוּ
f	עֲמֹדְנָה	חֲרַדְנָה	הֵעָצַבְנָה	הַאֲמֵנָּה		שְׁאַלְנָה	הִשָּׁאַלְנָה	מָאֵנָּה	מַהֵרְנָה		הִתְבָּרֵכְנָה
inf abs	עָמוֹד	חָרוֹד	נֶעְצֹב, הֵעָצֵב	הַאֲמֵן		שָׁאוֹל	נִשְׁאֹל, הִשָּׁאֵל	מָאֵן	מַהֵר		הִתְבָּרֵךְ
inf cs	(לַ)עֲמֹד	(לַ)חֲרֹד	(לְ)הֵעָצֵב	(לְ)הַאֲמִין		(לִ)שְׁאֹל	(לְ)הִשָּׁאֵל	(לְ)מָאֵן	(לְ)מַהֵר		(לְ)הִתְבָּרֵךְ
ms pt	עוֹמֵד	חָרֵד	נֶעֱצָב	מַאֲמִין	מָעֳמָד	שׁוֹאֵל	נִשְׁאָל	מְמָאֵן	מְמַהֵר	מְבֹרָךְ	מִתְבָּרֵךְ
f	עוֹמֶדֶת	חֲרֵדָה	נֶעֱצֶבֶת	מַאֲמֶנֶת	מָעֳמֶדֶת	שׁוֹאֶלֶת	נִשְׁאֶלֶת	מְמָאֶנֶת	מְמַהֶרֶת	מְבֹרֶכֶת	מִתְבָּרֶכֶת
mpl	עוֹמְדִים	חֲרֵדִים	נֶעֱצָבִים	מַאֲמִינִים	מָעֳמָדִים	שׁוֹאֲלִים	נִשְׁאָלִים	מְמָאֲנִים	מְמַהֲרִים	מְבֹרָכִים	מִתְבָּרְכִים
f	עוֹמְדוֹת	חֲרֵדוֹת	נֶעֱצָבוֹת	מַאֲמִינוֹת	מָעֳמָדוֹת	שׁוֹאֲלוֹת	נִשְׁאָלוֹת	מְמָאֲנוֹת	מְמַהֲרוֹת	מְבֹרָכוֹת	מִתְבָּרְכוֹת
ms pt pass	הָרוּג										
f	הֲרוּגָה										

Final Laryngal Verbs (§24)

HŎF'AL	HIF'IL	HIṬPA'EL	PU'AL	PI'EL	NIF'AL	QAL	
הָשְׁמַעְתִּי	הִשְׁמַעְתִּי	הִתְוַדַּעְתִּי	שֻׁלַּחְתִּי	שִׁלַּחְתִּי	נִשְׁלַחְתִּי	שָׁלַחְתִּי	1cs pf
הָשְׁמַעְתָּ	הִשְׁמַעְתָּ	הִתְוַדַּעְתָּ	שֻׁלַּחְתָּ	שִׁלַּחְתָּ	נִשְׁלַחְתָּ	שָׁלַחְתָּ	2m
הָשְׁמַעַת	הִשְׁמַעַת	הִתְוַדַּעַת	שֻׁלַּחַת	שִׁלַּחַת	נִשְׁלַחַת	שָׁלַחַת	2f
הָשְׁמַע	הִשְׁמִיעַ	הִתְוַדַּע	שֻׁלַּח	שִׁלַּח	נִשְׁלַח	שָׁלַח	3m
הָשְׁמְעָה	הִשְׁמִיעָה	הִתְוַדְּעָה	שֻׁלְּחָה	שִׁלְּחָה	נִשְׁלְחָה	שָׁלְחָה	3f
הָשְׁמַעְנוּ	הִשְׁמַעְנוּ	הִתְוַדַּעְנוּ	שֻׁלַּחְנוּ	שִׁלַּחְנוּ	נִשְׁלַחְנוּ	שָׁלַחְנוּ	1cpl
הָשְׁמַעְתֶּם	הִשְׁמַעְתֶּם	הִתְוַדַּעְתֶּם	שֻׁלַּחְתֶּם	שִׁלַּחְתֶּם	נִשְׁלַחְתֶּם	שְׁלַחְתֶּם	2m
הָשְׁמַעְתֶּן	הִשְׁמַעְתֶּן	הִתְוַדַּעְתֶּן	שֻׁלַּחְתֶּן	שִׁלַּחְתֶּן	נִשְׁלַחְתֶּן	שְׁלַחְתֶּן	2f
הָשְׁמְעוּ	הִשְׁמִיעוּ	הִתְוַדְּעוּ	שֻׁלְּחוּ	שִׁלְּחוּ	נִשְׁלְחוּ	שָׁלְחוּ	3m
אָשְׁמַע	אַשְׁמִיעַ	אֶתְוַדַּע	אֲשֻׁלַּח	אֲשַׁלַּח	אֶשָּׁלַח	אֶשְׁלַח	1cp impf
תָּשְׁמַע	תַּשְׁמִיעַ	תִּתְוַדַּע	תְּשֻׁלַּח	תְּשַׁלַּח	תִּשָּׁלַח	תִּשְׁלַח	2m
תָּשְׁמְעִי	תַּשְׁמִיעִי	תִּתְוַדְּעִי	תְּשֻׁלְּחִי	תְּשַׁלְּחִי	תִּשָּׁלְחִי	תִּשְׁלְחִי	2f
יָשְׁמַע	יַשְׁמִיעַ	תִּתְוַדַּע	יְשֻׁלַּח	יְשַׁלַּח	יִשָּׁלַח	יִשְׁלַח	3m
תָּשְׁמַע	תַּשְׁמִיעַ	תִּתְוַדַּע	תְּשֻׁלַּח	תְּשַׁלַּח	תִּשָּׁלַח	תִּשְׁלַח	3f
נָשְׁמַע	נַשְׁמִיעַ	נִתְוַדַּע	נְשֻׁלַּח	נְשַׁלַּח	נִשָּׁלַח	נִשְׁלַח	1cpl
תָּשְׁמְעוּ	תַּשְׁמִיעוּ	תִּתְוַדְּעוּ	תְּשֻׁלְּחוּ	תְּשַׁלְּחוּ	תִּשָּׁלְחוּ	תִּשְׁלְחוּ	2m
תָּשְׁמַעְנָה	תַּשְׁמַעְנָה	תִּתְוַדַּעְנָה	תְּשֻׁלַּחְנָה	תְּשַׁלַּחְנָה	תִּשָּׁלַחְנָה	תִּשְׁלַחְנָה	2f
יָשְׁמְעוּ	יַשְׁמִיעוּ	יִתְוַדְּעוּ	יְשֻׁלְּחוּ	יְשַׁלְּחוּ	יִשָּׁלְחוּ	יִשְׁלְחוּ	3m
תָּשְׁמַעְנָה	תַּשְׁמַעְנָה	תִּתְוַדַּעְנָה	תְּשֻׁלַּחְנָה	תְּשַׁלַּחְנָה	תִּשָּׁלַחְנָה	תִּשְׁלַחְנָה	3f
	יַשְׁמַע						juss
	הַשְׁמַע	הִתְוַדַּע		שַׁלַּח	הִשָּׁלַח	שְׁלַח	ms imv
	הַשְׁמִיעִי	הִתְוַדְּעִי		שַׁלְּחִי	הִשָּׁלְחִי	שִׁלְחִי	f
	הַשְׁמִיעוּ	הִתְוַדְּעוּ		שַׁלְּחוּ	הִשָּׁלְחוּ	שִׁלְחוּ	mpl
	הַשְׁמַעְנָה	הִתְוַדַּעְנָה		שַׁלַּחְנָה	הִשָּׁלַחְנָה	שְׁלַחְנָה	f
	הַשְׁמֵעַ	הִתְוַדֵּעַ		שַׁלֵּחַ	נִשְׁלוֹחַ, הִשָּׁלַח	שָׁלוֹחַ	inf ans
	(לְ)הַשְׁמִיעַ	(לְ)הִתְוַדַּע		(לְ)שַׁלַּח	(לְ)הִשָּׁלַח	(לִ)שְׁלֹחַ	inf cs
מֻשְׁמָע	מַשְׁמִיעַ	מִתְוַדֵּעַ	מְשֻׁלָּח	מְשַׁלֵּחַ	נִשְׁלָח	שׁוֹלֵחַ	ms pt
מֻשְׁמַעַת	מַשְׁמַעַת	מִתְוַדַּעַת	מְשֻׁלַּחַת	מְשַׁלַּחַת	נִשְׁלַחַת	שׁוֹלַחַת	f
מֻשְׁמָעִים	מַשְׁמִיעִים	מִתְוַדְּעִים	מְשֻׁלָּחִים	מְשַׁלְּחִים	נִשְׁלָחִים	שׁוֹלְחִים	mpl
מֻשְׁמָעוֹת	מַשְׁמִיעוֹת	מִתְוַדְּעוֹת	מְשֻׁלָּחוֹת	מְשַׁלְּחוֹת	נִשְׁלָחוֹת	שׁוֹלְחוֹת	f
						שָׁלוּחַ	ms pt pass
						שְׁלוּחָה	f

Geminate Verbs (§ 30)

HŎF'AL	HIF'IL	HIṬPOLEL	POLAL	POLEL	NIF'AL	QAL			
הוּסַבּוֹתִי	הֲסִבּוֹתִי	הִתְגּוֹלַלְתִּי	גּוֹלַלְתִּי	גּוֹלַלְתִּי	נְסַבּוֹתִי	קַלּוֹתִי		סַבּוֹתִי	1cs pf
	הֲסִבּוֹתָ	הִתְגּוֹלַלְתָּ		גּוֹלַלְתָּ	נְסַבּוֹתָ	קַלּוֹתָ		סַבּוֹתָ	2m
	הֲסִבּוֹת	הִתְגּוֹלַלְתְּ		גּוֹלַלְתְּ	נְסַבּוֹת	קַלּוֹת		סַבּוֹת	2f
הוּסַב	הֵסֵב	הִתְגּוֹלֵל	גּוֹלַל	גּוֹלֵל	נָסַב	קַל		סָבַב	3m
הוּסַבָּה	הֵסֵבָּה	הִתְגּוֹלְלָה		גּוֹלְלָה	נָסַבָּה	קַלָּה		סָבְבָה	3f
	הֲסִבּוֹנוּ	הִתְגּוֹלַלְנוּ		גּוֹלַלְנוּ	נְסַבּוֹנוּ	קַלּוֹנוּ		סַבּוֹנוּ	1cpl
	הֲסִבּוֹתֶם	הִתְגּוֹלַלְתֶּם		גּוֹלַלְתֶּם	נְסַבּוֹתֶם	קַלּוֹתֶם		סַבּוֹתֶם	2m
	הֲסִבּוֹתֶן	הִתְגּוֹלַלְתֶּן		גּוֹלַלְתֶּן	נְסַבּוֹתֶן	קַלּוֹתֶן		סַבּוֹתֶן	2f
הוּסַבּוּ	הֵסֵבּוּ	הִתְגּוֹלְלוּ		גּוֹלְלוּ	נָסַבּוּ	קַלּוּ		סָבְבוּ	3c
אוּסַב	אָסֵב (אַסֵּב)	אֶתְגּוֹלֵל	אֲגוֹלַל	אֲגוֹלֵל	אִסַּב	אֵקַל	אֶסֹּב	אָסֹב	1cs impf
	תָּסֵב	תִּתְגּוֹלֵל		תְּגוֹלֵל	תִּסַּב	תֵּקַל	תִּסֹּב	תָּסֹב	2m
	תָּסֵבִּי	תִּתְגּוֹלְלִי		תְּגוֹלְלִי	תִּסַּבִּי	תֵּקַלִּי	תִּסְּבִי	תָּסֹבִּי	2f
	יָסֵב	יִתְגּוֹלֵל		יְגוֹלֵל	יִסַּב	יֵקַל	יִסֹּב	יָסֹב	3m
	תָּסֵב	תִּתְגּוֹלֵל		תְּגוֹלֵל	תִּסַּב	תֵּקַל	תִּסֹּב	תָּסֹב	3f
	נָסֵב	נִתְגּוֹלֵל		נְגוֹלֵל	נִסַּב	נֵקַל	נִסֹּב	נָסֹב	1cpl
	תָּסֵבּוּ	תִּתְגּוֹלְלוּ		תְּגוֹלְלוּ	תִּסַּבּוּ	תֵּקַלּוּ	תִּסְּבוּ	תָּסֹבּוּ	2m
	תְּסִבֶּינָה	תִּתְגּוֹלֵלְנָה		תְּגוֹלֵלְנָה	תִּסַּבֶּינָה	תְּקַלֶּינָה	תִּסֹּבְנָה	תְּסֻבֶּינָה	2f
	יָסֵבּוּ	יִתְגּוֹלְלוּ		יְגוֹלְלוּ	יִסַּבּוּ	יֵקַלּוּ	יִסְּבוּ	יָסֹבּוּ	3m
	תְּסִבֶּינָה	תִּתְגּוֹלֵלְנָה		תְּגוֹלֵלְנָה	תִּסַּבֶּינָה	תְּקַלֶּינָה	תִּסֹּבְנָה	תְּסֻבֶּינָה	3f
								וַיָּסָב	*waw*-cons
	הָסֵב	הִתְגּוֹלֵל		גּוֹלֵל	הִסַּב			סֹב	ms imv
	הָסֵבִּי	הִתְגּוֹלְלִי		גּוֹלְלִי	הִסַּבִּי			סֹבִּי	f
	הָסֵבּוּ	הִתְגּוֹלְלוּ		גּוֹלְלוּ	הִסַּבּוּ			סֹבּוּ	mpl
	הֲסִבֶּינָה	הִתְגּוֹלֵלְנָה		גּוֹלֵלְנָה	הִסַּבֶּינָה			סֻבֶּינָה	f
	הָסֵב	הִתְגּוֹלֵל		גּוֹלֵל	הִסּוֹב			סָבוֹב	inf abs
	(לְ)הָסֵב	(לְ)הִתְגּוֹלֵל		(לְ)גוֹלֵל	(לְ)הִסַּב			(לָ)סֹב	inf cs
מוּסָב	מֵסֵב	מִתְגּוֹלֵל	מְגוֹלָל	מְגוֹלֵל	נָסָב	קַל		סוֹבֵב	ms pt
מוּסַבָּה	מְסִבָּה	מִתְגּוֹלֶלֶת	מְגוֹלֶלֶת	מְגוֹלֶלֶת	נְסַבָּה	קַלָּה		סוֹבֶבֶת	f
מוּסַבִּים	מְסִבִּים	מִתְגּוֹלְלִים	מְגוֹלָלִים	מְגוֹלְלִים	נְסַבִּים	קַלִּים		סוֹבְבִים	mpl
מוּסַבּוֹת	מְסִבּוֹת	מִתְגּוֹלְלוֹת	מְגוֹלָלוֹת	מְגוֹלְלוֹת	נְסַבּוֹת	קַלּוֹת		סוֹבְבוֹת	f

Nouns with Pronominal Suffixes

	§ 14–15		§ 25		§ 26					
abs s	חֲמוֹר	פָּרָה	דָּבָר	צְדָקָה	מֶלֶךְ	מַלְכָּה	סֵפֶר	מִנְחָה	בֹּקֶר	טֻמְאָה
cs	חֲמוֹר–	פָּרַת–	דְּבַר–	צִדְקַת–	מֶלֶךְ–	מַלְכַּת–	סֵפֶר–	מִנְחַת–	בֹּקֶר–	טֻמְאַת–
1cs	חֲמוֹרִי	פָּרָתִי	דְּבָרִי	צִדְקָתִי	מַלְכִּי	מַלְכָּתִי	סִפְרִי	מִנְחָתִי	בָּקְרִי	טֻמְאָתִי
2m	חֲמוֹרְךָ	פָּרָתְךָ	דְּבָרְךָ	צִדְקָתְךָ	מַלְכְּךָ	מַלְכָּתְךָ	סִפְרְךָ	מִנְחָתְךָ	בָּקְרְךָ	טֻמְאָתְךָ
2f	חֲמוֹרֵךְ	פָּרָתֵךְ	דְּבָרֵךְ	צִדְקָתֵךְ	מַלְכֵּךְ	מַלְכָּתֵךְ	סִפְרֵךְ	מִנְחָתֵךְ	בָּקְרֵךְ	טֻמְאָתֵךְ
3m	חֲמוֹרוֹ	פָּרָתוֹ	דְּבָרוֹ	צִדְקָתוֹ	מַלְכּוֹ	מַלְכָּתוֹ	סִפְרוֹ	מִנְחָתוֹ	בָּקְרוֹ	טֻמְאָתוֹ
3f	חֲמוֹרָהּ	פָּרָתָהּ	דְּבָרָהּ	צִדְקָתָהּ	מַלְכָּהּ	מַלְכָּתָהּ	סִפְרָהּ	מִנְחָתָהּ	בָּקְרָהּ	טֻמְאָתָהּ
1cpl	חֲמוֹרֵנוּ	פָּרָתֵנוּ	דְּבָרֵנוּ	צִדְקָתֵנוּ	מַלְכֵּנוּ	מַלְכָּתֵנוּ	סִפְרֵנוּ	מִנְחָתֵנוּ	בָּקְרֵנוּ	טֻמְאָתֵנוּ
2m	חֲמוֹרְכֶם	פָּרַתְכֶם	דְּבַרְכֶם	צִדְקַתְכֶם	מַלְכְּכֶם	מַלְכַּתְכֶם	סִפְרְכֶם	מִנְחַתְכֶם	בָּקְרְכֶם	טֻמְאַתְכֶם
2f	חֲמוֹרְכֶן	פָּרַתְכֶן	דְּבַרְכֶן	צִדְקַתְכֶן	מַלְכְּכֶן	מַלְכַּתְכֶן	סִפְרְכֶן	מִנְחַתְכֶן	בָּקְרְכֶן	טֻמְאַתְכֶן
3m	חֲמוֹרָם	פָּרָתָם	דְּבָרָם	צִדְקָתָם	מַלְכָּם	מַלְכָּתָם	סִפְרָם	מִנְחָתָם	בָּקְרָם	טֻמְאָתָם
3f	חֲמוֹרָן	פָּרָתָן	דְּבָרָן	צִדְקָתָן	מַלְכָּן	מַלְכָּתָן	סִפְרָן	מִנְחָתָן	בָּקְרָן	טֻמְאָתָן
abs pl	חֲמוֹרִים	פָּרוֹת	דְּבָרִים	צְדָקוֹת	מְלָכִים	מְלָכוֹת	סְפָרִים	מְנָחוֹת	בְּקָרִים	טֻמְאוֹת
cs	חֲמוֹרֵי–	פָּרוֹת–	דִּבְרֵי–	צִדְקוֹת–	מַלְכֵי–	מַלְכוֹת–	סִפְרֵי–	מִנְחוֹת–	בָּקְרֵי–	טֻמְאוֹת–
1cs	חֲמוֹרַי	פָּרוֹתַי	דְּבָרַי	צִדְקוֹתַי	מְלָכַי	מַלְכוֹתַי	סְפָרַי	מִנְחוֹתַי	בְּקָרַי	טֻמְאוֹתַי
2m	חֲמוֹרֶיךָ	פָּרוֹתֶיךָ	דְּבָרֶיךָ	צִדְקוֹתֶיךָ	מְלָכֶיךָ	מַלְכוֹתֶיךָ	סְפָרֶיךָ	מִנְחוֹתֶיךָ	בְּקָרֶיךָ	טֻמְאוֹתֶיךָ
2f	חֲמוֹרַיִךְ	פָּרוֹתַיִךְ	דְּבָרַיִךְ	צִדְקוֹתַיִךְ	מְלָכַיִךְ	מַלְכוֹתַיִךְ	סְפָרַיִךְ	מִנְחוֹתַיִךְ	בְּקָרַיִךְ	טֻמְאוֹתַיִךְ
3m	חֲמוֹרָיו	פָּרוֹתָיו	דְּבָרָיו	צִדְקוֹתָיו	מְלָכָיו	מַלְכוֹתָיו	סְפָרָיו	מִנְחוֹתָיו	בְּקָרָיו	טֻמְאוֹתָיו
3f	חֲמוֹרֶיהָ	פָּרוֹתֶיהָ	דְּבָרֶיהָ	צִדְקוֹתֶיהָ	מְלָכֶיהָ	מַלְכוֹתֶיהָ	סְפָרֶיהָ	מִנְחוֹתֶיהָ	בְּקָרֶיהָ	טֻמְאוֹתֶיהָ
1cpl	חֲמוֹרֵינוּ	פָּרוֹתֵינוּ	דְּבָרֵינוּ	צִדְקוֹתֵינוּ	מְלָכֵינוּ	מַלְכוֹתֵינוּ	סְפָרֵינוּ	מִנְחוֹתֵינוּ	בְּקָרֵינוּ	טֻמְאוֹתֵינוּ
2m	חֲמוֹרֵיכֶם	פָּרוֹתֵיכֶם	דִּבְרֵיכֶם	צִדְקוֹתֵיכֶם	מַלְכֵיכֶם	מַלְכוֹתֵיכֶם	סִפְרֵיכֶם	מִנְחוֹתֵיכֶם	בָּקְרֵיכֶם	טֻמְאוֹתֵיכֶם
2f	חֲמוֹרֵיכֶן	פָּרוֹתֵיכֶן	דִּבְרֵיכֶן	צִדְקוֹתֵיכֶן	מַלְכֵיכֶן	מַלְכוֹתֵיכֶן	סִפְרֵיכֶן	מִנְחוֹתֵיכֶן	בָּקְרֵיכֶן	טֻמְאוֹתֵיכֶן
3m	חֲמוֹרֵיהֶם	פָּרוֹתֵיהֶם	דִּבְרֵיהֶם	צִדְקוֹתֵיהֶם	מַלְכֵיהֶם	מַלְכוֹתֵיהֶם	סִפְרֵיהֶם	מִנְחוֹתֵיהֶם	בָּקְרֵיהֶם	טֻמְאוֹתֵיהֶם
3f	חֲמוֹרֵיהֶן	פָּרוֹתֵיהֶן	דִּבְרֵיהֶן	צִדְקוֹתֵיהֶן	מַלְכֵיהֶן	מַלְכוֹתֵיהֶן	סִפְרֵיהֶן	מִנְחוֹתֵיהֶן	בָּקְרֵיהֶן	טֻמְאוֹתֵיהֶן

INDEX

Unless otherwise indicated, all references are to sections. Superscripts refer to footnotes. Chapter and verse followed by *n* refer to matter in the Notes on the Hebrew Text of Genesis 37, 42–45 (pp. 180–192). Hebrew words are indexed in the Glossary (pp. 197–207).